FINDING A PLACE
IN THE PAST

A life-changing year in rural England

Moira Coleman

FINDING A PLACE
IN THE PAST

A life-changing year in rural England

First published in 2013 by
Barkers Print & Design
Attleborough, Norfolk NR17 2NP

ISBN 978-0-9926670-0-9

Printed in Great Britain by
Barkers Print & Design Ltd

Contents

Illustrations in full colour

Acknowledgements

Without the generosity of spirit of Lord Tollemache in permitting access to the Tollemache Family Archive for so many years, this book would never have been written. Without the enduring enthusiasm of Lady Tollemache for Helmingham Hall Gardens and her generosity in allowing me to pick the brains of her Head Gardener, Roy Balaam, the story of Helmingham would be incomplete and inadequate. Bill Serjeant and Vic Gray, respectively past and present Honorary Archivists at Helmingham Hall, and Dr John Blatchly, Honorary Librarian at the Hall, have guided me in my attempts to flail through the centuries. Without them and their professional generosity and courtesy, I would have given up long ago.

My neighbours and the courteous staff of the Helmingham Estate made my year at Framsden an unforgettable pleasure. Without them, and without the infectious enthusiasm and contribution of professionals at Strangers' Hall Museum, the John Innes Centre, the Institute of Food Research and in the Norfolk and Suffolk Record Offices, there would be no inkling of the loyalty or the excitement that Helmingham and its history can generate.

My American mentor, Constance Renfrow, has lived up to her name. Her constant commitment to reading and criticising my work as I attempted to articulate my place in the past was generously given and appreciated greatly. For those reasons, I dedicate this book to her.

Colin and Phyllis Barker at Barkers Print & Design have excelled themselves by doing what each of them does best. However, any historical howlers, grammatical errors or social solecisms must be laid at my door. If I have omitted to acknowledge anyone who has helped, supported or contributed to this book, I apologise unreservedly and assure you that any omissions are unintentional.

Finally, without Peter and Margaret Farmer, I would not be here to tell the tale at all. Thank you, as ever.

Above: Cottages of the Helmingham Estate in Framsden.

Below: Helmingham Hall viewed from the south-east.

Author's images

1: En route to the future

It is high summer, 2008. A 30-mile drive from south Norfolk to mid-Suffolk takes an hour. There is no alternative to this mercilessly slow route. After congested towns come minor roads forced into impossible angles by meandering rivers. But there are advantages, benefits and bonuses attached. Think of it as your investment; a little time in exchange for a lot of history. You are on a journey of discovery, something to be savoured and relished. Clear of the fast road linking Norwich and Ipswich, your pace will slow; you will open the car windows, feel the warmth of the sun, breathe deeply and catch the fleeting fragrance of wild rose and honeysuckle, and the unmistakeable, deeper one of grain warming as it swells towards harvest. As the seasons fulfil their cycle over the next twelve months, you will garner the history you have absorbed over a lifetime, the passion you cultivated and then abandoned in favour of your career. Research is your aim, discovery your objective; but their improbable potential is furthest from your mind on this first foray into your silver gap year, your self-constructed bridge between employment and retirement. This is a journey of intent. You have been careful to hedge your bets; but your future is not without risk.

❖ ❖ ❖

Attleborough, Norfolk, starting point of my journey, is predictably clogged with traffic. The cause lies a mile away at the railway station. Whenever the level-crossing gates are closed, traffic converges from four busy roads and grinds to a halt. The driver ahead of me switches off his engine. I do the same. There is no justification for impatience. The only deadline is a mid-day meeting at the cottage with the Helmingham Estate Office.

You've signed the tenancy agreement. Officially, you are a tenant of the Estate, even though you and your few sticks of furniture will not move in until tomorrow. Today is when you and your landlord check the newly-refurbished cottage; tick the boxes on the Schedule of Condition. You have hours to spare. It doesn't matter whether you unload your tightly-packed car before or after the meeting. Start as you intend to go on: use the delay to reflect on what has led to this journey. The route was winding and full of incident, just like the road ahead.

❖ ❖ ❖

Five hundred yards behind me, identified by its 'For Sale' sign, stands my Victorian mid-terraced cottage, free of debt or incumbrance. It has not been the hand of good fortune nor the salting away of salary that has brought me to this comfortable position at the age of 62. Rather, it has emerged from my knack for creating homes from houses, selling at a small profit and re-investing in the next move. In this way, property has been a source of personal pleasure and modest but reliable investment.

Upping sticks every few years has never concerned me. It began in my childhood and has continued unabated. The move ahead of me will be my twenty-first. 'HOW many?', gasps my friend Val, of whose rock-solid stability I stand in awe. She is perplexed by my capacity for enduring what she sees as the trauma of moving house. She suspects me, I have no doubt, of immature flitting at an age when I should know better. 'I've only ever lived in three houses in the whole of my life', she tells me. Val is well into her eighties. 'You won't be able to keep doing it, you know. It's fine as long as you are fit and capable but…' The rest goes unsaid. Val had a hectic professional career, too, and has developed into something of a modest property entrepreneur herself. She enriches her life, filling her personal time with family, swimming, a wide range of art, craft and cultural activities and a great deal of voluntary effort. Nonetheless, she is limited by recalcitrant joints, unimaginable less than twenty years earlier when she was the age I am now. Perhaps I should learn from her expressive concern before I reach my eighties. Meanwhile, I tell her that I consider house-moving to be a matter of strategy: organisation, planning and execution: paperwork, packing, more paperwork, unpacking.

However, with Val's words and the future in mind, I foresaw that my Attleborough cottage might well be my last move. With no Significant Other, no prospect of being anyone's beneficiary, I have to work at providing for my future. My strategy was to reach retirement with an asset and a house that I could call home. This property selection needed care. Measured by the yardstick of buying the worst property in the best street, the decision was sound. Fundamentally reparable, but neglected and filthy when I purchased it, the cottage and its garden have been transformed. Everything is safe and certificated. When the essentials were up to scratch, I took a risk, increasing the specification as work progressed, opting to build in as much comfort as I could afford but no more. This is risky because it has absorbed all of my small pension lump sums. But then, it is in my nature to see life as a process of managing. I am ever-cautious but readily satisfied as long as my outgoings never exceed my income: a veritable Mr Micawber. I think I have everything under control. What I am about to do is completely out of character.

❊ ❊ ❊

My reverie is interrupted as the vehicle in front comes back to life with a rattle and a dribble of exhausted fuel. We inch forward and continue at the same pace. Between here and the level-crossing there are two sets of traffic lights, two busy junctions where we have to give way, a one-way system that is constricted to single-line traffic much of the time, and five points where pedestrians can cross. Inevitably, the gatekeeper is closing the railway crossing as we approach. There are two keepers. One runs nimbly down the steps from his signal box to open the gates between trains, the other moves at snail's pace and keeps them resolutely closed for anything up to ten minutes. It's his day today. Those of us who can see that far ahead sigh and resign ourselves to another delay. Soon, there will be an automatic crossing here. Given the fickle nature of selective memory, I have no doubt that I will mourn the passing of both gatekeepers when the time comes. For now, I soliloquise on my own recent past.

✳ ✳ ✳

My Attleborough neighbours kept an interested eye on my progress as the cottage emerged like a butterfly from its chrysalis. Thanks to a long and glorious summer, my front door was open throughout most of the building works. I was happy for people to wander in and out, show them progress. I enjoyed the challenge of equipping and using what I called my field kitchen upstairs while the floor beneath was gutted and new services installed. All the same, I am relieved when I can celebrate my large, light kitchen with its view down the long, narrow garden; the smart downstairs cloakroom and sleek upstairs bathroom; the wood-burning stove to augment the brand-new gas central heating system. Getting there was not without the occasional drama but these trifles are soon forgotten. It takes over a year before I close my door to begin enjoying the fruits of all these labours.

Out for a walk one morning along the unpaved, grassy verge in our semi-rural road, enjoying the birdsong and admiring the tree-filled gardens, I am confronted by Carol, one of my neighbours. She is red in the face and fuming. 'Have you seen it?', she says angrily, dragging me by the arm to a large, detached bungalow two doors away from my cottage, 'There, on the gate. Look! It's a bloody planning application for six houses!'

I was irritated by the fact that a similar 'infill' development to the other side of the terrace was not revealed by the legal enquiries before I purchased but is now in build. I look at my road with new eyes, imagining the potential offered by extensive gardens and accessible driveways, by the ancient and narrow lane with its abundant hedgerows. I suspect this application to be the thin end of the wedge. If I had wanted to live on one of the established suburban roads throughout Attleborough, I would have done so. This site offered the best of all worlds. Location, location, location, as the saying goes. It seems my scrutiny was weak, my strategy flawed. I feel vulnerable.

There are over two hundred objections to the scheme, not just the predictable ones from immediately local residents but from wider community representation. Reeling but undeterred, the planning authority leaves the door open by inviting the applicants to reconsider elements of the design and re-apply. We wait, I wait, with baited breath.

The developers re-submit their plans, adding three more houses to the scheme, achieving space by proposing to demolish the existing bungalow. New objections are raised and the process grinds on as before. The next application was overturned resoundingly by the planning committee by ten votes to one.

But that was not the end, it was just the beginning of the end. As expected, the developers appeal against the decision. The appeal will take months to determine. I am not good at playing the waiting game. It gives me too much time to moil.

✳ ✳ ✳

The level-crossing gates open. Traffic flows. Attleborough's industrial outskirts recede as I speed on through open countryside towards Diss. The route is punctuated with hairpin bends and speed limits. Diss is a bottleneck most days, but delay is exacerbated today by road-works. Sod's Law, possibly, but in reality no more than a coincidental incident, as was my discovery of a cottage to rent for a year on the Helmingham Estate. 'Rent? Now? You? Why?' As I queue and endure the long wait imposed by the restrictive red light, I remind myself of the answers to this quartet of disbelief expressed by concerned friends. More alluring by far is the route leading to those answers.

❖ ❖ ❖

Stung by the prospect of unwelcome change around my cottage, I spend long hours weighing up the pros and cons of staying in Attleborough. The town was a good choice originally, well-placed on major transport routes that were essential to my work. I have made friends here, including John, with whom I am still working in partnership one or two days a week, and his wife, Sue. But otherwise, why stay? Despite Val's prognostications, I'm sure I have at least one more move in me. My heart is in the country and always has been but my choices have been ruled by the head. Why not see this obstacle as an opportunity? Whether or not development goes ahead, do I need to live here now? With the Internet and 'Rightmove' property search at my fingertips, I flit from county to county, from improbably remote location to impossibly expensive home. Unfailingly, my browsing draws me back to Suffolk, a county I lived in for 25 years and grew to love. In truth, I have deeper roots and more friends there than in Norfolk. But why is that every desirable Suffolk property is just a few thousand pounds beyond my reach?

Hindsight, they say, is the only exact science. In hindsight, I should have read more into the growing body of evidence. Property prices in Attleborough were falling, albeit gradually. Businesses were closing, some of them sizeable employers; and there were increasing numbers of unsold properties on the market, including several victims of mortgage repossession. In comparison with the green and pleasant rural locations I favoured, mostly in east and central Suffolk, Attleborough was looking distinctly low market. Prices were falling in Suffolk, too, but not at the same rate. Even though I had no concept of where this would end, I recognised with growing trepidation that if Attleborough prices fell much further, they would put a severe dent in my long-term plans. My future depended upon the value of my property – wherever it happened to be. All I had to do was live in it until values appreciated and then find a way to release capital equity should the need arise. After all, give or take the occasional dip, surely one could always rely on bricks and mortar to recover their value, couldn't one. Couldn't one?

In 2007, I enter my 60th year. Despite financial uncertainties, I want to recognise the milestone, do something memorable. I learn that Roy Lancaster, world-renowned plantsman, highly-honoured horticulturalist and well-loved raconteur, is to be at Helmingham Hall in Suffolk later in the year. The all-day event is costly but I can't resist it. I look upon it as an investment, which is my justification for any cultural indulgence, usually books. Helmingham Hall is the private residence of Lord Tollemache. His family has lived at Helmingham for 500 years. They raise the drawbridge over the moat every night, as did their ancestors before them, so the website claims. Opportunities for the public to cross that moat into the Tudor mansion are rare, but this is one of them.

There will be coffee in the Great Hall, Roy's talk and lunch in the Coach House, and then a tour of the gardens led jointly by him and Helmingham's professional garden-designing chatelaine, Lady Tollemache (Xa Tollemache, Landscape and Garden Designer). I know the Grade I Listed gardens well. Even now, I try to go at least once a year, one of thousands of visitors. But my attachment to Helmingham is much less casual. It was where I began to grasp the meaning and potential of history.

I went to Helmingham's Estate Office first in the 1980s, intending to do no more than enquire into the history of its Victorian model cottages. In the event, six centuries of accumulated archives proved to have a deep and abiding attraction for me. My research waxed and waned over the next thirty years but my quiet passion for Helmingham and its history remained undimmed.

I make the booking to attend Roy's event in 2007. Then my inquisitive eye alights on the 'Lettings' tab of the Helmingham.com website. Lettings? Really? What, to mortals such as I who have no connection with the Helmingham Estate? And in one of those model Victorian cottages that first caught my attention, with their arched front doors and an apple tree in every garden? For HOW much a month?

I can barely believe my eyes. For the price of a so-so semi on a forgettable street elsewhere locally, I could rent a piece of history in the place that ignited my love of history; and in an otherwise unattainable idyllic rural setting, to boot. In a moment of madness (or clarity), renting seemed to offer multiple opportunities. To rent at Helmingham meant that I would have no trouble filling my retirement with research activity. Simultaneously, I would buy time in which to re-evaluate my future while planning proposals and property values resolved themselves in Norfolk. The idea of the silver gap year emerged. Today marks the first step outside my comfort zone and into the unknown.

Where will it end?

❋ ❋ ❋

Contemplation carries me clear of Diss and on to the traffic-heavy arterial route linking Norwich and Ipswich. The journey becomes more purposeful because I have crossed the border, left Norfolk behind me. Shortly I leave the arterial route to the lorries and begin the westward leg of my journey into central Suffolk. Usually the winding minor road is relatively traffic-free. But I had not allowed for the unseasonably early harvest. There is nothing to be done but decelerate when I see the convoy ahead of me, escorting a massive combine harvester. The behemoth is so wide that it fills two-thirds of the road. Still, it pushes on to its destination, not too far distant, at a speed that would have been unthinkable in the days when my father drove an early version of one of these up and down the steep-sided Cotswold hills of my childhood. Meanwhile, I have to keep my eye on the road, especially now the road has reached the town of Eye.

Eye's medieval houses were built in the shadow of its Norman castle. Many survive, and now they crowd and crouch over the thoroughfare in a riot of colour and construction. A leisurely visit is long overdue to explore a town I know but not well enough. Now is not the time. The car is loaded to the gunwales with curtains and crockery, light-bulbs and linen, kettle and coffee. I am like a snail, carrying the essentials of life with me. I am in that vacuum between preparation and occupation, today and tomorrow, when a handful of my worldly goods will be carried across two counties in a hired van. For now, Eye Castle and the River Dove force passage and people into the narrow remaining space and I am forcibly reminded of this with a final nightmare bout of overtaking vehicles parked on a blind bend. Then everything changes.

The car lilts over the shallow humps of first one and then another bridge. To the left are the water meadows of the River Dove. The second crossing marks a distinct change in the landscape. A sharp bend and a short but steep ascent later and you are breasting the spine of Suffolk. The road is marginally less demanding now, a little wider, a lot more open, with fields on either side. Eye is glimpsed as a brief reflection in the rear-view mirror. The town is huddled behind you, with its church tower rising to a pinnacle of magnificence, facing off the ruined remains of that invading upstart of a Norman castle.

Now your shoulders drop a few inches and you ease back into the driving seat; but have a care, there are speed limits and warnings of hidden dips. There are sudden, sharp bends veering from left to right, right to left, as the road carries you through the villages of Occold, Rishangles with its imposing Baptist church, onward past the apple orchards of Aspall and from there to the town of Debenham. You don't know it yet, but Debenham will become your destination of choice. Here you will revel in its history, feel for its past, and delight in your acquaintance with its range of independent shopkeepers. You will learn that it takes exactly six minutes to drive from its centre to the new centre of your universe, the place you will think of as home for the next year, maybe longer.

Beyond Debenham, the road twists and turns as it climbs and descends. The views are arresting now; land gathers in folds descending to the valley bottom. In the distance, trees are so thickly spread that they resemble a range of blue-grey hills. It is as though another land has emerged. Your anticipation is heightened as you reach the sign that welcomes you to Framsden. You take a right turn: 'Helmingham Hall Gardens', indicates the brown-backed sign with its stylised white flower, a magnet for thousands of visitors annually. Your route will stop short of that attraction by a mile or so.

The road climbs sharply and veers to the right at an acute angle. You are truly in 'High Suffolk' now. This undulating part of the county lays claim to an agricultural prowess developed over centuries and maintained still. From this narrow limb of a road the land falls away steeply to your right, its tree-filled layers offering incomparable views. Fleetingly, you recall a childhood memory of your lengthy daily journey on the school bus crawling through the Cotswolds. You loved those birds'-eye views then. You love them still. They encouraged your early interest in maps, another passion you have nurtured and developed. You glimpse the surviving sails of Framsden Mill, the windmill, then the route demands all your attention. You obey the command to slow. The gradient is gentle but the road seizes you suddenly in a pernicious angle. Your foot rests permanently on the brake as you let the road guide you down and down again before it presents another sweeping bend.

The valley opens out before you as though spreading its arms in welcome; but now is not the time to let it embrace you. A Y-junction at the crook of the bend will take you into Framsden Street, with its inn, church and Village Hall. Not now. Later. Slowly, slowly now… The road straightens. Journey's end is in sight. To your right is the Hill Farm, with its long entrance drive, and a horse grazing peacefully in the field adjacent to the road. His name is Herbie, as you will discover.

A handful of yards beyond the farm brings the neat line of Victorian model cottages into view. This is St John's Row. You would be hard put to say what draws the eye first: steeply-sloping, protective roofs, warm red brick walls or soaring pattern-book chimneys. And then, suddenly, there it is: a break in the hedge. Your pulse quickens as you manoeuvre the car along the unmade drive, follow the loop around the group of trees and bushes that create an impromptu roundabout. You are alongside the wall of the cottage. There's the study window. Inch the car just beyond it. Stop. Engine off. Breathe out.

❋ ❋ ❋

I open the car door slowly. A venerable apple tree frames the view. My view, I think proprietorially. There is a quietness, broken only by birdsong and the buzzing of a bee. I climb out of the car gingerly, concerned that too sudden a movement will destroy the perfect summer stillness. The broad front garden spreads out generously before me, one of the largest in St John's Row. I turn my head slowly, committing this moment to memory. This is not a moment for the camera. This moment feels precious, inviolable.

I emerge from my transcendental state to look more closely at the compass of what I will be called upon to care for here. A spur of the entrance drive is edged with a massed border of 'Snow in Summer', its glaucous foliage set against a froth of snow-white flowers tumbling over from the lawn. I turn to the south, viewing the front garden through the contorted, fruit-hung boughs of the old apple tree. A neat and narrow path bisects two lawns. One is rectangular and occupied by the cascading layers of a mature deutzia which sits like a white crinoline on the grass. The other lawn is larger and triangular, interspersed with beds of perennial flowering plants and mature shrubs, including two buddleia thick with butterflies.

The path leads to a small wooden gate, freshly-painted in white. On either side of the gate is a mixed hedge of hawthorn and bramble, a thorny barrier against the world. From here the passing road is barely visible and the eye is drawn beyond it to the fields opposite, rising gently from the valley bottom. This scene will fill my view and my senses in the coming year.

From the gate, the lawn slopes upwards to the cottage and is separated from the adjoining neighbour's garden by a thick hedge. As I turn my attention to the building, I catch the heady fragrance of rose. A golden-yellow rambler reaches to a substantial front door, arched to a rounded head. No-one enters via their front door here. Everyone uses the back way, as I must, because that is where the keys have been concealed by the Estate staff. We're done with all the legalities, the deposit has been paid and now begins the bond of trust that will link me to my landlord for the next twelve months. I dispense with dreaming and call myself out of somnolence.

Pauline, from the Helmingham Estate Office, will arrive shortly to take me through the checklist, sign off the Schedule of Condition. Before then I want my solitary moment of possession inside the cottage. I drag myself away from the view, almost unable to believe it will still be there later, tomorrow, the next day and all the days after that. I lift the string that secures a wide gate into the rear garden. I go to where 'X' marks the spot and feel in the appointed place. My fingers make contact with a plastic bag in which the keys to my future are neatly secured by tape. I can't resist a glance to the right, to the large external workshop. Mentally I designate it as tool-store, wood-store, coal-store and freezer space for all that produce I will be able to raise here. Beyond, there are two more gardens and a field to explore. I am itching to go and look. But not now. Not yet. It's time to go inside.

Last time I visited the cottage it was in chaos and painted blue, a colour I love in sea, sky and many kinds of flowers, but dislike in décor. Every inch of inside and outside space was filled with men and materials. The Estate's building team was there in force, upgrading the cottage ready for its next occupant. This is how it works here. When any one of the hundred or more properties becomes vacant, the Estate seizes the opportunity to undertake works.

Please don't let it be blue, I think, turning the key in the well-oiled lock of the rear door. The portents are good as I step into the lobby, with its cloakroom and WC off to one side. I see this as a useful space for storing coats, muddy boots and a handy supply of logs and coal. The floor is surfaced with a washable covering in cream and ochre colours. Not blue. Good. The walls are creamy white. Even better.

The three remaining keys are large, dark and patinated with decades of use. One belongs to the outdoor workshop. Another fits the enormous keyhole of the kitchen door - the rear external door of the cottage before this lobby was added. The new, cream-coloured kitchen is smart and well-planned, a galley layout around three sides with spaces for appliances. One will be filled tomorrow by a small fridge, the other by a cooker. I grimace when I remember that it is a beaten-up old thing which I bought in haste and feel sure I will repent at leisure. I love to cook, but because I am offering my Norfolk cottage for sale complete with its appliances, I could not bring my coveted eye-level oven and five-burner gas hob with me. The dishwasher remains in Norfolk, too, more's the pity. I cheer myself by opening cupboards, smelling their newness and admiring their potential to absorb everything I have carried with me today and more.

Directly off the kitchen is the newly fitted bathroom. This arrangement is not favoured by anyone who has a choice, but tenants don't, I remind myself. I must accept that the Estate has done the best it can within reason.

I lift the latch on a stripped pine door leading from the kitchen into the living room. There's not a bit of blue in sight. I smile with relief when I see the soft caramel colour of the new carpet and creamy white of the walls. I feel relaxed now in the certainty that this neutral palette will continue. Light pours in through the south-facing window. I'm delighted when I think how well my curtains, bought on a whim at auction and sitting outside in the car, will match this décor. What luck!

The large multi-fuel stove is in place. New copper pipes emerging from its side tell me what I need to know: whenever the fire is alight, I will have hot water. That, and the electric shower, will help to keep the utility bills under control. With two homes to juggle, that's no mean consideration. Practicalities satisfied, I want to roll on my back and whinny in this field of dreams with its soft light, gentle colours and promise of comfort.

A narrow space alongside the Living Room, the 'study' could be anything I want it to be. It has a window looking east on to the entrance driveway. My car is just out of view. I can see across to the next pair of cottages and wonder who lives there. This room will be ideal for the tall, walnut wardrobe I bought with the cottage firmly in mind. It is fitted with deep drawers and pull-out shelves as well as hanging space. It will serve as a multi-purpose store, housing a few clothes and much else besides. My small writing desk with its pull-out top should fit neatly beneath the window. There's just enough room for a slim bookcase, too.

Returning to the Living Room, I find it hard to tear myself away from the window and that view. I imagine all those sunrises, sunsets, changing colours, textures, crops and creatures that are to come. It is close to mid-day now, and the room is soaking up warmth and light as the sun reaches its zenith. I would be content to perch on the window sill until the sun moves out of sight; but there is upstairs to explore yet, with the promise of even better views.

The Living Room opens on to a tiny front hall and the beautiful arched door leading into the front garden. The largest key, a shapely piece of Victorian ironmongery, slips readily into the lock and turns with a satisfying smoothness. I open the door to reveal a picture of perfection. Here I am, the model tenant in the model cottage, surrounded by grass, hedges, trees and flowers. There are bees buzzing and birds singing and, in the distance, I hear chickens clucking contentedly. With my measuring eye I estimate that there is enough space to fit another slim bookcase behind the front door, at the foot of the stairs. I can live without many comforts but not without books.

The staircase is steep and narrow. Why did I not recall this from my first visit? How on earth will I bring a bed or even a chest of drawers up here? I make a mental note to ask Pauline for an answer, for there must be one, surely. I think ruefully of the downstairs bathroom and its distance from the upstairs bedroom. Then I have a eureka moment: one of the pieces of furniture that will arrive tomorrow is a sofa-bed, destined for the Living Room. At night I can open it out and sleep on it. The so-called study can double as a dressing room because the wardrobe will be in there, and the bathroom is adjacent. I have come armed with tape-measure and a notebook full of furniture dimensions. I will began plotting and planning as soon as I have hung those curtains. But first there are the two bedrooms to explore.

By now, I have reached the top of the stairs. Here I am well and truly under the eaves and every space has steeply sloping ceilings. Even so, there is a useful area on the landing for excess clothes if I'm canny with the hanging of them. There is a radiator up here, too. Not one of the fixed electric storage heaters but a hot-water radiator. This is unexpected, and I make another note to ask Pauline whether it is obsolete or functional.

The large front bedroom lies directly above the living room and offers a glorious aspect. Its window is deep, fitted into a dormer projecting from the roof. I sit in the alcove and revel in the panoramic view. In the foreground, a stream courses through the valley bottom, edged with willow and alder trees. A slope rises to the horizon, with a grazing meadow at its foot and small hedged fields beyond, one of them suffused with pale gold and almost ready for harvest. Westwards, the stream runs parallel with the road, which skirts the remainder of St John's Row and then curves out of sight, heading for Helmingham. Framsden Street, the heart of the village, lies to the east. I cannot see the Dobermann Inn or the church from here, but I will find them later when I begin to explore my surroundings. I smile with satisfaction at the thought of having nothing opposite but fields and sky.

This large, light-filled room, I decide, would make an excellent study, allowing me to make the most of that inspirational view. My antique mahogany pedestal desk comes to pieces. Each section will fit easily up the stairs. That would leave ample room for a bed, if I can ever get one up here, and I can use the smaller bedroom as a general-purpose work and storage room.

The thought goes with me into the small bedroom, which is narrow but useful. There is enough space for low bookcases beneath the eaves. I envisage a workstation along the one wall that is unhampered by a sloping ceiling. This will accommodate the unlovely battalion of computer equipment that I will not want in the study/bedroom next door. Something prompts me to open the window, and I look down on to the roof of my car. Only then do I discover that when I arrived and began this pleasurable exploration, I left my driver's door wide open to the world.

I run clumsily down the narrow stairs, reproaching myself at every step. What a careless thing to have done! Just because Framsden is in a peaceful rural setting does not render it immune to opportunists. In fact, on top of the litter of junk mail that someone has left in a neat pile for me in the kitchen, I noticed a circular from the local police. It is a stark reminder of what rural life can be: it warns that heating oil is being siphoned from external storage tanks. Many of the Estate cottages have oil-fuelled heating systems and, with their secluded gardens and remoteness from one other, they are a prime target. I fly out of the front door. When I reach my car, I'm in for a shock. Nestled in the footwell is a chicken.

My introduction to my neighbour, Jo, begins with the altercation between this feathered intruder and me. It eyes me warily. 'Shoo!', I say sternly. It makes a dismissive noise but stays put. I try a range of other persuasive noises and flapping motions, but nothing works. And then a voice says 'Hello there. Are you our new neighbour?' Jo is smiling in welcome. A little girl tags along behind her. Mother and daughter are followed closely by a pair of inquisitive cats who waste no time in wrapping themselves around my ankles to give me a good rub of welcome.

I laugh with relief, we introduce ourselves to each other, and I introduce Jo to the chicken. She claims it as one of hers and wastes no time in removing it from the car and sending it home. 'I hope it hasn't pooed in your car' she says as the bird rises with a squawk of indignation and scurries off in the direction of its siblings, murmuring anxiously in the distance. It hasn't left anything more onerous than a few feathers, but this isn't going to be my last encounter with it or its compatriots. Jo says she would love a peek inside the cottage but not now when I've got so much to do, maybe next week when I've settled in a bit more. She leaves me to it, generously offering her husband Ben's help when the van full of furniture arrives tomorrow, or hot drinks, tools, anything I need.

'And just ask', Jo says, 'if there's anything about the Estate or the village that you want to know.' It has been so good to meet her, and valuable to know that she will be watchful as I trek back and forth between here and Norfolk for work and property management. But it will be up to me to remember to close my car doors in future.

Pauline is late. There's plenty of time to unload. I have used every inch of capacity and then some, achieving a load that puts the rear end of the car well down on its springs. Unpacking would be quicker if I didn't keep stopping to admire the view, both outdoors and from inside, but eventually the car is empty, and, ironically now there isn't a thing left in it, the doors closed and securely locked.

I hang curtains in every room. They transform the house into home. I relish being a home-maker, even on a tight budget, or perhaps especially on a tight budget. One of my artistic and perceptive friends calls it 'set-dressing'. To augment what I am bringing from Norfolk, the furniture and curtains for this cottage have been bought for a song, either from local auctions or charity shops. And they do look perfect here. There is still no sign of Pauline. Kitchen cupboards and drawers fill quickly as I unpack linen, crockery, cutlery, glassware, cooking utensils, all bought for pennies or a few pounds from boot sales. These are almost an industry in this part of the world, a combination of recycling and recreation, especially on Sunday mornings. Occasionally, I have set up stall myself, shedding surplus books to make room for more. There are never enough bookcases in my life. I pause briefly to contemplate the prospect of having two houses with all that potential for bookcase space; then my ambitious dream of a library in each county is interrupted by a timely knock at the door.

Pauline, standing in for Jane, who is on maternity leave, arrives with her clipboard for the Schedule of Condition visit on behalf of the Estate Office. She admires the curtains, congratulates me on all the unpacking. She doesn't know the answer to the question about the radiator on the landing or how to get a bed up the stairs but promises to find out. She takes photographs, notes the few items still needing attention and says that she'll pass the list to Rob, who is the Estate Foreman. Jobs will be dealt with as soon as practicable. This is a new experience for me and oddly disconcerting for someone used to making decisions and solving problems.

'What should I do if something urgent happens outside your office hours – say, water starts pouring through the ceiling in the middle of the night?'

'Oh, I'll give you Rob's mobile number.' Pauline writes the number and hands me the slip of paper.

I say: 'Ah! I see. Thank you'; but think: 'Poor Rob'.

As to the immediate jobs, we agree that if I am working in Norfolk when Rob needs access for his team, I will leave a key in the appointed place and they will lock up afterwards. It is only when Pauline leaves and I escape for a walk to explore the rambling rear gardens that I stop to think about the nature of trust. It has taken me less than three hours to break the shell on a lifetime of measured isolation. It strikes me as ironic that it has taken isolation to give me the hammer.

The extensive rear garden is contained by tall hedges offering privacy on all sides, and is arranged in three tiers. Steps and a path offer alternative routes from a paved lower area up to a formal garden, roughly oval in shape, lawned in the centre and edged by well-stocked but overgrown herbaceous borders. Beyond, screened by mature trees, some of them fruit, the second level is unkempt now but might do for vegetables because it is open to plentiful light. An enormous compost heap sits here, topped incongruously by an abandoned bicycle. From this level a grassy path leads to the gentle rise of the long, narrow field. This holds the promise of walks cut through swathes of wild flowers and more; but it needs some attention, and soon. The grass is knee-high and ankle-deep in traps for the unwary; the brambles are thigh-high and vicious; there are trees that need cutting back. I was optimistic to think that I could manage all this alone. Tight budgets notwithstanding, I will have to draft in some help. Reality is beginning to impinge on romanticism.

I return to the cottage and renew my optimism at the window of the front bedroom.

In the foreground are the meadows that will flood with water in February and wild flowers in March. Rare, spotted Jacob sheep will flock and give birth there. Rising to the middle distance are neatly hedged fields. These will form the stage on which I'll watch the ever-changing performance of boxing hares, browsing rabbits and strutting pheasants. To the left and extending to the horizon are arable cultivations. I will see them turn from pale to deeper gold. I will be able to watch the combine-harvester and then the tractors crawl like green-wheeled insects through the seasons, working with headlights at night to capture every precious ear of grain, every moment of clement weather.

It will be as though I am watching my rural childhood played out before me, sixty years on, from a position of security. I can see it all.

I am surprised to find that in the space of a few hours, I have formed a strong attachment to this place. Everything that can be prepared is prepared. I am organised. That is how I like my life. All here will still be here tomorrow, waiting for me when I lead friends and furniture in the hired van.

I leave reluctantly. I stop the car before reaching the road. I take a last look at the peaceful garden and the tranquil scene across the valley where the sun is just beginning its pyrotechnic display, its dip and blaze. Leaving is harder than I thought. I want to stay here. This is visceral. Is this, I wonder, what people mean when they talk about being rooted in a place? As someone who is embarking on her 21st house move, this is a question I had not expected to ask of myself, let alone answer.

It has something to do with a feeling of familiarity, of knowing where I am in life, of knowing what to expect. I have not felt that for a very long time, not since I lived in a place remarkably similar to Framsden in another life called childhood and on the other side of England, embraced by the Cotswold hills.

I drive, questions and sensations competing for attention. I am already at my Norfolk cottage when I remember that I had planned to stop in Eye for a pleasurable, unhurried visit. But it was late and growing dark by the time I reached Eye. In any case, Eye has been there for over a thousand years and it isn't going anywhere. Indeed, the self-drive furniture van and I opt to avoid Eye the next day, our convoy taking the wider, faster but longer and less picturesque route to Framsden.

The van carries only what I need. My friend John, his sturdy grandson Josh and I form an effective chain-gang, unloading in under half an hour. Josh shifts heavy boxes of books for me while John connects the cooker, slots the fridge and freezer into place. We share a celebratory picnic lunch outside and tour the gardens. Then with hugs and kisses of good luck, they are on their way back to Norfolk. This is no mournful parting: I'll see John regularly because we still have work to complete together before I retire from the business formally, and because he and his wife Sue live less than a mile from my Attleborough property.

'In any case', says John reassuringly from the window of the departing van, 'you're not that far away. Ring us if you feel homesick! And any problem, let me know and I'll come straight over.' He means it. John is eminently dependable. I wave him off but watch as he stops the van, part-way down the drive. He extends an arm in the direction of the fields: 'Fantastic view', he says thoughtfully, 'you'll love it here…'

It does not take me long to arrange the furniture because there is little of it. Then, the flurry of activity over, I make my way around the cottage, locking doors, switching off lights, noting the boxes still to be unpacked, drawing up a list of things to do, oddments to buy, a reason to see what Debenham has to offer. Then comes the sensation that I associate always with the end of a house-moving day. It is familiar because I have moved house so many times, felt this feeling every time. It is a mixture of anticipation and slight unease.

I find contentment in a last look at that gloriously unpopulated view before I close the curtains. Pinpoint stars are visible. Dusk has gathered up her vibrant sunset skirts; now she conceals them beneath a cloak of darkness, released softly through the night.

Meanwhile, I sleep a dreamless sleep on a sofa-bed bought for a song.

Next morning I awake at daybreak to the sound of one of Jo's belligerent cockerels. I am up and alert, filled with the spirit of discovery.

Above: small mower facing a big challenge.

Below: Galega (goat's rue), an inspirational plant.

Author's images

2: Holding the live end

The day has that freshly-washed look: there has been rain overnight, but the sky is cloudless and the sun is up. My first day as a resident of St John's Row will be spent in the garden where I can enjoy that spectacular view while I work. My phone is connected but broadband is a few days away yet. Television reception is abysmal. There is an aerial on the chimney but no more than a vestigial fuzz where channels ought to be. I can survive without TV, but I confess to feeling remote without e-mail. Communications have been part of my life for so long that it is hard to rid myself of the notion that I am disconnected from life because I am without access to the Internet. I check my mobile phone. There is no signal inside the cottage. Outdoors, I discover one spot in the rear garden, midway between the greengage and the Victoria plum, where reception flickers to life.

Today's priority is grass cutting. I unlock the workshop: the mower faces me, glowing in its umbral surroundings, cheerfully orange and innocently new. It stands ready for action, pristine, unbloodied, its cable wound neatly around its handle. It looks more prepared than I feel.

'Get a Flymo', my grass-experienced friends advised me.

'Why?'

'It floats over uneven ground and rough grass, which yours probably will be, and you don't need to bother about collecting the clippings.'

Schooled in the art of using cylinder and rotary mowers with grass-boxes, I am perplexed by the prospect of green deep litter; but on the other hand there is a lot of rough mowing in view here.

Strong morning coffee in hand, I make an early reconnaissance visit to the front garden; at least, that is the intention. At first, I am little short of poetic as I breathe deeply of the fresh air, soak up the stillness, strain to hear anything but birdsong and silence. By the time I have noted all that needs to be done, I am rather more prosaic. Despite periodic attention by the Estate while building works were in progress, intermittent rainfall and a few weeks of neglect have raised the grass to ankle-height. The boundary hedges have had no attention since the previous tenant vacated. Now, towering above those of both neighbouring properties, the hedges are thorny thugs that will need bringing down to size. I doubt that my lightweight hedge-cutter will cope with more than the younger, sappy outbursts of fresh growth. I add to my growing list headed 'Organise reinforcements'.

My few garden implements barely make a dent in the generous space of the workshop. Later in the year, it will fill with bags of coal and half a ton of logs. But today the sun is shining and I am not looking that far ahead. Instead, I think how rewarding it will be to fill that capacious and empty freezer which lurks in the corner. I open its lid, picturing layers of home-grown bounty: sliced courgettes, tiny French beans, baby broad beans by the bag-full, tomatoes, made into purée with and without garlic and shallot, savoury delights there for the taking. Then there will be fruit: individually-frozen raspberries, apples many ways, ready for transformation into sauce or pancake fillings at the drop of a pip. Optimism restored, I carry the surprisingly light Flymo to the front garden and set it down to prepare it for our first challenge. I feel I have an ally now.

Two hours later, already hot and bothered after only half the lawn is cut, my main achievement is that I have been greeted with smiles and waves by three tractor drivers and two bus-loads of passengers travelling in each direction. Welcome to the public face of St John's Row; and to the realities of a large garden. Ever the recorder, I take a photograph to mark the occasion of half a lawns-worth of mowing. Later, I will swear that the grass put on a spurt of growth in the space of one half lawn and the next. That might have been so. My estimates of how long this job would take are short by a country mile.

Four hours later I am pouring with perspiration. The Flymo is definitely not up to this task. A bad workman may blame his tools, but it was my foolish decision to cut the grass while it was still wet. Untidy lumps of compressed grass litter the surface of the lawn. Some have even made their way into the flower beds where they sit and gloat as they dry out in the rising heat of the sun. The Flymo is belly-up more often than not, being cleared of blockages. Come to think of it, were all those travellers smiling or laughing? I can't bring myself to leave the front lawn looking like a waste site, so the fold-up canvas wheelbarrow is pressed into service. Soon, the barrow collapses into a heap. It endures only so many trips up and down the long, bumpy route to the compost heap before its wheel parts company with its axle. Country Living, Lesson One: ensure that you have the right tools for the job. I come out in sympathy with the wheelbarrow and collapse into a heap indoors, skin glowing, muscles screaming and pulse bouncing. Time to cool down and be tactical.

I phone John with a progress report and a plea.

'My broadband isn't connected yet, so could you be a pal and go online, see what's in the Diss auction catalogue for me. I need a bigger mower.'

'I wouldn't buy one at the auction if I were you', says John, 'because you might find yourself throwing good money after bad. Why not get yourself a bigger Flymo with a grass-box then you won't have to worry about collecting the grass. They're not that expensive.'

Telephone calls to three garden centres and even somewhere that sells seriously large reconditioned mowers reveal the awful truth: they *are* that expensive and well beyond my budget. Country Living, Lesson Two: always travel with a contingency sum in proportion to the magnitude of the task. Mine is found wanting and I've been here for only half a day.

A frugal and shamefully lazy supper of beans on toast tastes better for being eaten at the table against the backdrop of that view. My optimism waxes as the light wanes and sunset takes to the stage. I watch the last act upstairs, sitting on the wide sill of the bedroom window. I take a photograph. It is a little hurried and somewhat blurred. I'll do better next time. What a warming thought: there are plenty of next times to come and digital photography costs nothing. I feel up to unpacking some books now.

I made a careful selection of books to bring with me to Framsden. Hundreds more remain in Attleborough. As the bookcases fill, they reveal an eclectic mix. Why is it that the face of a book is infinitely more appealing than its spine, even when it lacks a dust-cover? I lift *Liberties and Communities in Medieval England* from the box. A slip of paper invites me in. The author, Helen Cam, opens with a spirited essay 'In Defence of the Study of Local History'. Professor Cam explains that 'He [the local historian] starts from a present-day objective reality, whether building, boundary, name or custom; he holds the live end of an unbroken thread running back into the past that he is exploring. He takes for granted the continuity of history, and it is in that continuity that not only the fascination but the justification of such researches... lies.' Her words fill me with pride that I am one of these doorstep-seekers-after-the-truth, a passionate amateur, here to renew my own particular connection with 'the live end' of history.

If you want to look into, rather than just look at the relationship between the English and their land, you need to delve into the roots that bind them. To understand what you find when you get there, you will need a good grasp of the law. In my hand, I hold a dog-eared copy of *Mozley and Whiteley's Law Dictionary*. Finding myself needing to understand the history of law was unexpected. But then if you're holding the live end of history you must be prepared for a few shocks.

My greatest shock, I recall now, was to recognise the difference between the version of history I was taught in my disinterested youth and the history I absorb from local records. Gradually, mediated versions and popular myth are demolished, falling like chess-pieces as I step warily across the board of local history. Speculation is anathema to its experienced practitioners, generalisations unwelcome. It is all too easy to fall off the board when it tilts dangerously in the direction of either. There must be some very good reason why I find myself wanting to clamber back on to that unforgiving incline. Surrounded by unpacked boxes of books, I open the album of my mind to view the reasons. The lens is more prismatic than magnifying, the image not always edifying. As the boxes empty and the book-cases fill, I recall my first ignominious arrival at Helmingham Hall in the early 1980s and what happened in the 27 years that followed.

❀ ❀ ❀

I approach Helmingham Hall from the main gates, drive along its imposing, tree-lined avenue. The experience was unforgettable, but for all the wrong reasons. This journey is my first as an independent driver, and coincides with my first visit to the Hall. The winter fog lifts to reveal the building against a clear blue sky. With its tall, twisted chimney stacks and warm red brick walls reflected in the still waters of the surrounding moat, Helmingham Hall is the epitome of serenity. I hold my breath briefly, position my front wheels on the wooden drawbridge spanning the moat. And then, discarded L-plates notwithstanding, I lose my nerve. The arched opening beneath the gatehouse looks impossibly narrow. I can see into the courtyard but getting there is beyond me. Gingerly, I reverse the car off the drawbridge and manoeuvre myself into a parking position on the grass. I climb out of the car and take a photograph of the Hall in this picture-perfect setting. And then the spell is broken.

A Land Rover approaches at high speed and comes to a halt alongside my car. It is only now that I notice the criss-cross of tyre marks imprinted on the frosty grass, and others revealing my thwarted approach and hasty departure from the drawbridge.

'Can I help you?' asks a voice from inside the vehicle.

'Oh, good morning. I have an appointment to meet Bill Serjeant in the Estate Office. Er, to look at some archives.' The hesitant offer of additional information is superfluous: Bill is Lord Tollemache's Honorary Archivist.

'That's fine. Just follow me in your car, would you? We normally expect our visitors to use the other entrance' – an arm through the window indicates a distant lodge cottage I had passed *en route* to the main gates.

'Ah', I say, weakly. At least I would know which entrance to use next time – if there is a next time, I think ruefully.

Landed estates rely upon their muniments: they may be meat and drink to historians but they provide families with essential, tangible evidence of title spanning centuries of right and responsibility, privilege and duty. The privilege for me is to be granted access, which not all family estates are willing or equipped to permit. Until the first decade of the 21st century, Bill Serjeant is Lord Tollemache's Honorary Archivist, lending professional support to the ongoing task of cataloguing and maintaining the Tollemache Family Archive. Bill is the retired Suffolk County Archivist and will be my mentor today and for many years to come as I step cautiously into the family's past. I am in an enviable position.

These days, I smile as I watch wide-eyed celebrities being supported at every step as they attempt to answer the question: 'Who do you think you are?' Archivists and specialists are on hand when they arrive at each specialist repository, ready and waiting with all the evidence and the hard work of cross-referencing and interpretation complete. Nonetheless, my smile is due more to a feeling of slight envy than to snobbish skepticism: local archivists in Suffolk and Norfolk confirm that the appetite for family history has increased exponentially as a result of the programme and its offshoot projects. There are many routes into history. Once in transit, few who begin the journey will choose to exit, as I am about to discover.

As I leave my notebook and pencils on the desk and look out to get my bearings, there, visible beyond the moat, is a clear view down the magnificent oak avenue lining the main drive. I blush at the thought of my arrival. Anyone working in this wing of the quadrangular Tudor building would have had a grandstand view. And word would travel fast along this narrow suite of rooms. Little wonder that one of the Estate staff came out at all speed to prevent me making an even bigger fool of myself.

Mid-way through that first morning, Bill introduces me to Lord Tollemache. The rest, as they say, is history. The catalogue comes to life as Bill and I follow this scion of a centuries-old family through an enfilade of elegant rooms on the ground floor of Helmingham Hall. It seems to me, nervously inquisitive as I am, that the rooms offer enticing glimpses of successive changes in architectural taste. Lord Tollemache pauses before a portrait of a flame-haired beauty wearing a shimmering, pale blue gown. The Countess of Dysart was a leading light in the Society of the Sealed Knot. As I struggle to put dates to events, and significance to both of them, Lord Tollemache goes on to explain that the Society's headquarters were here, at Helmingham Hall. The Countess was clever. She gained the trust of Oliver Cromwell. As a result, neither Helmingham nor the family's other property, Ham House (Richmond), was damaged, let alone confiscated. And a few steps later, in another room, this sudden immersion into the dangerously polarised world of the 17th century is confirmed. Lord Tollemache indicates a letter protected inside a glass case: 'That's the letter the King wrote to her later to thank her for all her efforts on his behalf. He was in France at the time, of course...'

Of course. In that moment, with dappled sunlight reflected off the barely ruffled waters of the moat, I begin to grasp the significance of what I am seeing and hearing. In the space of a few rooms and the span of a few ancestors, English history emerges through Tollemache family lives. Charles I, executed. With his head went the head of state; England had villified and ultimately destroyed the monarch who took liberties with theirs; a monarch who was seen to overrule rather than rule. Lord Tollemache's commentary breaks into my dawning recognition as he goes on to explain that the Countess wrote letters in code to other royalist supporters. They all did. Some of those letters survive in the family archive, as Bill shows me later. The Society's aim was to restore the monarchy and the monarch. And they succeeded. The exiled son of Charles I returned from France to become Charles II in 1660. This was how families like the Tollemaches shaped the course of history. Of course.

I return, wide-eyed, to desk and Victorian documents. With Bill's calm encouragement and expertise to guide me, I view a limited range of archives that will introduce me to the 19th-century model cottages built to house Estate employees. Soon, there is a pile of documents beside me and the day in which to enjoy them. The time passes all too quickly. This was to be the first of several visits, all of them memorable. Gradually, over a period of years, Bill introduces me to the complex, multi-volume catalogue of the Tollemache Family Archive. If I thought the house was old, I was in for a shock. The Tollemaches didn't settle in Helmingham until the late 1400s, but they had been in Suffolk since the 12th century. Their archive embraces more than 800 years of history. Theirs. Mine. England's.

Over the next twenty years or so, I find good reason to continue consulting the archive. In the late 1970s, I tuck my coveted Open University BA (Hons) in Humanities under my belt. The achievement came a bit late in life but it was worth every one of the six years of slog that led to it. I celebrate by joining the WEA [Workers' Educational Association] as a part-time tutor. I feel my way, guided (and frequently goaded) by locally-organised Branches whose members have an insatiable appetite for the history of Suffolk.

To begin with, I am loath to budge from what I know, which is broadly the history of town planning. I have a fascination for rural planning and development, especially any example that predates statutory provision. It is the presence of the many groups of Victorian estate cottages provided by the first Lord Tollemache that drew me to Helmingham. Once enthused, Suffolk WEA groups want to know more. Gradually, I feel my way back through 18th, then 17th-century emparking and landscape improvement schemes – anything that led to the creation of a 'model' settlement. I find fashion and philosophy, and much to challenge me, let alone my WEA groups. I know my limits. I reach them at Helmingham in the 16th century. What I find succeeds in shifting my perspective.

I have my first sight of Catherine Tollemache's 16th-century manuscripts. One of these contains recipes for food, perfume and colours. The instructions are offered with such clarity and economy of language that I am drawn immediately to their author. I work my way through only two-thirds of her manuscript before my world changes out of all recognition. From being a part-time tutor running a full-time, small business, and juggling the two to make ends meet, I become a full-time employee of the WEA. The role is new and organisational, designed to support Suffolk Branches. Teaching is not part of my remit, but I continue offering courses in my free time. This does not last. The responsibilities of the full-time role expand. As the Hale-Bopp comet streaks across the sky, I blink, reach my 50th birthday and find that I have a career, not a job; it takes me over because I allow it to.

Something had to give. I gave up teaching and put my research papers into storage. What others might have predicted, I could not see. It took almost ten years before I realised that this peremptory setting aside of my slow-burning passion for history had robbed me of something valuable, something humanising. I become as robotic as the technology that absorbs me and, increasingly, dominates my work. A rare visit to Helmingham one day brings this into perspective. I am there at one of the popular 'Plant Heritage' sales hosted in the park. The gardens are open to visitors. As I cross the garden from the causeway and walk into the parterre, I find myself recalling Catherine Tollemache's 16th-century recipes, and how her unequivocal instructions sprang to life when they were shared with visiting WEA groups and would emerge fresh and bright at the end of their searching questions. The recipes rely heavily on fruit and the productive garden at Helmingham remains full of it. Modern varieties of apples, apricots, peaches, pears, plums, cherries, figs and grapes mentioned in the 400-year-old recipes still cling to the sheltering walls and scramble up archways. Soft fruits – strawberries and 'respes' (her rapsberries) fill the beds.

What had happened to me since those days of shared discovery? Had the live end gone dead? It would be another decade before that chance encounter on a website prompts me to restore the connection. The silver gap opens just in time. And here I am, sitting on the floor of one of Helmingham Estate's model cottages, attempting to build a future through the past.

❋ ❋ ❋

The Framsden bookcases take no time at all to fill. This was a good way to end a physically challenging day: Tomorrow, I will begin to think how I should reacquaint myself with the Tollemache Family Archive.

The weather pattern of night-time wet and daytime dry persists. It puts paid to any hope of research activity. I fly the wretched mower over the burgeoning sward at least twice a week. And I have barely touched the back garden, giving it a cursory cut now and again, the equivalent of a lick and a promise. The promise remains unfulfilled. The neglected edges sprout six inches of spiky growth in a wayward green tonsure. Weeds flourish, taunting me every time I open the kitchen door. I am praying that the Estate Office does not plan to make an inspection visit. I have launched an initial attack on the front hedges and, as expected, progress is thwarted by inadequate tools. John has promised to bring Sue for a social visit next weekend, offering hedge-cutting services in return for a good lunch. It is an offer I cannot refuse.

It strikes me one afternoon as I de-clog the underside of the Flymo for the umpteenth time that I don't recall lifting my eyes to the beautiful landscape once in the past four hours. What happened to eulogy and poetry? Country Living, Lesson Three: if you must be a country gardener, then you must be prepared for nature to dictate the rules of engagement. A garden is like a domesticated animal: if you abandon it, it will revert to the wild and may even come back to bite you.

I am aggrieved that my headlong rush back into history has been stymied at the first hurdle. What an irony: where history is concerned, there is no bar-code, no sell-by date. Repetitive mowing might force my eyes down to the ground, robbing me of that view, but it does offer ample opportunity for self-scrutiny. If I want to make best use of this silver gap year, then it is time to put my passion to the test. I need to invest my energy into a piece of research that is achievable under the circumstances. But what?

At least I have established a mowing strategy. Today, the easy area is done; now comes the tougher, larger one. It is full of obstacles like trees and island beds. Persistence is essential. As I set off along the triangular route of the garden's boundaries, I ponder my research options: return to something I am familiar with or start anew? I swipe the Flymo along the 'Snow in Summer' border, carelessly lopping flower-heads. In the midst of a thicket of overgrown shrubs and plants, I stop the mower to clear a way. A plant seems to have sprouted overnight. What's this? I don't recall seeing this before. Its leaves resemble those of wisteria and pale mauve flowers are emerging in profusion. The plant is rampaging its way through the bed and threatening to swamp everything in its path. The sight of it triggers a memory, dim but insistent. Obstacle cleared, I frown as the Flymo glides effortlessly over the smooth, downward slope from the apple tree towards the path. There is something about that plant and the Tollemache family: something to do with recipes. Swish-swishing around the fading deutzia, hoovering up its spent confetti of fallen blossom, it comes to me. The plant resembles milk vetch. I feel sure there is some connection between Catherine Tollemache, her 16th-century recipes and milk vetch.

As dusk falls, the grass lies uncollected in heaps: it is dead anyway. A small part of the half-millennium of Tollemache history, on the other hand, has just come to life with a vengeance.

The scent of garlic and rosemary lingers in the kitchen. A casserole of lamb with cannellini beans, leeks, tomatoes and herbs, prepared in advance of the garden onslaught, has been eaten and enjoyed. Now I can search out my 30-year-old notes. Catherine Tollemache's prodigious output, and my laborious transcription of her recipes, fills and enriches my senses. Fruit, hundredweights of it, finds its way into her pastes, preserves and conserves. Flower-petals, roots and seeds are crystallised patiently over many days, some of them used to decorate her home-made marchpane. Then I find the reference I seek in her recipe 'To make wallnutts artificiall'. Sugar dominates, as it does in most of her high-end foods to impress; but in addition to those mind-boggling 'like [equal] quantities of sugar and cinnamon', the Renaissance lady instructs her acolyte to: 'Mix with gum dragon steeped in rose-water'. And there, in my girlish 20th-century hand is a note reading: 'gum dragon = tragacanth = (probably) *Astragalus gummifer* (RHS New Encyclopaedia of Herbs & Their Uses, pp 136-7)'. Needless to say, the *Encyclopaedia* is to hand. I note with interest that there are 2000 varieties of milk vetch but I need not pursue them. Despite similarities, my plant is not one of them but galega (goat's rue); that is immaterial now. Its inspiration was all I needed. I settle in for a long night with Catherine Tollemache and her gum dragon.

It is 2 am. My eyelids are drooping but my spirits are high. By then, I have found gum dragon throughout the 16th-century recipes. It is the essential fixative in her sugary conceits. Without it, her 'wallnuts artificiall' would sink and sag, and her wide range of 'artificiall fruites' would be nothing more than a mass of shapeless sugar. Tragacanth finds its way into her household commodities, too: she adds it to starch, washing balls and candles before she perfumes them... Perfumed starch to sweeten the deeply layered ruff that adorns her neck in a 1597 portrait... washing balls, her personal soap, applied to those noble but hard-working hands, their finger-tips scorched by the constant testing of heated sugar... no wonder she wears gloves in that portrait; perfumed candles to burn in a chamber, to mask the unavoidable odours of life... In my chamber, achingly tired, I stretch out where I sit, fully clothed, lacking the energy to transform the sofa into a bed. The lady's transformational achievements are scattered all around on the floor. Catherine Tollemache would have been appalled at such slovenly behaviour.

Next day, the sun is out. I am yawning but full of conflicting and exciting ideas about how to re-visit the 16th-century recipes in a way that will celebrate their writer and her remarkable skills. Today marks the connection of my broadband service, too. I am tempted to linger over my e-mail but dry days cannot be wasted, so I celebrate with loud huzzahs and an attack on the neglected rear garden. Armed with the Flymo, which is so grass-spattered and mud-speckled as to be unrecognisable, I step out purposefully for a morning of restitution. It doesn't last. The Flymo wreaks its revenge for my careless treatment of it yesterday. Just before mid-day, I cut clean through its electrical cable and my labours come to a precipitate conclusion with a loud bang. The mower sits smugly in the middle of the oval lawn with a foot of cable attached. I, meanwhile, stand disconsolately with the other eleven feet in my hand, breathing a silent prayer of gratitude for the circuit-breaker that has undoubtedly saved my life. Restoring life to the Flymo necessitates a thirty-mile round trip to the nearest supplier of Replacement Cables for the Careless. And so passes another day at Framsden.

When dusk falls, I turn to the Internet for solace, intent on nothing more than an evening of restorative calm. My bank account, on the other hand, is about to get the shock of its life.

With no expectation of finding anything, I enter 'Catherine Tollemache' as the search term. Google takes me by surprise, tells me there are 'about 126,000 results'. Really? I opt not to Follow Catherine on Facebook or Find Catherine on LinkedIn or buy her from Amazon; but I do find something that shames my ignorance. Before my disbelieving eyes, and the silent 'O' of my open mouth, I read of a volume published by the Roxburghe Club in 2001: *The Tollemache Book of Secrets: A Descriptive Index and Complete Facsimile with an introduction and transcriptions together with Catherine Tollemache's 'Receipts of Pastery, Confectionary &c', by Jeremy Griffiths, completed by A.S.G. Edwards.*

I access the homepage of the Roxburghe Club website. The Club is, I learn, 'the oldest society of bibliophiles in the world', founded in 1812. It is exclusive. Membership is limited to 40, chosen from among those with distinguished libraries or collections, or with a scholarly interest in books. Each member is expected to commission a presentation volume at his or her own expense. Beyond those for members, 300 further copies may be produced for circulation; sales are limited strictly to this number. Seven years ago, *The Book of Secrets* was Lord Tollemache's presentation volume. I read on: members' copies are bound in half-calf, with the individual recipient's name printed in red within the list of members. Copies produced for public consumption will be bound in cloth. I learn that I may buy a new (cloth-bound) copy for an eye-watering sum from Maggs Bros. Ltd., book-sellers of Berkeley Square, 'By Appointment to Her Majesty the Queen, Purveyors of Books and Rare Manuscripts'.

Alternatively, a secondhand copy is available from a dealer in rare books for £375 plus postage and packing. I e-mail him and plead eloquently. Is there, perhaps, a volume of *The Book of Secrets* that one might describe as… I struggle for the words… a working copy? I explain my particular interest. I wait. I dare not call up my spreadsheet of living expenses, constructed and calculated to ensure my survival as I sustain two properties until one of them attracts a buyer. I know the limitations of my budget only too well. I toss and turn, sleepless from dark till dawn, plagued by images of recalcitrant mowers, collapsing compost heaps and the bank foreclosing on my Norfolk cottage, which is wrapped in blue cloth.

Next day, I crouch over my computer until a reply from the book-dealer drops insouciantly into my e-mail account. The courteous respondent is sorry, but no, this is the only copy in stock and it is in perfect condition. It would be. What else did I expect. 'However…' I seize on his 'however', hope rising… However, given my scholarly interest, he would be willing to waive the cost of postage and packing. Do telephone, he invites, if I would like to pay him by card. How can I refuse?

I live on permutations of eggs and baked beans for the next panic-stricken three days. It seems appropriate somehow to do penance in advance of the deed. That way I can better endure the guilt when my purchase arrives.

On the fourth day, the postman arrives. I watch, spellbound, as he opens my gate and walks up the path. I rush to meet him.

'Hello', he greets me cheerily, 'I need a signature for this one'. I'm not surprised. I am tempted to prick my arm and sign in blood. Is that shaky inscription really mine?

'Thank you, thank you SO much', I say to a surprised postman.

'You're welcome! Hope you have a lovely day'.

Oh, I will. And a lovely few days after that.

Unpacking the *Secrets* is akin to anticipating first sight of the Holy Grail. Layers of significance waft through my sleep-starved brain, doubtless fuelled by guilt, inadequate calorie intake and heightened expectation. The packing is exquisitely done and there is much of it. I almost don't want it to come to an end.

But suddenly, there it is. I lift the book from its final protective bed. The first thing I recognise, with a tingle of anticipation, is the half-calf binding. This extends to the inner edges of front and rear covers, the remainder of which are covered in darkest blue cloth. I hold my breath: this was never a public sales copy. This is a Roxburghe Club member's copy of the finest quality. Emblazoned in gold on the front cover is the familiar Tollemache family fret contained within a shield and surmounted by a winged horse. The spine reads simply 'The Book of Secrets'. The words are inscribed in gold. I tilt the top of the book towards me. The mid-morning sun catches the glint of more gold: the top of each page is gilded.

I open the cover and turn to the list of members. There, inscribed in red, is the name of Lord Wardington, who died in 2005. The 2nd Lord Wardington was a leading English bibliophile.

I have never owned such a beautiful book in my life. I doubt that I ever will again.

I am right about the first, wrong about the second.

Perfidy follows my over-indulgence; duplicity becomes second nature; withdrawal of social contact follows.

'Are you alright down there in the depths?'

'Yes, yes, fine, thank you.'

'I just wondered… I've left three messages and you haven't returned any of my calls'.

Of course not, you foolish person, you called me from your mobile phone and I have absolutely no intention of putting my bank-balance at further peril.

'Ah. I've been out a lot.'

'Oh? Where?'

'Walking'.

'Walking? Is there something wrong with the car?'

'I don't have to drive everywhere, you know…'

'Yes you do! You can't do anything except post a letter in that place. Come on, what have you been up to?'

'Gosh! I must go – I can smell my dinner burning!'

'Dinner? It's only four o'clock!'

'Ah! Yes! I'm going out shortly. Must dash. 'Bye.'

I can't bear to go online to check my bank balance unless night has fallen and the curtains are closed. The glare of the monitor is the stark light of truth. I can't think why I bother: I know my outgoings to the penny. But the reality check is essential to remind me of the magnitude of what I have done. I console myself: it's all a question of cash-flow, which can be controlled. I manipulate the spreadsheets – again. Perhaps if I reduce the amount I budgeted to spend on winter heating … and if I shop only once a month then my petrol will be less… and as for birthday and Christmas gifts – well, they will be infinitely more modest this year.

Little by little, I inch the total savings up to about two-thirds of what I need to close the gap. I am about one hundred pounds short. There is nothing for it, I will have to go to Norfolk and scour my house for things to sell.

The next Saturday morning finds me in Diss at dawn, my car loaded with what I hope will be irresistibly saleable goods. The queue inches along to the auction house valuer, a patient soul who must disabuse people of their belief that 'this is worth something'. They always know, they tell him, because they've seen one just like it on e-Bay, Bargain Hunt, Antiques Roadshow – and it was worth THOUSANDS. I want to turn tail and run, but suddenly I am at his table, clutching two carrier bags full of portable items and waving a hand in the direction of my car filled with small pieces of furniture. One item, a book, needless to say, is earmarked for the 'Special Antiques' sale, two for the 'Modern and General', one is consigned to the 'Outside Pens'. The valuer tells me kindly to take the rest home.

Items are catalogued by Wednesday, viewed on Thursday and sold on Friday. I expect to make about £150 so I'll have a little in hand.

The entire haul yields £94.78 after vendor's costs.

Fondling the *'Secrets'* one evening, and wondering whether or not I am yet certifiably insane or on the rapid route to book-addiction, I have a phone call from John in his capacity as my business partner. We met and worked together on a high-profile WEA project. When that came to end, we harnessed our skills and set up a small business together in Attleborough. John is an innovative bespoke software developer and I am the buffer, the communicator, working front of house. Not everyone can think in code. Sometimes our clients need help in articulating what it is they think they want their programme to achieve. Since the move to Framsden I contribute only the occasional day as I withdraw gradually from the business. John has news.

'Do you remember that charity we worked for in Ipswich a couple of years ago? We developed a diagnostic programme for them so they could tailor learning materials. Well, they've been on the phone today. They've got a bit of a problem. They think you might be able to help them out.'

The bit of a problem proves to be a panic to complete some unfinished research into local community needs and write a report on the findings. The consultancy fee offered is £500. The completion deadline is less than four weeks away. I discuss it with John. We agree that this is not a piece of work for the business, but a personal commission for me. I go to Ipswich the next day, sign a contract, get on with the job.

The grass grows unheeded. The cottage and the *Secrets* gather dust. I throw myself into the challenge. The report is submitted on time. At the end of it, I am physically and mentally drained but my finances are buoyant. The penny drops as the consultancy fee reaches my bank account. Repeat after me or write out five hundred times: I must NOT do this again. For 'this' read 'put my already perilous existence at risk'.

At least now I can indulge in the *Secrets* without suffering palpitations brought on by excessive guilt. I get as far as the Foreword, written by Nicolas Barker, member of the Roxburghe Club, eminent and acknowledged authority on antiquarian books. In a scholarly commentary, Mr Barker introduces the Tollemache family and their 800 years of association with Suffolk. This is familiar territory. He outlines the building of the Hall, explains how it was altered subsequently, but without losing its 'distinctive early Tudor character'. And then, just as I think I am safe from the world of the bibliophile, he invades my resolve with another Roxburghe Club delight, the one he wrote in 1988, a volume that provides not one but two facsimiles. *Two East Anglian Picture Books* compares a pair of illuminated medieval manuscripts that once belonged at Helmingham Hall. More than that, they were, in all likelihood, commissioned by the Tollemache family at around the time the Hall was built. If so, they were there to greet Catherine Tollemache 70 years later when she came to the Hall as a young bride. The association is enough to have me alert and excited; the topic has me on the edge of my seat: one of the medieval manuscripts is known as the *Helmingham Herbal and Bestiary*. The other is held by the Bodleian Library and is catalogued as a *Tudor Pattern Book*. This is a manuscript that provided source material for tapestry, embroidery and other forms of applied decoration.

Enthused, I perceive how to draw together a small part of the immense riches of the Tollemache Family Archive and share them within a broader church. I see a route mapped out ahead: extract the recipes from the rarefied air of the privileged bibliophile and present them in their domestic setting. I will use the herbal and other household evidence to give them substance. This should make it possible to interpret the recipes in the round, revealing everything from their raw materials to their use at Helmingham Hall. There will be something of interest for historians of many persuasions, including those keen to find authentic evidence of domestic and culinary activity, irrespective of its regional provenance.

Inspiration is everything. I know I will be inspired if I can get a look at the contents of at least one of those medieval manuscripts described so invitingly by Nicolas Barker.

Before I run headlong down the path in mind, I write a formal letter to Lord Tollemache seeking his permission to work on the recipes with a view to presenting them for publication, eventually, in a culinary and domestic context. He replies generously, has no objection, is happy for me to proceed.

I contact the Bodleian Library. Yes, the Tudor pattern book volume is accessible but it would be best to make an appointment. Alternatively, if I know what images I would like to see, they could photograph them for me and transmit them by e-mail.

I re-read Nicolas Barker's introduction to the *Secrets*. He describes how he was tempted by an image in the Bodleian volume; he believes the illustration, made in or around the late 1400s, may represent the Hall, newly built. I contact the Bodleian Library. Yes, they can locate that image readily. Would I like a photograph of it? I am putty in their hands. The dithering and delay only increase my anticipation. I am not disappointed.

The image arrives and I cannot quite believe the beauty of it, the depth and richness of its colours. The original illustration is at least five hundred years old. It is illuminating, and no mistake. The Bodleian has been generous: there were three images on the same page. They have sent the entire page, revealing that the fanciful medieval house is not the main subject, but part of its border design. The page is dominated by two plants: despite their stylised design and the archaic presentation of their names, both are instantly recognisable. Rushes: they grow abundantly in damp patches in the park surrounding Helmingham Hall. Ramsons, wild garlic. It grows abundantly here in the local hedgerows.

I launch myself into a frenzy of fact-finding. What is the train fare from Ipswich to Oxford? And is it more or less costly to travel from Norwich to Oxford? And how many trips might it take me to view *Ashmole MS 1504*, the *Tudor Pattern Book*, the single volume of these Helmingham-related illuminated manuscripts that the Bodleian holds in its care? I doubt that I could do justice to such a volume in a day. I would not be allowed to take photographs myself, but the bill for just one digital image made me wince. I learn from the Bodleian catalogue that the volume contains 98 illuminations. I add it all up. The cost is prohibitive, even if I select only a few images to be photographed. In any case, it still leaves me without a view of that other volume described by Nicolas Barker, a close copy of the Bodleian manuscript, the one known as the *Helmingham Herbal and Bestiary*. Unless…

I send an e-mail to my worthy book-dealer friend. He replies promptly. He does, indeed, have a copy of *Two East Anglian Picture Books*.

The postman comes up the path with another parcel a few weeks later.

Don't ask.

Above: Hoar-frosted Estate land, Framsden.

Below: Memorial in St Mary's church, Helmingham, honouring three generations of Tollemache gentlemen in the lower arcades, and the 1st baronet above them.

Author's images

3: With all due respect

My reacquaintance with the world of Helmingham Hall and its Tollemache family in the 15th and 16th centuries is coloured, inevitably, by the beautiful books that I have risked so much to acquire. But the investment repays me handsomely every time I open either volume. Nonetheless, I feel the need to come back down to earth. Nothing is more grounding than historical research. It is detective work, a painstaking journey from questions to answers through evidence. Sometimes the route is tortuous and filled with temptation, a veritable *Pilgrim's Progress* of obstacles and pitfalls, byways and cul-de-sacs for the unwary traveller. I am beginning to recognise already that I am in danger of attempting to follow too many routes. Despite my avowed intent to concentrate on the household, I cannot ignore what is evident every time I open my curtains here at Framsden. Inevitably, it is the quality of the surrounding countryside, all part of the Estate, that delights me on a daily basis. I ask myself what makes it palpably different from any other slice of productive Suffolk agricultural land. The simple answer is that the same family has owned, controlled and cultivated its resources for over 500 years. Now, as one of their tenants, I have become one of those resources. As a result, I feel I owe a debt that outweighs my monthly rent, yet if pushed to qualify or quantify this debt, I would find it difficult to explain; but I do know that it relates to my environment and my appreciation of it.

On an early foray into the village, no more than an exploratory stroll, I look more closely at my surroundings. This is a working landscape. Farming is what keeps the environment looking as it does, but it is a particular kind of farming, one that puts stewardship high on the list of priorities. The fields are relatively small. Hedges are laid in the traditional way, encouraging them to grow and flourish. Their health and vigour is apparent. They provide varied and reliable habitat for wildlife; they, and the wide grass verges that are a feature of St John's Row, are rich in flora. I see a Robin's pin-cushion for the first time in years. Simple discoveries like this please me, cause me to be grateful that I am here. I used to revel in looking out for these mossy red tufts in the hedgerows when I was a child. The fact that they are caused by a gall wasp that lays its eggs on the wild rose makes them no less attractive to me – then or now. The recollection reminds me of something I read in my cherished copy of the *Secrets*, in one of the medieval manuscripts collected and cherished by Catherine Tollemache. These documents were at least a century old by the time she read them and several relate to colours, which seem to have fascinated her. One manuscript describes how to make a variety of coloured inks. Black ink relies on oak gall. I wonder, did she collect any from the hedgerow oaks that flourish in the vicinity of Helmingham?

As I climb the last few yards to the Y-junction, the chimneys and roofs of St John's Row come into view. I pause before I cross the road. As I recall the impact of the proposed, ill-considered infill development that prompted my flight from Attleborough, I wonder whether Victorian Framsden people were appalled at the intrusion of St John's Row, perhaps seeing it as a waste of good agricultural land; or did they stand in awe, envious at the thought of all the modern conveniences that the occupants of the new cottages would enjoy? And what of relationships with their landlord, who would be rewarded for his commitment with elevation to the title of 1st Lord Tollemache?

As I unlock the cottage door, I think about the Tollemache line and its presence here from the House of Tudor to the House of Windsor. The imperative for the Hall's late medieval builder, and his successors, was to ensure a future for their heirs. How did they do it? A good place in which to remind myself of the family and its long history is St Mary's, the parish church at Helmingham. Here, generations of Tollemaches are remembered.

✿ ✿ ✿

Dominating the south side of the nave, four generations of public service are reflected in a soaring, colourful, arcaded memorial. At the top is the first baronet, Sir Lionel, who commissioned this monument prior to his death in 1612. Below are three generations of his ancestors: father, grandfather and great-grandfather respectively, dating back to the early 1500s. All served variously as Justices of the Peace, Sheriffs of Suffolk, Earl Marshall of Norfolk and Suffolk. Public service is in the blood. The present (5th) Lord Tollemache is Lord Lieutenant of Suffolk.

✿ ✿ ✿

Prompted by my visit to the church, I eschew my Roxburghe Club beauties and turn instead to my copy of *The Tollemaches of Helmingham and Ham*, written in 1949 by Maj.-Gen. E.D.H. Tollemache. He traces the story of his ancestors from their 12th-century arrival in Suffolk from Normandy. They settled at Bentley (south of Ipswich), less than 20 miles from Helmingham. In the 1480s, one of the Bentley Tollemaches married into a Helmingham family. He and his heiress wife built Helmingham Hall on the site of her family's older house some time between 1487 and 1510, but the Bentley estate was retained. The Major-General's narrative leads and guides through the family's consistently loyal support of crown and country, through lives lost and fortunes forged. However, he mentions a 'spendthrift' descendant, who is never identified by name. It seems that at some point in the 16th century, a bet was made and lost; as a consequence, much of the Bentley estate was lost with it, except for some areas of woodland. I am intrigued. This is a byway I cannot ignore.

✿ ✿ ✿

An Internet search of The National Archives confirms that they hold copies of the wills of the three earliest 16th-century Tollemache gentlemen whose memorials I admired in the church. I begin with the most recent will (1575) and work back through the next (1572) and end with the earliest (1552). This approach enables me to develop more familiarity with handwriting and terminology, which, in turn, gives me more confidence to cope with the increasing challenge posed by earlier wills. I may not be quick but I have the luxury of time. I favour working in short bursts and keeping careful notes. Some weeks I have to spend more than one day at work in Norfolk as well as keeping the garden under control here at Framsden, so by restricting myself to small pieces of transcription, I do not feel discouraged by my slow progress.

Inevitably, questions abound. I answer some of them by spending my Saturday mornings in the Suffolk Record Office in Ipswich. The proximity of this resource is another bonus of living at Framsden, which is barely ten miles away on a pleasant rural route: this compares with 50 miles each way and much of those on thundering main roads from my Norfolk cottage. I browse reference works on the open shelves of the public Search Room. Inevitably, I decide to buy some books that I think are essential. Several are handbooks designed for quick reference and their titles force me to admit that I have forgotten much of the learning I did years before. The selection particularly useful for this piece of work includes: *Words from Wills and other probate records* by Stuart A. Raymond; *Simple Latin for Family Historians* by Eve McLaughlin; and, indispensably, *Reading Tudor and Stuart Handwriting*, produced by the British Association for Local History and written by Lionel Munby, Steve Hobbs and Alan Crosby. I add them to my existing collection. The Framsden bookcases begin to sag.

What I learn is that 16th-century wills are concerned with the bequest of portable goods. Items of jewellery, wine, clothing, linen, especially bedding, all are described and their distribution stipulated carefully. Often, there is little or nothing to describe the extent of what the heir will receive by way of land and property. This was taken for granted and mentioned briefly, if at all. It will be a long time before I discover other ways to find out more, but that time will come.

I discern an image of gentlemanly generosity amongst the 16th-century Tollemaches. Some express their bequests in ways that reveal touches of thoughtfulness, both to family members and to servants. I am particularly taken by the 1572 will of Lionel Tollemache 'the Elder', gentleman, of Helmingham. He paid particular attention to the gifts intended for his unmarried female beneficiaries, bequeathing money to enable them to make their own choice of coverlets for the beds he bequeathed to them. Not all of my friends share my point of view, but I think of the immense pleasure I derive from book tokens, garden gift tokens, anything that delivers that precious gift of choice. The pleasure is doubled in the choosing and, I feel sure, this was as true in the 16th century as it is now.

What becomes obvious from the dates of the wills is that the Tollemaches lost four generations of male heirs in the space of 60 years. That was not all they lost. The 1572 will is hedged around with stringent conditions imposed on the heir. These include the occupation of Helmingham Hall by a pair of trusted gentlemen for one month immediately after the testator's death. The heir was forbidden to lay hands on a single item of household goods until the trusty watchers had drawn up a detailed list of everything portable. That done, their watchfulness was to extend until the heir had properly executed his responsibilities as executor of his father's will. Furthermore, the heir would be 'bownd in the sum of one thowsand pounds' to these gentlemen until he had completed the task. One thousand pounds in 1570 is worth roughly £174,000 sterling (in 2005). The will undoubtedly reveals a level of mistrust between father and son.

I catch sight of the heir through his own will. When I add up the gifts of gold rings, each specified by weight, and the extensive bequests of cash, I see a man who likes to spend freely; is, perhaps, generous to a fault. But there is a problem. During his lifetime, this Lionel Tollemache, constrained by the enduring limitations of his father's will, is not permitted to raise money from all but a small portion of the Helmingham estate. The exception is to ensure a satisfactory settlement of 'joniture and dower' for his wife. My trusty *Mozley and Whiteley's Law Dictionary* confirms legal definitions for both jointure and dower. In a nutshell, when the phrase is used in a will, it refers to the financial provision for a widow. The restricted Lionel Tollemache did predecease his wife and only outlived his father by three years, dying in 1575. On his deathbed, he made hurried arrangements for his widow and in so doing, left a massive debt for his son.

The evidence, a document dated just eighteen days before he was buried, bears Lionel's tortuous signature, striking evidence of his proximity to life's end. *In extremis,* and citing the burden of restriction created by his father's will, he signs away to his wife's brother the right to receive income from 800 acres of prime agricultural land. In return, his brother-in-law agrees to settle 'all outstanding debts to diverse men' and also to pay his sister, the soon-to-be-widow, an income for her natural life. Where was the land? It is part of 'the manor of Framsden'. Now I am even more intrigued. History is on my doorstep and no mistake.

What was the brother-in-law, Robert Jermyn, to pay for these 800 acres of Framsden? 'Twelve pennies of lawfull money'. Twelve pennies in 1575 are roughly equivalent to £8 now. In return for this derisory sum, the 1575 income for Robert Jermyn would be in the region of £164 per annum in rents payable by tenants of the land. How long was this to go on before it was deemed that the debt was settled?

'Twenty-and-one years from the date hereof', which would be at the end of 1596. The debts Jermyn cleared, and the payments he made to his sister, must have been considerable because £164 in 1575 is worth in the region of £29,000 now. The value of money fluctuated considerably over the 21 years of the agreement, reducing to an equivalent of around £16,000 by 1596. By then, the heir to Helmingham, another Lionel Tollemache, had reached maturity, accessed his inheritance when he married at the age of 18, had been married for 17 years and had 7 children of his own. No wonder the family showed signs of celebration the next year, 1597, marked by the painting of a portrait of his wife, Catherine (the recipe writer), and the making of some modest alterations to Helmingham Hall. The challenge they faced during those 21 years lends a new perspective to my view of what Catherine achieved. The household had to be managed to maintain a balance between high-status hospitality and strict domestic economy. I can see that finding the right context in which to explore and share the story of life in the 16th-century household is not going to be straightforward. But then history is like that.

❀ ❀ ❀

Returning to St Mary's church, Helmingham, weeks later, I gaze up again at the great family memorial, feeling renewed respect and sympathy for the man at the top, created Sir Lionel in the year he died, the first man in his family to achieve a title. Who would guess that this image of familial piety and honour conceals years of accumulated debt and bad feeling between at least two of the gentlemen beneath his feet? Who would imagine that he and his wife did not have full enjoyment of the Helmingham estate for the first two decades of their marriage, carrying a burden of debt created by an earlier generation? But that's the point: the sweeping rhetoric and representation of solidarity expressed by the monument are meaningful. 'Look at us', it proclaims, 'we are united; between us we served crown and country, remained loyal to our monarch no matter what, and we will continue to survive and serve through successive generations. We stand for, and by, our family, no matter what; and we honour them, no matter what.' Unlike Sir Lionel, who had to work for it, his son inherited the title in 1612, and with it an estate unencumbered by debt. It helped that he married an heiress, but, as I was to discover, he also had support from his remarkable mother, Catherine, the recipe writer, whose other achievements I hope to bring to light, eventually.

I walk the few yards through the nave and into the chancel. I look up at Catherine Tollemache's modest and delicately decorated memorial. I can't read the inscription from ground level, so I take a photograph. A preview of the digital image reveals two words heavy with significance: 'loved and honoured'.

Honour. What defines it? I leave the church weighing up the complex demands of financial debt and debts of honour, asking myself how they differ fundamentally from the simple expressions of respect where nothing is owing yet much is due.

I feel in need of inspiration. I find it, yet again, in an association with plants.

❀ ❀ ❀

The gardens of Helmingham Hall are as magnetic as its archives. Even when they are closed to visitors, I can invoke their beauty at any time thanks to a large collection of 35mm slides and digital images. It is while I am admiring an image of the rose garden, part of the modern, historically sympathetic development spearheaded by Lady Tollemache in the 1980s, that I recall an odd association between roses and honour, and, more specifically, red roses demanded in lieu of rent. My slides include an image of the tomb of William Clopton, white and alabaster-cool, at rest in Long Melford church, with a red rose laid on his armoured breast. I find my notes: Clopton is honoured annually with this presentation of a red rose by the residents of Hadleigh, Suffolk. The ceremony derives from an agreement of 1436 when Clopton permitted the use of land in Hadleigh for a market. There was to be no payment of rent in cash but a red rose *'sy pytatur'* – if demanded. I browse the Internet, using 'rose in lieu of rent' as the search parameter. I set myself a simple first task: find out how frequently similar demands are mentioned in surviving records. History is eloquent in its reply.

I scour The National Archives and British History Online, both unquestionable sources of authentic records. The results are astonishing: I find over three thousand surviving documentary records dating from 1200 onwards in which a red rose at Midsummer is accepted in lieu of a year's rent, or a rose and more. This is history as theatre because I am forced to suspend my disbelief in the face of hard evidence. Payments in lieu of rent are made with everything from 'a snowball at midsummer' to 'a red rose at Christmas'. Really? I delve further and find the range and combination of tokens to be almost beyond belief, including 'One red rose garland and one barbed or broad arrow, with two rosebuds at the Feast of John the Baptist'.

My next task is to analyse the examples to see what they reveal. Quickly, I detect a clear pattern. There are symbols related to battle where the token rents are paid in the form a sparrowhawk, a pair of spurs, a pair of gilded spurs, one white glove, a gauntlet, a pair of gauntlets, a pair of gloves or even a right-hand glove or a left-hand one; barbed arrows, a point of steel, a catapult. Then there are the floral ones, the most intriguing of which demands 'four odoriferous flowers, a marigold at Christmas, a violet at the Anunciation, a red rose at St John the Baptist [Midsummer] and a carnation at Michaelmas'. The rose recurs: one rose, one white rose, one fresh rose, a chaplet of roses, a wreath of roses, a garland of roses, a red rose at Christmas, a rose at Pentecost, and a very reasonable 'rose at the time of roses'.

Then I find that one 12th-century deed demands a rent of 'One rose valued at one penny'. This suggests that sometimes a cash value can be ascribed to tokens of honour. I look again at the analysis and find a group of sought-after and expensive commodities. Unlike the red rose, which seems blatantly symbolic and not commercial in its own right, these commodities do have economic value. The range is diverse: a gallon of wine at the Feast of St Michael, 3 hens, 2 capons, a pound of wax, a root of ginger, a clove, a clove of garlic, a grain of wheat, two pounds of pepper, half a pound of cumin, a pound of cumin, a dish of honey, and even 'a flask of lamp oil and a rose'.

It seems clear that the symbols related to war can be interpreted as a measure of the honourable recognition between serving or fighting men. The floral ones, most especially the rose, are an acknowledgement of loyalty. The commodities, somewhere between the two, are more difficult to place but suggest that effort and some expenditure is required even if the payment is not handed over in hard cash. Cash, it seems, is the last thing being demanded. It is the expression of honour that is valued. When I feel I have scraped the surface as far as I dare without compromising the evidence with some ham-fisted interpretation, I seek help from Susan, a respected archivist friend of mine in Norfolk. What I'd really like to know, I tell her, is how long this has been going on and, if possible, why it began at all.

What Susan confirms is that before the time of written records, or 'deeds', a transfer of land demanded the presence of both parties, one of them often a monarch, to acknowledge the status of giver and receiver. At this time, cash was not at issue. The exchange was confirmed by giving land in return for services – what we have come to understand as the feudal system. However, if the high-status giver could not attend in person, there needed to be a symbolic recognition of his presence. In recognition of his hand in the time-honoured, deal-sealing act of a handshake, the symbol was a glove. The rose was a symbol of investiture, or perhaps better described as invesment: the rose declared loyalty. Later in time, cash replaced labour services as the currency of exchange, and handshakes were replaced by written agreements, signed and sealed. Nonetheless, in situations where cash was of little or no importance, the old symbols of recognition became potent symbols of honour. Their presence in a written agreement speaks volumes: 'I have no need of your cash but I demand your recognition, which you will present to me in a tangible form'.

The picture then becomes clear: all those 'odoriferous flowers' and the combinations of other commodities demanded effort, not money. To present a snowball in midsummer (demanded and deliverable in areas such as Derbyshire where there are deep, cool caves), or a rose at Christmas (entirely possible and often demanded by landlords in balmy Cornwall) meant making effort. Effort, or evidence of it, proclaimed respect. Respect was more valuable than mere cash. Respect is synonymous with honour. A demonstration of honour may be demanded.

Convincing myself that this sojourn in medieval England was time well-spent, I convert what I have learned. Without doubt, I have a better understanding of the currency of honour. Equipped with this, I feel ready now to reacquaint myself with the Tollemache Family Archive. Here, I want to learn more about the relationships between privilege and duty, right and responsibility. In particular, I want to see how they manifest themselves in that all important 16th century, 32 years of which were occupied by Catherine Tollemache in her role as mistress of the house at Helmingham Hall, and the last of those as wife of the 1st baronet.

❀ ❀ ❀

The process has not changed in thirty years. Every visit to the archives is preceded by a catalogue search. There are numerous volumes relating to this branch of Tollemache family history alone. Browsing the catalogues can take a day and I do this preparatory work at the Suffolk Record Office in Ipswich. Armed with a list of the references to documents that I would like to view, I write to Bill, who is now in his eighties and still serving as Lord Tollemache's honorary archivist. Bill checks that my cited references are correct and that documents are accessible, then he seeks Lord Tollemache's permission on my behalf. Sometimes the documents are sent to Ipswich on temporary loan, and I return there to the Record Office at intervals over a month or so to view them. But today is special, because one document I have asked to see can be viewed only at the Hall.

Deer lift their antlered heads lazily as I park the car and walk to the Hall, concerned to carry on browsing, as am I. They are certain of what they will find. I am not, and that is the feeling I relish. I leave my own life behind as I cross the moat on the east side of the house: this is more than metaphor. I am treading from present to past. I encourage the sensation, choosing to stop briefly at the mid-point of the drawbridge, taking a deep breath and enjoying the panoramic view of the modern knot gardens behind me, the park stretching to the horizon on either side. This is a moment of anticipation. By the time I return to cross the drawbridge, I will be richer, more rewarded, more fulfilled than I can imagine. However, this step is not taken without trepidation. The history I seek is all there. Extracting it is another matter. This is the primary reason, as much as any other, why I have decided to work no further back than the 16th century.

As I reach for the bell, I spare a thought for Catherine Tollemache, the recipe writer, the lady whose memory is 'loved and honoured' across the park in the church, who lived and worked here. Today, though, it is not her but her mother-in-law who is the focus of my attention.

❖ ❖ ❖

Window shutters are closed to protect the room's contents from the glare of sunlight; a letter is removed from a protective glass case. I hold my breath.

The writer is Lady Susan Spring, previously Susan Tollemache, widow, but now married to her second cousin, Sir William Spring. The letter is written to her son, Lionel Tollemache, addressed to him at Tilbury Camp. The date is 10th August 1588. Few English children can get through to adulthood without some knowledge of Queen Elizabeth I and the culmination of her rout of the Spanish Armada in August 1588. Facts may be fuzzy, strategies unrecognisable, ship names muddled beyond belief. Storms and storm-troopers may be entangled hopelessly, Drake and Raleigh may be credited as heroes and villified as murderous pirates simultaneously. However, one thing is certain: we grow up knowing that Elizabeth I proclaimed herself at Tilbury Camp to be a weak and feeble woman who had the heart and stomach of a king. Lady Susan Spring shows spirit, too. In clear, firm handwriting, she makes no bones about the purpose of her letter. Lionel is there to fight. What he must remember, she emphasises, is that 'it hathe pleased the Lord to chuse yow out amongst the rest to fyght his battell'. No pressure, then.

Lady Susan warms to her theme, telling her 'goode sonne' that she does not 'fear any want of valour in you' but is writing 'the more to stir yew up to the same'. She begs him to live with honour, follow a life that is unquestionable, and perform his duty to God and country. Here it is again – honour – measured in what Lionel owes and how he must demonstrate his recognition. She leaves no room for doubt about the risks if he fails in any respect, the danger hissing palpably over four centuries. The intolerable alternative, she says, would be life under 'those wicked miscreants and filthy idolaters'.

The letter ends with a lighter touch: '…I bid yow farewell; not forgetting my harty commendaciouns unto you, with your daughter Susan's, who prayethe yow to pray to the Lord to bles her'. Susan is Lionel and Catherine's eldest daughter. I wonder why she is mentioned but not her three younger sisters, nor, indeed, Catherine, Lionel's wife. It will be more than a year before I discover the answer to this: Susan has been staying with her grandmother for months, perhaps offering Lady Spring hope for the future while the men of the family do their duty and risk their lives.

As I transcribe the letter, it occurs to me that Lionel Tollemache must have gone to face the prospect of war with some concern about the fate of his family line if he failed to return. He had no son, at least no son living. He and Catherine had nine children. Seven of them reached adulthood. Their first-born was a son but he did not survive beyond infancy. He is buried not at Helmingham but at Catherine's family home, North Elmham, in Norfolk. There, the span of his short life is measured in a single line entered in the parish register that records his burial on 26 November 1581. The Tollemache line might have ended there, and perhaps Lionel feared that it would. By the time he served at Tilbury Camp in July and August 1588, eight years into their marriage, Catherine had produced four daughters. It would be three more years after the failed Spanish invasion before they welcomed a son.

The Spanish were routed; Lionel never had to face them. He was home by September. In 1591, his first son was born, followed by two more sons. The estate he left on his own death in 1612 remains in the hands of his descendants over four hundred years later. Where I stand now, in this house, he and his wife and their family lived and breathed. The letter is replaced under its protective cover. We leave the room. In the next, light is shifting and shimmering, reflected off the moat. The agitation reminds me of a similar experience on my first visit to the Hall almost 30 years ago. Today, I glimpse a prospect of a future dread articulated by Lady Susan Spring. I have seen something else, too: an example of unquestioning loyalty by the women behind those dutiful men bred for active service and public duty. Lady Susan Spring, despite her personal terrors, writes to her son of duty, valour, honour.

By the time Lady Susan's letter was written, let alone reached its destination, Elizabeth I had been reassured that the danger was over, was triumphant, even as she stood and addressed the troops on or about 8th August 1588. The Spanish Armada, or what was left of it, was fleeing back to Spain. In Suffolk, starved of news, Lady Susan Spring could not have known that orders were being given for men to stand down from the 10th August. The significance of the date of her letter was clearly recognised by her son, Lionel, who retained his mother's impassioned plea. His successors have preserved it ever since. Its power is undiminished, four centuries on. It is a declaration that honour is a duty.

❋ ❋ ❋

At home in Framsden, cookery and contemplation are the evening equivalent of mowing and musing, especially after a rewarding day of research. With a pot of home-made vegetable soup simmering, I make some croutons while I wait for the pearl barley to soften. These simple tasks remind me how much it is possible to achieve as a result of electricity on demand. Apart from any other advantage, its instant provision of light extends the day immeasurably. How much harder life was when these cottages were first built. Everything took infinitely longer, demanded more effort, more patience. The potential to do as much as I have achieved already today was unthinkable. Life was still hard in the late 1950s, when I was growing up in the Cotswolds. Our experience of rural life was by no means unusual. My mother cooked on a range that bears no relation to the must-have kitchen accessory of today that borrows its name. Our range was cast iron, had to be kept clean with black-lead polish and had an open fire-grate, a single oven and a hotplate above. The cycle of lighting, coaxing, cleaning, emptying and refilling with fuel was relentlessly unavoidable. When the weather was still, so was the fire. Cooking was protracted, tempers were short.

I return to the softly-lit living room, where glowing flames are visible through the glass door of the stove. Behind the curtains, the Victorian windows are augmented by sliding panels of secondary glazing to help reduce the inevitable draughts. When these cottages was first built, this room would have been similar to the one in the agricultural tied cottage in which I grew up. 'Living' meant that almost every household and personal function took place here in its turn: cooking, eating, bathing, and laundry-drying in wet weather. There wasn't much time or space for any other sort of living, although we did have a radio around which we gathered in anticipation of hearing something, anything, as my father twiddled the dials with his brow furrowed in concentration. The room used here now as a kitchen, beautifully fitted out by the Estate, where my soup simmers and will soon satisfy me, would have been the scullery, little more than an outhouse. We had one of those, too; and outside there was a cold, dank lavatory situated a long walk away at the end of the garden.

After supper, I read more about my landlord's 19th-century ancestor, who was energetic in improving the lot of his Estate staff. He was disappointed that having provided a school in Helmingham, his labourers were reluctant for their children to attend. This sounds familiar: less than a century later, there was similar resistance within my own family to 'the kid reading too much', 'getting above herself'; rank disbelief when I passed the Scholarship, known later as the 11-plus; and a chorus of satisfaction when I was removed summarily from Grammar School at 15 years of age to go out and earn a living so that I could contribute to the household 'like she ought to'. Low expectation has a long reach.

I was led to believe that I owed it to my parents, so I did my duty with gritted teeth, despite protestations and attempts at intervention by my school, who thought my removal was a waste prompted by the prospect of short-term gain. They had me down as a UN interpreter on the basis of my English and French language skills and my liking for geography. I can remember long discussions with the Headmaster and Headmistress, who spoke to me of university, of opportunities to work abroad, the means by which to invest in a new life, all the prospects I had fathomed out for myself when I was 7 or 8 years old. It was all to no avail. I was not the one who needed convincing. My school did not abandon me. They refused to countenance the idea that my first taste of working life would be in the local blanket factory. They used their influence to secure an interview for me with a firm of local solicitors whose office was practically at the foot of the school drive. I left school on my 15th birthday and began work the following Monday. There was little honour or respect involved, as I remember it. The experience drove a wedge between me and my past. As soon as I was legally able, I moved as far away from my roots as I possibly could. I suspect that is why I have been rootless ever since. I wonder whether any of Helmingham's 19th-century labourers' children felt similarly cheated when they were robbed of their opportunity to attend the school provided on the doorstep with their futures in mind? Were they keen to break the mould of limited ambition? I wonder whether their families, like mine, dismissed anyone in a position of responsibility and authority, however visionary or well-intentioned, as 'them interfering buggers'?

Later, I will try to find out what was expected of the first model tenants here and how the 1st Lord Tollemache treated them. For now, I show my respect by paying my rent on time and abiding by the terms of my lease. Despite some close calls, I am never behind with my rent at Framsden nor have I failed to pay any of the outgoings on my Norfolk home. On all counts, I tell myself, I have got the balance about right. The research is eminently satisfying and challenging. My days are full to bursting. I love my surroundings. Despite my expensive excursions into rare book-buying, I am not flat broke. My silver gap year investment is beginning to reward me. I am feeling reasonably smug and self-satisfied, Micawber-ish.

Then, out of the blue, I am called upon to do something honourable. I would find it preferable to deliver a snowball in summer than to do what is being asked of me. The demand is complicated. It involves losing control of my Norfolk cottage and adopting a cat.

At a stroke I become pleading tenant and diffident landlord.

Above: the new tenant installed at Framsden.

Below: Autumn flowers prepared for the boot sale.

Author's images

4: Home truths

Debts of honour can be burdensome, demanding a lot more than a red rose to keep both sides satisfied. There are some situations when you know that you owe. I face two of them in quick succession. I am enjoying my dual existence, soaking up history like a sponge in my Framsden cottage and treating my Norfolk home as a hotel for short breaks after spending a day at work with John and our clients in the software development suite. I relish the contrast: in Framsden, I have history and blissful rural isolation, and manage on very little. In Attleborough, I use the washing machine, wallow in the luxurious warmth of my cosy, centrally-heated bathroom, trim the undemanding garden and deal with anything that arises, ever hopeful that this might include meeting potential purchasers, who never come. Instead, what does come is a very unexpected request.

John and Sue are stalwart friends of many years to whom I owe a great deal. I return from a visit to them to find a string of anxious messages on my answering machine at Framsden. 'Please call us', they say, 'as soon as you get in'. Moments after I left Attleborough, they heard from their daughter, Annie, who was in great distress. Annie, her husband Toby and their two small children are being forced by a less-than-considerate landlord to vacate their rented house at short notice. The landlord is acting within the law. The landlord is also a member of a complicated extended family on the husband's side. Acting out of kinship, he charged the couple a relatively low rent at the outset of their tenancy. The arrangement suited both sides at the time. With the tenancy due for renewal, the landlord wants to charge at a level well beyond their means. With the couple out, he can draw up new tenancy arrangements at a higher rent. Recriminations fly and tears flow.

At any other time, John and Sue would not hesitate to accommodate their family's needs. They are open-minded and generous people. They have just bid farewell to another daughter and family who were housed temporarily with them. However, John has committed to a major building project. The recently vacated annexe to his large Edwardian house is full of building materials, being stripped out and doubled in size to create a separate dwelling for sale or rental. Worse still, John is doing all the work himself. He and Sue have enough on their plates and attics full of things that four married daughters couldn't quite manage to find house-room for as each flew the nest in turn. And there was I, sitting pretty, apparently, with not one but two roofs to choose from, one of which was at my disposal.

Would I help? Would I let Annie, Toby, two small offspring and one large dog occupy my Norfolk cottage temporarily? It would be only for a few months, just to tide them over until they found somewhere else to rent. After all, I didn't need the house, did I? The family would be classified as homeless if no-one could help. Yes, they had already asked the local authority, and no, there was no housing available, not unless they were prepared to be separated and accommodated in hostels. My mind was reeling. The likelihood of selling a two-person cottage crowded with a family of four and hound was negligible: I confess I did feel emotionally blackmailed until my conscience rebuked me fiercely and I heard myself saying yes, yes, of course, let them come.

Rent was out of the question; any arrangement was to be on a friendly basis, giving the family use of my roof and floors as guests. Privately, my risk-averse hackles rose at the prospect: in law, neither of us had a leg to stand on if problems arose.

'It'll be alright, really', said John. 'I'm only half a mile away; if anything should crop up, Annie can ring me and I will go and sort it out'.

This was all about trust. Quite right, too, I told myself. It's time you started to consider the needs of others above your own and, just for once, you have the gift within your grasp. But what about utility bills? Everything is at a minimum because I'm not using the house apart from those laundry visits. I can't subsidise them. No, no, of course not. No-one expected me to. If I could just see my way to be generous, perhaps to charge them enough to cover what I thought they would use by way of electricity, gas, phone, water, septic-tank emptying and all the rest? Trust notwithstanding, cost-covering was not only sensible but essential, so I did a pessimistic calculation based on double my use. It proved naïve: I had not guessed at the hours of laundry, the gallons of hot water for baths, the blocked drains and pressure on the elderly septic-tank (no, honestly, we meant it when we said please do not put disposable nappies down the loo), the peak-rate phone calls. In short, I was pathetically unprepared.

Planning for their move-in was a baptism by fire. I was one and they were four in number. My Norfolk cottage had only two bedrooms. Not to worry, the children were tiny, one was a baby: they could share the big back room. Big back room? That was my bedroom, filled with my favourite bits of antique furniture. Toddlers in there? Well yes, because husband and wife will take your study as their bedroom. My study? My inner sanctum? The place occupied by my shelves full of books, my cupboards full of research papers, my desk… Well, come on, be reasonable, it would be best if you had all of those with you now, wouldn't it? After all, you are at Framsden for research, aren't you? And then there was the dog to consider. I winced at the thought of paw-scraped paintwork inside and furious digging out in my well-stocked, regularly-tended garden.

Readjustment would follow, I told myself; but first there was the little matter of physically moving them in. There were long faces when we made a joint visit to assess how much of their own furniture they could bring with them and how much they would have to put into storage. I found myself apologising for the size of my front door (just too short and narrow for their massive modern couch to squeeze through); the available space in the kitchen (not quite wide enough to accommodate their American fridge-freezer), and the capacity of my garden shed (for their family bikes and the mountain of outdoor toys). Speaking of outdoor toys, the 120-foot long garden was considered totally inadequate because it was so full of plants that there was nowhere for children to play. Play? The grandparents were unequivocal. I was dealt that pitying look that becomes familiar to the hapless and childless.

The parents sulked. The children whimpered. Even the dog sighed in that resigned fashion in which only Labradors can sigh. I could see that one of us was going to have to give some ground and I knew that it would have to be me. I offer to cover part of the garden with a play-friendly surface… even though it means digging up my Jerusalem artichokes and the asparagus bed… John and Sue, ever positive, suggest kindly that maybe it wouldn't be a bad idea if I moved out a lot more of my belongings to Framsden… After all, with the little ones, and the dog… It was akin to opening the floodgates. Ah, yes. If I could just take that, and that, and those, and clear my shed, and take my washing machine because they'd really rather use theirs… and on and on it went. I hired yet another removal van and, with the help of the long-suffering John and Sue, proceeded to move my entire household contents, including those from the garden shed, from Norfolk to Suffolk. Again. I hardly dared contemplate the prospect of a repeat performance within the next few months.

This time when the self-drive van disappears down my driveway with a stressed John at the wheel, I feel drained and dispirited. The effort was doubled because I have spent days helping to move the youngsters and their furniture out of one house and into two others. Despite being surrounded by rooms full of building materials and tools at their own home, John and Sue agreed reluctantly to act as a storage facility for anything that their offspring could not accommodate in my Norfolk cottage. John drives away to face countless black sacks filled with toys and clothes, two enormous couches that weigh a ton, as well as piles of 'treasures', nameless and bulky. Waving the van out of sight, I feel for him as he returns to Sue and a sea of chaos, but only as long as it takes to close the door and face my own.

I have, at least, reclaimed the bedroom for my bed. There was a simple solution, explained patiently by Rob, the ever-helpful Estate Foreman. The bedroom window can be removed easily, thanks to the presence of an internal security bolt. The bed is duly hoisted up the cottage's front wall and in through the enlarged window opening. The spectacle provides a few moments of farce enjoyed by a bus-load of passengers bound for Ipswich that morning. The desk stays, and much other furniture joins it. Research papers stored so carefully in the adjoining small room are lost beneath lumber.

Downstairs, the cottage overflows with furniture and hastily-packed belongings. The excess is contained only because one item is piled on top of another. I trip over boxes, cursing at every collision. The kitchen is a nightmare, although I do now have my washing-machine connected, giving me cause to raise a wan smile. Snap out of it, I tell myself. It's not going to be all beer and skittles for the youngsters, either. Four of them are crammed into your single-person cottage, and it doesn't even have a satellite dish to serve their overweening TV. Ha! Brimming with evil glee at the thought of this painful blow to their cherished routine, I open a bottle of Merlot and spend the next few days in feverish activity and a semi-stupor. I storm around the cottage arranging, re-arranging, unpacking, discarding and storing. It takes days of effort but the sun shines and I have my garden in which to spread a tarpaulin and sift and sort to my heart's content in the fresh air. By the end of the week, I am halfway to feeling triumphant and seriously considering my next piece of research work. Then I have a phone call.

Life is impossible without a satellite dish. The little boy is pining, can't function without his diet of Sky TV. They have a friend – no, rephrase that – another member of the extended family - who installs satellite dishes. If I'd just say it was OK for him to shin up a fragile part of my roof – no, no, don't worry, he does this all the time – and it would be at the back so it wouldn't show… Yes, yes, we know the TV aerial point is at the front of the house but it doesn't matter because he'll just dangle the cable over the roof, bring it down the front of the house, knock out your air vent in the front wall and poke the cable through. Easy. See? I beg John to be there to supervise. He agrees but says he can't see what I am fussing about. After all, I'm going to end up with a satellite dish that I won't have to pay for! I should be grateful! My trips to Debenham Co-Op to stock up on anything red and drinkable increase exponentially over the next few weeks. The irony of it is that I have a TV aerial perched temptingly on the chimney at Framsden but absolutely no TV reception. I have stored away my TV and rely entirely on the Internet. I open another bottle and raise a toast to broadband.

Over the next few weeks, Framsden becomes home by default. I forget that it is not mine. I am in nesting mode. I abandon any attempt at research and wander about listlessly, sketchbook and tape measure in hand. I contemplate shifting a wall here, a door there; replacing the electricity-hungry storage heaters with a more efficient central heating system to warm every inch of space. I go so far as to assess space for storing LPG (gas) bottles outside so that I can heat with gas, cook with gas…. I am propelled by so much hot air that in retrospect I will blame all that red wine. In reality, what I felt was an urge for possession out of all proportion to the reality of being a tenant.

One thing I had to do, tenant or not, was solve the problem of the ice-cold landing radiator, especially now that my bedroom was reinstated to purpose. Rob had assured me that when I lit the stove, water heated by its back-boiler would feed not only the domestic hot-water system but was fed into separate pipes designed to heat the radiator. *Ergo sum*, there would be a nice warm lump of metal just where I needed it most. Sadly, the radiator had not read the script and remained resolutely icy. As the year inched its way closer to winter, I lit the fire earlier and earlier every day until it became essential to keep it permanently alight, closed down sleepily overnight and then raised to a lively state of combustion the next day. Balancing the airflow was an art I discovered soon enough. I remember sharing this scientific fact with my friends John and Carolyn. John nodded but Carolyn frowned, whether in disapproval at my dishevelled state or at the idea of handling this black beast lurking on the hearth, I can never be sure. 'It's easy', I crowed. 'Air makes the fire burn. Close off this little vent and the fire dies down but doesn't go out.' I live to eat my words.

I wake suddenly, feeling unnaturally hot, to hear and see the water-pipes rattling ominously beside the bed. I dash downstairs like the proverbial scalded cat and open the living room door to find the stove emanating enough heat to warm St John's Row. I can barely get near it, let alone touch it, but one thing is certain: I have to run off as much hot water as possible. My poor neighbour, Ernie, must have wondered what on earth was happening, since each of us could hear the other's gurgling water systems fill and empty on a daily basis. And here I was at two in the morning, running a bath… or three. Steam is spurting out of the kitchen, bath and basin taps with terrifying power. I open them all fully and hare back to the stove armed with thick protective oven gloves so that I can handle the air vent which, surely, I must have left open. But no. The vent is securely closed. There is nothing for it, I will have to investigate in the morning when the fire is totally depleted. After several hours of running water and reassuring myself that I have done all I can possibly do, I return, puzzled and frazzled, to bed. I put a hand on the landing radiator. It is as cold as charity.

The problem with the stove is resolved easily: the air vent was fully closed but there is a decorative motif in its centre, fixed with a screw. My fussy housekeeping routine means that every time I wipe the stove with a damp cloth, I loosen the screw ever so slightly. It was terrifying to see the effect of that tiny influx of air. Maybe Carolyn had a point. Perhaps I wasn't as up for all this as I thought. I have to admit that I did give more than a passing thought to the reliable gas central-heating system currently warming my non-tenants back in Norfolk. Flick a switch for warmth. I can hardly bare to think about it as I trudge back and forth from workshop to outer lobby to living room with muscles stretched taut by the weight of incoming coal and wood, outgoing buckets of ash. And that wretched radiator sits there, resolutely cold, leering at me every time I drag my weary bones up to bed. I become resolute, too. It's me or the radiator. The time has come to call for help.

I phone the Estate Office and explain. Rob comes to investigate. When he arrives, the stove's fire is burning brightly. 'You should have heat in the radiator', he says, puzzled. He follows the route of the pipes, examining the visible ones for obvious problems. 'I think there must be air in the system somewhere because water isn't even reaching this radiator: it's empty. I'll get a plumber in to bleed the system.' A plumber is duly sent in and much banging and thumping ensues. I escape to the garden and pray. Hope spring eternals but the radiator does not. The plumber is summoned again… and again. Exasperated, he concludes that there has to be a problem somewhere in the concealed pipes. There is no other explanation.

'And?' I ask cautiously.

'And we're going to have to take up the fitted carpet in the bedroom, and raise the floorboards right across the room in order to find out what's going on.'

I groan, mentally putting myself in the Estate's position. 'I can't go ahead without the Estate's permission', he says, 'but if you want that radiator to work, there is no other way'. Suddenly I feel the weight of tenancy settle like a stone. Should I bother? Should I just let it be and not cause any more problems? But then again this isn't about me and my tenancy: I am a temporary fixture, there will be other tenants facing this problem. As I prevaricate, I think of how life was when my parents refused to raise problems with their landlord, even when he was not their employer. Their lethargy was justified by 'Ah, them buggers'll only blame us and then they'll put the rent up!' I tolerated the lack of a bath for weeks then broke the stalemate by writing a grimy explanation to the landlord myself. Despite the unleashing of vitriol within the household when my subterfuge was discovered, I believe, all in all, that my parents were relieved; but perhaps not quite as relieved as they were when I left them and 'them buggers' to their own devices. I moved to Birmingham, a better job and a tenancy of my own, followed swiftly by my first property purchase and tentative renovation project (supported by a loan from my employer, the University of Birmingham), and began sending money home. There was no doubt in anyone's mind that I was a lost cause, destined to become 'one o'them buggers'; but the money was welcome, all the same.

The plumber is frowning, waiting for my response. 'I do want the radiator to work', I say decisively.

A few weeks later, the bedroom is cleared and the carpet lifted carefully. The floorboards are raised to reveal sagging pipes: there was no way that the water could get beyond the centre of the room, let alone reach the radiator on the adjacent landing. With the room in chaos, the plumber asks me to make a decision.

'The easiest solution would be to close off these pipes and to run new ones around the wall. The trouble is they will show. Do you want that?'

What a question! This is not my house. The decision is not mine to make, although my answer would have been a resounding 'yes, please'. The plumber calls the Estate Office. And so it is that the chilly lump of metal becomes my best friend. Better still, the copper pipes running around the bedroom wall at skirting height give me additional heat in the bedroom. I dread to think how much of my rent has been committed to achieving this outcome. But that is not my problem. My problem is thirty miles away in Norfolk, simmering to its own boil.

My next visit to the Norfolk cottage convinces me that I should take my cottage off the market. The careful photographs taken by the Estate Agent months before were unrecognisable. The garden was a lost cause. And the utility bills were going through the roof, which was the reason for my visit. I have kept my distance since they moved in, not made unscheduled visits, even when I am working half a mile away. This one had to be planned, and I had to be well prepared. As kindly but firmly as I can, I go through the figures: what I'd budgeted, what they were using, and the increasing gap between the two. There were yet more long faces and threats of tears as I explain, uncompromisingly, that their payments will have to increase by 60% to meet the shortfall.

It had to be done, but it wasn't comfortable, and now, having withdrawn the property from the market, there is no doubt that my Framsden days are numbered. I can sustain the rent until the end of the one-year initial tenancy and cope, just about, with the dual outgoings now that my non-tenants are to contribute a more realistic amount. But a plan had been materialising into a strategy during the last few months, one I felt confident that I could achieve. This relied on selling my house and investing the capital sum to fund an extended tenancy on the Estate. As I grew older, I surmised, I might have to consider other options. I thought that was the only risk. Perhaps it was just as well that I had to abandon the dream when I did: I could not foresee that interest rates were set to tumble to levels below those of my most pessimistic spreadsheet. I would have been lucky if my investment had sustained me beyond ten years.

The immediate priority was to let the Estate know where I stood. But not before both of us have faced another challenge. With the awkward discussions about outgoings concluded, I visit John and Sue. In amongst the piles of furniture and building materials, I see Jeremy. And Jeremy sees me.

❈ ❈ ❈

I had met Jeremy previously, but he had not been in a sociable frame of mind. In any case, I was warned, do not attempt to touch him: he is tetchy at the best of times and always wary of unfamiliar human contact. Jeremy was one of two semi-feral orphaned kittens found and adopted by another of John and Sue's daughters, the one who had vacated their annexe recently. Jeremy had been neutered, had been taught a few social graces (not many, it has to be said) and had lost his sister to cat 'flu. Subsequently, he lost his place in the pecking order, usurped by the arrival of a new human baby. To add insult to injury, his keepers had upped and left him. The stories of failed attempts by vets to handle Jeremy were legion. I should have listened. This cat's only virtue, it seems, is that he does not hunt at all.

On this visit, however, I find Jeremy diminished, less assured. He sits outside the door to the annexe as if expecting to be let in, as though there will be a welcome for him. I turn to join John and Sue. Jeremy follows. I sit a chair. He sits on the floor at my feet. 'They couldn't take him down to the new house in Ipswich… the landlord won't allow pets. And in any case, he doesn't like the baby at all', explains Sue. 'She grabs at him and he doesn't understand, so he lashes out.' Jeremy moves his head between the two of us, following the conversation, catches my eye and blinks very slowly. 'And the trouble is', continues Sue, warming to her theme and reeling me in at the same time, 'we're trying to feed him and Tabitha sees him off every time he tries to get near the dish'. Tabitha is their elderly and practically toothless cat but she is still fiercely territorial. She has been known to kill pheasants and to carry home half-dead rabbits twice her size.

Jeremy sighs audibly, and surveys me, wide-eyed, then lifts a paw in supplication. I pat my knee. He pauses briefly, and then, all of a sudden, there it is, that familiar soft thud as he lands on my lap. Many years ago, I had a cat of immense character. My Birmingham cat was legendary: he used to wait at the bus stop to meet me from whichever bus carried me at the end of the working day and escort me home, chattering animatedly, much to the amusement of my fellow travellers. He was at once a fearsome mouser and dedicated companion, refusing to move from the foot of my bed for almost twenty-four hours when I succumbed to a bout of 'flu. In the days before I could afford a telephone, it was the absence of the cat that alerted my very good neighbour, an elderly lady on his daily visiting list. She came to the rescue but we both thought it was the cat who deserved a medal. When he died of old age, I never felt able to replace him. And after all, cats are such a tie. And then there are all those food bills, vet bills, fur balls and worse. And I am house-proud, especially so in a house that is not mine. It is all to no avail. Jeremy lies in a purring coil of contentment. John and Sue can't believe their luck. And, if I am honest, neither can I. By the time I leave for Framsden, I have agreed to adopt Jeremy, subject, of course, to having permission from the Estate Office. I feel sure they are field sportsmen, dog lovers to a man, and it crosses my mind that they may not agree to admit this clawed invader. Before I leave to return to Framsden, I give Jeremy a talking to. 'Now listen', I say firmly; 'I may be able to take you home. We'll have to see.' He blinks knowingly and purrs. He knows the outcome before I do.

Pauline is cautiously optimistic when I phone the Estate Office to ask, diffidently, about the potential for adding a cat to the household bearing in mind that I am, sadly, going to be a very short-term tenant. A few days later, she has news. 'You can have a cat but we'll have to amend your lease for the remainder of the term. It won't affect the rent but there will be new conditions'. The Cat Clause, as I insist on calling it, duly arrives. It is nothing worse than I expected. 'Do not allow the animal to foul the carpet'. Good grief! Of course not. 'Any mechanism for allowing access and egress is to be lockable in both directions'. No question about it. I don't want any old Tom breaking, entering or leaving a calling card. 'Carpets must be steam-cleaned on vacating the property. The Estate's designated cleaning contractor must be used and a receipt produced by way of evidence'. Fair enough. That would have to be done anyway, but it did make me smile as my mind drifted back to another Estate cottage I had declined. Its tenant (or its tenant's cat) had clearly not read, or perhaps not behaved, quite in the spirit of the lease. I hoped the smile would not be on the other side of my face when I became a cat-owning, departing tenant.

Over the next few weeks, as autumn runs headlong into winter, I prepare for the lodger. In accordance with the Cat Clause, I buy a two-way lockable cat flap and call Rob to ask if it is alright for a friend (the long-suffering John) to fit it. 'No need', he says, 'I'll come and do it'. I suspect Rob blanches at the thought of DIY installations on the Estate and this is the lesser of two evils. We crouch on the chilly floor of the outer lobby, trying to make sense of the badly translated instructions accompanying various bits of plastic. Jointly, we fathom which bit goes where, and Rob proceeds to cut a hole in the lower half of the door. We fit the flap and I play cat so that we can test it from both sides. Rob hands me the circular bit of wood that has been cut from the door. 'You can burn that on your stove', he says. I am puzzled. 'But it says in the Cat, sorry, Pet Clause that I must reinstate the door when I leave, so how do I do that if I burn this piece?'

Rob says: 'Are you planning to leave, Moira?'

'It's not through choice but necessity, Rob. I have told the Office.'

Pause, then 'I'm sorry to hear it. We had hoped you would stay. We will be sorry to lose you as a tenant.'

Rob pauses again, then says pragmatically 'But when you do go, if the next tenant doesn't have a cat we'll just replace the whole lower section of the door.'
I stand there nonplussed, clutching a useless bit of door, thinking what a lot of trouble I have given the Estate in so short a time. And I am not even going to stay. I add up to a pretty poor return on their investment.

I prepare for cat-dom well in advance, leaving nothing to chance. I have checked on Jeremy's eating habits and am glad to learn that he favours dried food and an ever-ready bowl of water. I stagger out from the Co-Op store in Debenham with packets of the stuff in one of each flavour. Henry Abbott's Hardware, that purveyor of all things useful and conveniently next door to the Co-Op, provides the bowls for food and water, a large bag of cat litter which the staff carry out and load in the boot of the car for me, together with a generous litter tray and, most important of all, a cat-carrying basket. This is capacious in size, woven in wickerwork and equipped with a wire grille that can be secured with stout leather straps. Next day, with cat basket and the car suitably protected with newspaper and absorbent padding, the stove lit and shut down so that all will be warm and welcoming on our return, food and water dishes at the ready, I set off on my 60-mile trek to bring the lodger home to Framsden.

I was forewarned that Jeremy did not care for baskets, much less travel. As is my way when I am a house guest, I remove my shoes at the entrance to John and Sue's home and pad about behind the cat in my carpet slippers, trying not to appear nervous or predatory. Eventually, he gives in to hunger when Tabitha is out of the way and I pounce on him while he is eating. Jolly bad sport, I know, but the hours are ticking by. In the next few minutes of furore, I discover just how strong Jeremy's back legs can be. Eventually, with much howling and cursing from all involved, we succeed in closing the basket door on something approaching a wild animal. Jeremy's pupils are dilated to black saucers. He flattens his ears to his head and makes menacing noises that disintegrate, finally, into a continuous, blood-curling, gut-wrenching yowl. There is no time for polite farewells. 'Get him into the car now', urges John, 'he'll settle once you're moving. Go, go go!'.

He doesn't settle. It is a good ten miles later before I realise I am driving the car in my carpet slippers. Worse than that, the only way I find to pacify Jeremy is to drive in third gear and with only one hand on the steering wheel. My left hand is bent double, poked through the slats of the wire grille to stroke and reassure him. Gear changes and stops at traffic lights and junctions are best forgotten. I'm not sure which of us is the more stressed and distressed when we arrive at Framsden.

With the door and the cat-flap locked securely, I release Jeremy from his prison. Wild-eyed and confused, he makes a dash for the cat-flap and howls in disgust when he finds it unyielding. He turns tail, gives the food dishes a fleeting glance en route to the living room. There he hides himself, flattened against the wall behind the sofa bed.

I expected all this. He might hide for hours. I go about my chores, close the curtains to the outside world and liven up the stove to give the room warmth and a nice cheery glow. And wait. After about an hour, a somewhat dishevelled creature emerges from his hiding place, gives me a glowering look as he heads off to explore dining and bathroom facilities. Tour of duty over, he reappears, eyes still like black-lined saucers, but slightly calmer. I say nothing. I toss on to the rug a large, grey-coloured fish made of a soft fabric suffused with catnip. This, his welcome gift, evokes a response. He stalks past me and pounces on the fish, grasps it tightly with his front paws, holds it tightly to himself and proceeds to knock seven bells out of it with his back legs, his teeth clamped to its head. Am I to believe this is a non-predatory cat?

Suddenly, toy abandoned but his mouth still open, Jeremy's attention is fixed on the dancing flames visible through the glass door of the stove. I realise that he has never seen fire before. I hold my breath as he steps gingerly on to the brick hearth to give this great black but glowing beast a closer look. As the heat hits him, he jumps back slightly. He sits, head slightly extended, sniffing and observing, ready to take evasive action if this thing rears up to attack. Occasionally he gives me a glance, then looks quickly away. Then, satisfied that this creature is not about to retaliate, he takes up residence on the rug and begins to groom himself fiercely. Only then does he deign to stalk over and give me the merest rub of recognition before he heads off to reunite himself with his supper dish.

Within a short time, Jeremy makes it plain that I may after all, be trusted, climbs on to my lap and sleeps the sleep of the exhausted. Later, he follows me up the stairs and climbs on to the foot of the bed where I have placed a folded blanket, just in case. He stays there contentedly for the rest of the night and most nights from then on.

Needless to say, all is enchantment to begin with. Then Jeremy shows his complete contempt for the Cat Clause in the lease, throwing up at regular intervals and using the carpet as a highly satisfying alternative to any other scratching post. I solve one problem by addressing his digestion, changing his food to a more expensive, meat-based alternative. When I mention this to John and Sue, they confess to being aware of this tendency. So much for honour amongst friends. The clawing habit is more difficult to overcome because he ignores the brand new scratching post I buy for him, sniffing it and looking at me disdainfully. He has long since abandoned his furry fish toy, but I learn two things: when indoors, he becomes bored and that is when he claws. Energetic activity is supplied simply with a piece of string that he favours over any purpose-designed toy. Most important of all, he loves to be brushed. The discovery amounts to cat heaven and tenant relief, even though I spend almost as long tending the carpet as the cat.

With the decision to opt for expensive cat food comes an increase in the grocery bills that I am finding it hard to offset with reductions anywhere else. With the creeping onset of chill winter, I know I must budget for increased electricity bills, more coal, more wood. It is time to take stock and start using my wits. A browse of potential car boot sales on the Internet shows that there are some good opportunities locally. I book pitches, enter the dates into my diary and begin scouring my bulging bookshelves, removing a couple of hundred volumes to sell, as well as maps and a few good-quality surplus household items.

The garden is ripe for exploitation, too. Both apple trees are laden with fruit, much of it falling and being attacked by wasps even before I can gather it. And there are flowers galore, needing no more than a little artful presentation to make them appealing. I spend the whole of one Saturday evening trimming and arranging bunches of them. I experiment with colour combinations: shocking pink nerine with anything grey-green is a winner. I tie the bunches with green twine and try them in various containers, including galvanised buckets and watering-cans lurking in the workshop, which look very chic. I sort and weigh bags of apples, some cookers, some eaters, and label everything with a price writ large on brightly-coloured cards. Next, I experiment with how to make my stall attractive. Digital photography is a boon: quick to achieve and simple to view, the results show clearly where I can improve. I cover my table with a textured cream cloth to conceal packaging and all the unlovely things that no-one wants to see.

I learn the tricks of the trade. Look cheerful but don't be pushy. Never eat or drink at your stall but disappear discreetly into the car with your Thermos flask and keep an eye on the stall at the same time. Never put all your wares on display at once. Engage with people if they show interest. Let them ask, then tempt them a little. 'Oh, you're interested in Ordnance Survey maps. Well, it just so happens that I have more in the car…' Or 'Let me look: I might just have a few more apples. Yes! Here we are! How many bags would you like?' Crucially, I learn never to say no. If a reasonable offer is made, I accept. I watch and learn the importance of refreshing my stall. People circle a boot-sale like predators, eagle-eyed and ready to snap up a bargain. If the stall is modified, even slightly, they will home in on it to see what they might have missed the first time. All it takes is a subtle shift here, a book displayed open there. Unexpectedly, I enjoy this stress-free retail experience, especially when it adds up to a stall emptied in record time and a stallholder driving home with a satisfyingly heavy wallet. The cat and I will eat well for a while.

As winter gathers, my homespun economic strategy will take another battering as I face a choice of heat or eat. But for now I am optimistic and eager for a return to that other source of enrichment. It is high time I returned to my research.

Above: View of the avenue, looking south from Helmingham Hall.

Below: Deer browsing in Helmingham Park.

Author's images

5: Rooted in history

The silver gap is narrowing. What seemed at the outset to be an open, infinite opportunity is now delineated and constrained. It is important that I make best use of the remaining time here. With issues in Norfolk resolved, at least temporarily, the cat settled and the garden marginally less demanding, life at Framsden can revolve around my research again. In this way, ritual becomes more important than routine. My research efforts may keep me pinned to my desk, begin with the lark at dawn and end with the owl in the hours darkened by insomnia, which seem to be increasing. Alternatively, opportunities may be seized briefly in the space of a few precious hours in Ipswich, at the Record Office, or at Helmingham Hall itself. The pattern is immaterial: it is restoring my intensity of focus that matters. Living on the spot, so close to the live end of history, I continue to be drawn by what is visible as much as what is recorded. My focus now is on timber. It seems to me that Helmingham is rooted in its timber.

The gently undulating, wooded surroundings of Framsden and Helmingham prompt this new search for understanding about the relationship between the family and their land. The parishes occupy prime positions in the central belt of predominantly clay land known aptly as High Suffolk. Oak is synonymous with High Suffolk because the tree thrives on clay. In moments of despair at my futile efforts to re-stock the garden, which is substantially clay, I think perhaps I should plant oak there, too.

Oak is nowhere more apparent than in the 400-acre Helmingham Park, most notably in the stately approach to the Tudor mansion. Believed to have been planted in the 1680s, it is not difficult to imagine the impact of this as an imposing carriage drive, nor to see how the family's visitors throughout the centuries would have been impressed by it. I was, and and still am, although these days I am wise enough to know that public visitors like me should exit, rather than enter the park along the avenue. Beyond the avenue, oak extends as far as the eye can see. Trees stand sentinel singly, or in small clumps and groves. Red, fallow and roe deer and rare breed sheep and cattle browse and graze beneath their canopies.

Some oak trees in the park are venerable specimens, recognisable by their stag-headed, leafless crowns clawing at the sky. Then there are delicate saplings whose tender limbs are protected from the nibbling attention of deer by tree-guards. What intrigues me, on a walk through the park, is the frequency with which small ponds intersperse the planting.

They are one of many forms of water at Helmingham. Primarily there are two moats, one surrounding the house and, unusually, another surrounding the productive gardens to its west. There is a pair of substantial fish ponds close to the church, once an important source of food. Throughout the 400-acre park, there are also narrow watercourses, evidence of the ditches that once bordered hedges, long since removed. But in addition to all these forms of water there are numerous small ponds, irregularly-shaped and of varying size. One, in particular, looks as though it provides a looking-glass for the somewhat contorted oak that leans over as though admiring its own reflection. It is one of many. What were they for? And why are so many of them close to oak trees? I find the answer in 1708, and it turns out to be worth a fortune, but I have to go back to the end of the 16th century to find out why this was so. Gradually, the archive leads me from acorns to warships.

Although I would like to know whether timber had any direct bearing on the life and livelihood of Catherine Tollemache, who arrived in 1580 and died in 1620, temporarily that remains an unfilled gap. Better to leave the gap for the time being than speculate on how to fill it. It will be filled, but not yet. Instead, I take her husband's service at Tilbury Camp in 1588 as my inspiration. Although he was a soldier, not a sailor, the sea and ships were central to the events of 1588 and ships depended upon timber.

Elizabeth I's strategic advisers informed her that England was short of ships. Anything that was seaworthy, and much that was not, was pressed into service. Towns and cities were asked to provide money, men, ships, or, in the case of the maritime counties, all three. Some, including Suffolk, dug in their heels, because the demands on them were three times more onerous and the more unwelcome for that. The organisation, successes and shortfalls of the 1588 engagement with the Spanish Armada fill thousands of pages of State papers and thousands more of retrospective scholarly commentary and academic argument. I learn from these sources that beyond the matter of seaworthiness there was a victualling nightmare well hidden by the propaganda of victory. Ships were provided with barrels of stinking fish, casks of weevil-ridden flour, sour, undrinkable ales and wines and worse. For every flag waved in procession, every knee bent in praise, there is an unpaid seaman, many of them ill-equipped, if equipped at all. It was a navy all at sea, so to speak. The long and short of it is that we did lose ships, and this left England vulnerable. We had denuded our fishing fleets, our boatyards and, inevitably, our stock of suitable timber. I learn from an 18th-century treatise that it takes approximately 46 mature oak trees to provide enough timber for a warship. Timber takes time to grow, and the exigencies of one century become the economic bounty of another.

The Helmingham archive yields bounty of its own. I read an agreement, dated May 1708, between 'Richard Burchett, Shipwright of London', and the Earl of Dysart, a title first acquired through marriage by an astute Tollemache gentleman ancestor in the 1640s. They seem to have done well from their marriages over the centuries, with more than a sprinkling of heiresses in the mix. I learn that Burchett buys not only 400 'standing timber oakes' from the 'Olde' and 'Newe' Helmingham parks but another 661 from selected sites nearby, all belonging to Lionel Tollemache, 3rd Earl of Dysart. Burchett agrees to purchase all this timber at the rate of 'six and fifty shilllings of lawfull money of Great Britain per load'. He is to make an advance payment of £500 by way of security before lifting a twig, followed by further instalments of £500 whenever he comes to collect another load. In all, he commits to taking 1,061 oak trees over a period of four years. This amounts to 5000 loads at a total cost of £14,000. In today's terms, roughly speaking, that sum equates to £1.2m sterling. This represents a signficant deal, and a timely one for the next generation, because the 3rd Earl dies in July 1712.

Taking the timber in loads of 'forty foot guirt measure', was a painstaking business over those four years between 1708 and 1712. The agreement includes for the purchase of existing fallen timber. This, and each of the 1,061 trees, had to be measured accurately before removal. Burchett was to come in with his band of men, equipped to fell the larger trees and saw up any existing fallen timber of the right size. He agrees to provide 'workmen and labourers, with carts, wains, carriages, working tools and implements' for the purpose. This army of men and battery of equipment will 'hew, cutt out, dig saw pits, saw, convert and have, take or carry away to and for their own use all the said timber oakes'. The park, and every other site they attended, would have been left cratered from the activity. Burchett's sawyers work in pairs, using axes and massive double-ended saws to fell and process each tree. Branches are cut off and graded, so there would have been piles of undersized timber heaped and left around the park to provide useful sources of firewood and fencing, pea-sticks or park paling for the Estate. Next comes the bigger business of stripping most of the bark from the main trunk of each felled oak. Then each piece of timber is split into lengths suitable for carriage by horse and cart, travelling by road to the nearest port for onward transportation by sea to London.

The sawing was done over a pit, dug for the purpose, and was a two-man job. Spare a thought for the man beneath, probably choked and half-blinded by sawdust as he wielded his half of the double-ended saw: he was the under-dog. It doesn't take much imagination to work out who was top dog. By the time I reach the end of the agreement, I realise that it is probably these saw-pits, together with the craters left as each felled oak yielded its ground, that account for the many small ponds scattered throughout the park.

When I drive slowly down the formal avenue of oak trees for the short drive home to cat, cottage and casserole, I am aware of a scene unimaginable a few hours earlier. Is it my fertile imagination or can I see, smell and hear the furious activity, the muscular men, teams of patient horses and carts, the noise, sweat and probably blood that accompanied the felling, sawing and splitting? And what of the 'Olde' and 'Newe' parks after these lengthy visits? Did they display a pock-marked surface of ruts, craters, pits, piles of small timber and sawdust? How many of the Earl's men had to be deployed in coping with the aftermath? There must have been collateral damage everywhere Birchett's men went, not just here in the park. And where did this labour force live, eat and sleep during the collecting periods? Were they billeted locally or quartered on site? How long did they stay? And were the roads between Helmingham and the nearest ports rendered more rutted, more crowded, less passable as a result of these transfers of timber that were taking place on an industrial scale? And did the Hall, its staff and the villagers breathe a collective sigh of relief as the last load trundled its way down to the sea and ships?

❋ ❋ ❋

Over the coming weeks, I begin to wonder what happened after Burchett had taken his 1,061 'standing timber oakes'. I should be returning my attention to the 16th century but the temptation is too great. I walk the park, pore over maps and pester Bill, who knows the catalogue intimately. As ever, he leads and guides me through all that is available, including correspondence between the next, (4th), Earl of Dysart and his Estate Steward, Thomas Brereton. A steward has overall responsibility for running an estate on his master's behalf, particularly when his master spends a good deal of time away from home at his other family seat, Ham House. Twelve years after Burchett dealt and bargained at Helmingham, Thomas Brereton writes to his master. When I handle his letter, I come to recognise the value of paper, both in this and earlier centuries. Writers frequently fill every available space, adding or continuing their commentary along the margins, at right angles to the main letter, or squeezing words tightly into corners. Brereton's letter has all these idiosyncracies and more because one side shows curious sketches of straight and dotted lines which make no sense to me at first. Then I turn the document over.

The letter is dated 22nd December 1720. I can picture Brereton preparing his sketches in the teeth of a chill winter wind. I picture him on the roof of the house, because that is where he says he has been. The vantage point gave him a clear view out to the north of the park to 'view the intended planting'. But there's a problem: what Brereton discovers from his rooftop perch, and by careful measurement on the ground, is that the 'visto' (or vista) is going to look all wrong if it is planted in a straight line running northwards from the house. The reason, he explains, is that the moated site is not set square and, in addition, the moat is wider on one side of the house than the other. I realise then why he has made two sketches, and what the Earl was supposed to do when he received them. Brereton had run out of paper before he could complete the full plan to scale, so he drew a second sketch that could be tacked (mentally) on to the first. Join up the dots, so to speak, in order to see the full picture.

The upshot of it was that if 'Yr Hon. approve on it', the avenue would have to be planted running at a slight angle away from the house. On plan, this looked odd, but he was at pains to explain that on the ground, it would look right, or, as he put it, 'be nearer a truth... and in my opinnion look much ffiner'. This would have been quite an avenue: he reckoned it should be 240 or 250 feet wide because that would match the width of the moat. He has drawn the plan to a scale of 100 feet to the inch. I measure with my ruler: his avenue was to be about 1000 feet long. He recommends incorporating existing trees into the new planting in order to improve and extend the 'visto'. What stops me in my tracks as I pace out the park in my mind and think how fashionable all this will be, is his reminder of the genuine imperative behind this proposal: 'the design being chiefly to raise timber'.

Helmingham, like many hundreds of English country estates, did not receive the attentions of prominent landscape designers between the 17th and 19th centuries. There was no grand plan for Helmingham set out by Capability Brown, no Red Book of 'before' and 'after' transformational proposals by Humphrey Repton. The fact is that both these great men, fashionably sought-after and influential in their time, were also supremely well informed about timber – and economics. Their skill was in taking a commodity like timber and exploiting its capacity to lend elegance to a landscape. The two things are perfectly compatible. Brereton's letter confirms that men like him, estate stewards with a depth and breadth of practical experience, were the unsung heroes of landscape improvement, equipped to keep one eye on fashion and the other on economics. The Helmingham Estate was not immune to fashionable trends: it just kept them in their place, which was a discreet second.

While I am musing on how big these trees will be when Brereton plants them out, and whether they are already being raised in a nursery bed somewhere, I read that if the Earl agrees, Brereton says he will be 'Starting on the work, digging the trenches and sowing the Akerns which we shall begin soon after Christmas if the weather continue open, else as the season shall allow'. It seems the Earl did not approve because, as far as I can ascertain, the avenue was never planted. Yet I cannnot resist looking out to the north side of the park and picturing this practical man supervising the planting of acorns in a post-Christmas icy blast. Had the Earl 'approved on it', planting would have been for the benefit of generations of Tollemaches who would live here centuries after Brereton and his master, neither of whom would ever see the trees reach maturity.

All the same, Brereton's fascinating and revealing letter prompts me to pursue fashion where there is rare evidence of it in the park. On my next walk, I head for the Mount. This man-made feature, is, as its name suggests, a hillock and is clearly visible from several points in and beyond the park. My OS map confirms that the Mount occupies a commanding position on the 60-metre contour line, which is one of the high points locally. As I approach, I can see immediately that the ascent to its peak is not smoothly steep but distinctly dimpled. At its foot there is a shallow depression, deep enough to hold water when there is enough rain to fill it. The closer I get, the more intriguing the Mount becomes. Its grassy, striated face reveals a vestigial spiral path. And what looks to be a gradual incline from a distance becomes steeper in closer proximity. Now I am excited.

Instead of attempting to scramble up one side of the slope, I do my best to follow the line of the spiral, which has collapsed in places to become a bumpy path. Despite this, I recognise the bones of a formal landscape feature beneath my feet. Until now, I have only read about these in the garden history books that line my shelves back at the cottage. Mounts, or mounds, were a popular feature of the 17th century and were associated with ponds, canals or other formal water features. It makes sense: you dig out a quantity of earth that you pile up to form your ornamental mount and then you re-shape the area you have dug and let it fill with water. At a stroke, you have two garden features for the price of one. When you have exerted yourself following the spiral, you are rewarded with a panoramic view of the park, and reflections of it in the pool at your feet. My climb is mildly exhilarating and the view, when I am brave enough to lift my eyes from the irregular ground, is an ever-changing revelation as the path spirals towards its peak.

From the platform at its top, occupied now by a brick obelisk, it is the Hall that takes pride of place in the view. This presents the house as I have never seen it before. The building is not in a direct line with the Mount, which lies well to its west, and this leads me to wonder how visitors were led from one to the other. It is time to delve into the dusty documents again.

Establishing when the Mount was first constructed is elusive, but there is ample evidence of what stood on it in the 18th century. One set of accounts shows that a thousand bricks were delivered there in 1750. Then, less than twenty years later, an account of 1766 is for 'repairs to the summerhouse on the mount'. Next comes a truly exciting find because it provides so much detail about the Mount, the park and the Hall's gardens. This is an agreement for the employment of a gardener, also dated 1766. The gardener, William Dimmock, is from Twickenham in Middlesex. This is where the Tollemaches, thanks to their marriage with the Murray family, Earls of Dysart in the mid-1600s, held Ham House. Now a National Trust property, Ham House stands on the banks of the River Thames close to Richmond (and not far from the world-famous Kew Gardens) and is a by-word for 17th-century fashionable taste, both inside and out. Walking Ham's grounds now is to walk through garden history, particularly that of the 17th century. There are broad, high-hedged walks called *allées* which cut diagonally across the garden and lead to neat and secluded little summer-houses. This area is known as the 'wilderness' and was intended to instill a frisson of insecurity into the walker: no doubt a perfect excuse for a ladylike fit of the vapours and a gentlemanly offer of support to help the dear lady overcome her disposition.

Wilderness planting continued to be fashionable through the 18th and even into the 19th-century. Such wildernesses were, of course, anything but; they were features deliberately orchestrated to provoke a reaction. The wilderness was a shrubbery within which the walker was relatively concealed from view. This seclusion was suggestive of all sorts of exciting social possibilities – a veritable wilderness of uncertainty. Dimmock's agreement shows clearly how he was required to maintain the one at Helmingham in 1766:

> To take care of and keep clean the wilderness work about the Mount in the Park, as also the Mount and Borders round it.
> To keep the grass close mown, and the edges of all the walks and borders about the wilderness and Mount cut twice a year if necessary, and the whole, with the trees, forest plants, flowers and flowering shrubs well taken care of.
> To keep the basin [pond] within the said Wilderness clean from weeds.

Taking the two sources together – the 1766 accounts and the agreement dated the same year – persuades me that the Mount and its surrounding wilderness were well-established by the time Dimmock arrived at Helmingham.

The areas described in Dimmock's list of labours suggest how walkers might have reached the Mount from the Hall. His responsibilites extend beyond what we take to understand as the 'garden' today, and one of them was 'to keep clean the white thorn walk and the cinder walk from ditto to the further corner of the Bowling Green'. It takes a bit more searching and mulling over old maps to fathom out where these existed, but there is a   Thorn Walk still identified by name on a map of 1830, a feature that has disappeared by 1880.

Thorn triggers something in my memory, so I delve into my now relatively accessible paper filing system and the stock of images – some still on 35mm slides and others digitised – that I accumulated during my thirty-year old research. I am looking for anything that relates to thorn and am pleased when I find it. In the late 18th and early 19th centuries, Humphrey Repton, self-styled 'landscape gardener', wrote almost as much as he designed. In detailed notes appended to some of his schemes, he advocated that hawthorn should be planted in groups around newly-planted hardwood trees. The idea was to deter predatory deer, tempted by the succulent bark and shoots offered by young trees. The hawthorn was the equivalent of a living tree-guard. As hawthorn grows quickly relative to most species of tree, the young hardwood it protects has an opportunity to mature to the point where it is out of danger, no longer being palatable. At that point, advises Repton, the hawthorn should be grubbed out. In Suffolk, in parks where Repton was paid handsomely to advise and produce his famed 'Red Books' of before and after views, ingeniously operated by hinged pieces of paper, I found evidence of where his advice was taken but not followed through. In Culford Park, not far from Bury St Edmunds, and in Shrubland Park, not far from Ipswich, the hawthorns were never removed. There they stand, overgrown sentinels, some almost as large as the trees they were planted to protect. It is a reminder that many landowners commissioned Repton for his detailed proposals but few engaged him to supervise the schemes he designed, and fewer still adopted his recommendations thoroughly.

When I first see the 'Thorn Walk' on a map of Helmingham Park, it occurs to me that this might have been a similar protective barrier, but a closer look at all the garden and park features mentioned by name in Dimmock's agreement makes me realise that the Thorn Walk was exactly what it says – a walk, or avenue. Rather than being constructed to protect hardwood plantings, in all likelihood it protected walkers as they perambulated from one formal garden feature – the Bowling Green – to another – the Mount. To reach the Thorn Walk from the Bowling Green there was the 'cinder walk'. The scene this conjures up is elegant in its simplicity. A gentle game of bowls on the lawns to the west of the Hall comes to an end. It is followed by perambulating a dry and firm 'cinder walk' leading from the edge of the Bowling Green to the start of the rougher, infinitely more exciting path through the Thorn Walk. Just imagine: there might be snuffling animals out there beyond the hedge, or, worse still, peasants going about their daily routine. The senses heightened, the peak of excitement would be reached when the Thorn Walk reaches the wilderness, complete with its less-than-wild surround of trees, shrubs and flowers, its reflective pool and its demanding spiral climb to the top of the

Mount. Once there, the delicately breathless ladies and their sturdy gentlemen companions could sit in the summerhouse and survey the route of their outward adventure, and anticipate the homeward return.

Faintly breatheless myself after this burst of romantic fantasy, I concentrate on Dimmock's agreement to understand what else was required of him, and what his Lordship agreed to do, too. Taken together, it looks as though Helmingham's grounds were somewhat neglected by 1766. Dimmock, no doubt familiar with the well-regulated and up-to-the-minute gardens at Ham, was well-placed to bring Helmingham up to scratch. The Earl of Dysart's part of the bargain involved spending money on labour, particularly for thinning and felling trees, because he agrees to 'first clean the plantations in the Park'. His Lordship will, in addition, select and pay for 'all such trees, evergreens and shrubs' and put all 'glass and framing' into good condition. Having done his bit, his Lordship then expected a lot in return from Dimmock. Apart from his work out on the walks, the wilderness and the Mount, Dimmock signed his mark, 'X', to signal his agreement to a demanding list of other responsibilities. But I am not misled by that 'X'. William Dimmock was no fool. Judging by an obvious alteration to the sum he would be paid, he negotiated himself a handsome increase from pounds to guineas, substituting £52. 10s. 0d a year for £50. In return, this is what else he agreed to do:

To undertake the management of his Lordship's Garden at Helmingham in the following manner: To keep it well planted with variety of the best Kitchen Stuff and to raise such a quantity thereof as shall be necessary and sufficient to serve his Lordship's family while at Helmingham, with all kinds that shall be wanting and according the proper Seasons of the year.

To keep the said Garden clean, as well within as without side [outside] of the Garden walls, together with all the walks and slopes round the Hall and Garden Moats, as also the Bowling Green and the Grass where the Walnut and Chestnut Trees are planted, well rolled and close mown.

To keep the Hall and Garden Moats clean from weeds, as also the Plantations in the Park. To take care of the Trees in the Plantations in the park and to thin or prune them all every year if occasion require, at reasonable times of the year.

To keep all the borders in the said garden fully planted with variety of flowers.

To keep the Fruit Trees in and about the Garden and Hall well cut and nailed.

To keep the little Box yard by the Cellar Stairs clean, and the borders of the little garden by the Parlour planted with Flowers, as many as are necessary.

There is more responsibility: Dimmock is to provide his own tools, seeds, nails, threads and 'materials of all kinds' and all the flowers 'as shall be sufficient and proper' for the flower beds – all at his own expense. If there were subsequent glass breakages once His Lordship had put the glass and framing into good condition, then repairs were also to be at Dimmock's expense. Nonetheless, £52.10.0 was a good annual wage, and the things that Dimmock was asked to provide were probably no more than any competent gardener would expect. The knack, born of experience, was to be canny and careful; to gather seeds, propagate plants, hoard bits of string and nails and do everything possible to keep outgoings to a minimum. Dimmock was not permitted to sell or otherwise dispose of anything he had raised in the garden 'without leave from the said Earl of Dysart for so doing'. It does not mean that he was forbidden, only that he should ask first.

I ponder the relationship between William Dimmock, uprooted from Twickenham, and the Earl of Dysart who uprooted him. This, the 4th Earl of Dysart, was born at Helmingham in 1708. He was 68 by the time Dimmock agreed to work at Helmingham. This made sense to me: if Helmingham had stood neglected in favour of the more fashionable house at Ham, so close to London, what the Earl needed in Suffolk was an experienced gardener, someone he could trust to reinvigorate the gardens at his Suffolk seat. I look at a genealogical table: the Earl died four years later, here at Helmingham, and was laid to rest with his ancestors just across the park at St Mary's church, that protective repository of so much Tollemache family history. I close my eyes and imagine the elderly Earl and his trusty Dimmock, doing the rounds of the extensive gardens, noting what needed to be put into good order. And then I imagined how things might have evolved over the next four years, precious final years for the Earl. I could envisage the garden coming to life and supplying its seasonal bounty of fruit and vegetables. I could imagine the scene beyond the garden, how Dimmock would have worked every hour possible to bring some order to the shaggy shrubbery around the Mount. Walks along the Thorn Walk to the Wilderness might have been taken less frequently as the Earl aged; but nonetheless he would want to see the transformation for himself, I have no doubt of it.

The transformation was not about remodelling or flinging aside the old to introduce something new-fangled; it was about making good, restoring order, leaving things in good heart for the next in line. The next in line was 35 years old when he inherited the title, and the extensive estates at Helmingham and Ham, from his father. And so the pattern would continue through lean times and plenty, through periods of neglect and restoration, always guided by a commitment to ensuring continuity. Moderation, it seems to me, has been the watchword at Helmingham for centuries. The more closely I look at the records, the more I see this mixture of aspiration and thrift. Come to think of it, this is something I recognised when I first struggled to transcribe one of Catherine Tollemache's 16th-century recipes.

In this circumlocutory fashion, I am returned, at last, to the subject I still believe should lie at the heart of my research. Some days later, I retrieve my notes and recall the conflicting emotions I felt on first sight of Catherine Tollemache's recipe book.

❋ ❋ ❋

My initial response was one of anticipation: what might I learn about the food of four hundred years ago? The second was a sensation of slight disappointment that this was such an unprepossessing little volume. I don't know what I expected, but at the time I had been so busy with the documents of later centuries, often beautifully drafted documents in clear, copperplate handwriting, or elegantly illustrated surveys and hand-coloured maps, that I never stopped to think about what came earlier. I handled the little manuscript volume carefully; its cover told me that this was 'Catherine Tallemache's Receipts for Pastery, Confectionary, &c' a title post-dating the contents. Within, each page is lined to provide margins, space for a title, and the largest area for the instructions themselves. If the recipe is short, two are written on one page so that paper is not wasted.

Titles made my life easier, so my first task was to copy each one. I sit back at the end of this to count and consider: there are forty-two recipes in all and they are grouped together, like with like, showing evidence of forethought. First, fruit pastes, fruit conserves, fruit preserves. Then different techniques for drying, which include candying and crystallising as well as storing bunches of fresh fruit for a year in pots made airtight with clay seals. Then come almond and sugar pastes. Next, flour-based pastes, pastry to us. Perfumed items follow. A quince recipe appears out of sequence and then, as a finale, 'To make flowers grow of any colour'. Some recipes are theatrical: 'To make wallnutts artificiall', others practical and more economically produced: 'To drie pippens or pares without sugar'. The perfumed items include household and personal commodities such as 'washing balls'. I face a veritable feast of opportunities. I re-read the titles, stop to think how I might use them. At the time, in the 1980s, I was asked to develop more courses on Suffolk garden and landscape history. How could I incorporate this valuable early resource? The answer seemed obvious: concentrate on fruit. Everybody recognises it, we still eat it, and, most importantly, the fruits mentioned by Catherine Tollemache can be seen growing at Helmingham, where she wrote her recipes. What better way to bring a garden's history to life? Motivation was not the problem. My lack of skill in those early days was the real challenge: transcribing the recipe 'To preserve cher[r]ies' almost drove me to distraction.

I copied the recipe painstakingly. Where I couldn't recognise a letter, I attempt to recreate it. Sometimes, the physical act of moving the pencil up or down, shaping a curve here or a loop there, was enough to provide a solution. That long curving 'f'-like letter is an 'f' sometimes, but only when it has a horizontal line through it. When it doesn't have the crossed line, it's an 's'. These were simple enough exercises, straight out of palaeography for beginners, but as the recipe wore on, I encountered more and more unrecognisable letters. After three more recipes I remember that I went home to brood. There, I realised that the way to make progress was to look for resemblances. If this letter was an 'n', then so was that. Soon I began to recognise the tricky 'gh' combination. At first sight, neither of the letters looked familiar but common sense often provided an answer. Words emerged.

Eventually, I made a reference alphabet of my own, a crib related directly to the handwriting in these recipes, so that I could refer quickly to individual letters and pairs of letters. It felt like code-breaking and I loved it. Very slowly, gaps were filled and I began to 'get my eye in', referring to my home-made alphabet less and less. After several hours spread over several days, I had managed to transcribe the whole of the cherry-preserving recipe bar one word. This was frustrating because the word occurred in the very first line and was repeated further down. The first few lines, which I copied out in a second, modernised version, read: 'Take some of your [?] cherries and boil them in spring water, then strain the thinnest liquor from them and set it by.' I modernised the next couple of lines: 'Then take a pound of your best cherries and a pound of fine sugar and beat it very small.' That made sense. Sugar didn't come fine and sifted but in huge, cone-shaped loaves. Bits were cut from the loaf and transferred to a mortar where they were beaten into submission with a pestle.

Consider: if she's using her best cherries at the second stage, what would she be using to make that 'thinnest liquor' at the first stage?. Light still failed to dawn so I read on. What happens next is that the best cherries and the sugar are layered in 'a preserving pan' until all the best cherries are used up. We still call it a preserving pan today. Then what? 'Then put in the liquor you made of the [?] cherries and then boil them as fast as ever you can...' I stop, force myself to refer back to my home-made alphabet. It would be lazy not to go back to base, after all. Surely that first letter is a 'w'? And the final letter a 't'? And that's got to be an 's'? Of course. String them together and the word is 'worst' (or, in her version, 'worste'). How obvious: this is the lady being economical, using the 'worst' or imperfect cherries to make the cooking liquor for the best ones. Importantly, the recipe makes an ideal introduction to the walled gardens at Helmimgham. There, groups could see for themselves how sweet and cooking (morello) cherries grow at Helmingham now, soaking up the heat of the brick walls against which they are trained. Any of us who garden (I didn't then, as it happened) and all of us who raise fruit know that the birds are likely to get to the cherries before we do. But nothing was wasted in the 16th century. I recognise this again and again as I work through other recipes. At a time when an overt show of wealth was displayed as theatre on the dining table to amuse and delight guests, Catherine Tollemache succeeds in maintaining a fine balance between luxury and economy, show and substance.

❋ ❋ ❋

I have spent several hours immersed in this thirty-year reverie, most of them on the floor of the study, surrounded by my notes. Jeremy has taken the high ground and has curled up on my chair to sleep. Not two miles away stands the house that continues to fuel my interest: the same house in which Catherine Tollemache had not only preserved her cherries but where she kept a private collection of medieval manuscripts and modern books of her own. One of her descendants lives there now. He is a bibliophile, too. I wonder if she would be surprised to find that he treasures her manuscript of recipes? I wonder if she would grasp the significance if she knew how far her manuscript had travelled from her home before it was brought back, and the reasons for its outward journey? Many years before the present Lord Tollemache inherited his title, during one of those periods dominated by those dual adversaries, death and taxes, Helmingham Hall stood on the brink of decay. Tough decisions had to be made. The recipes, along with other fine manuscripts, books, silver and works of art, were sold. Decades later, Lord Tollemache made efforts to bring Catherine's writing home from America, a land that was, even by her time, still thought of as 'new'. This manuscript's journey through time and space is measurable, quantifiable; but for me, the value accruing from its return to

Helmingham Hall is incalculable. Historians are the beneficiaries; in return, they have a responsibility to look into history rather than look at it.

This mental soliloquy is the place I reach through my transcription of the gardener's agreement. This is the gift of my silver gap. I begin in one place and am led, willingly, to other places, other times, other levels of understanding. Sometimes, answers are elusive but clues accumulate. It is important, I realise, to keep track of everything I discover. As with any evidence, it is the sifting, sorting, cross-referencing of facts that contribute to clarity. This is the mental prompt to organise my notes before I go to bed. I attempt to dislodge a disgruntled Jeremy from my office chair. We compromise: he clambers up behind me and stretches into more than his share of space, his paws pressed firmly against my back. Before me, the cursor blinks expectantly. I type 'References and Bibliographic Sources' and begin to cut and paste from earlier versions, sifting and sorting, sub-dividing and incorporating annotations and web-links. I think of it as the first step in creating information from data. I am enthused when I see how extensive it is, how firmly the roots of history are embedded, how deep they are and how far they run.

❂ ❂ ❂

As I fall asleep that night, my thoughts return to William Dimmock and his task in caring for the gardens. Inevitably, I compare him with Roy, the Head Gardener at Helmingham Hall now. Roy is the William Dimmock of his day. But unlike Dimmock, who was transplanted, Roy belongs here, is rooted here. He was apprenticed to the previous Head Gardener at the age of 13 or 14. He has been here ever since, clocking up a total of some sixty years, with a small and dedicated team to assist him, some of them volunteers. I recall catching sight of him on an earlier visit at the far end of the walled garden, his tall, rangy frame bent double over the fine tilth of a seed bed. He waves a greeting to me and returns to his labours. He was planting radish seeds, I recall. As I drift into sleep, the image of another gardener and the Lord he served comes into my mind. In the span of a moment, I recognise the power of continuity. The business of planting the 'best Kitchen Stuff as shall be necessary and sufficient to serve his Lordship's family' remains as essential at Helmingham Hall today as it was in 1766.

I awake next morning to find Jo's chickens wandering and clucking around my own bit of kitchen stuff. My neighbour's fowl are something of a recurrent theme. They bring me down to earth in no uncertain terms.

Above, November 2008 fuel deliveries; Below: the next day.

Author's images

6: Speaking for myself

I find a trio of fowl digging up the remnants of my vegetable plot in the rear garden. Jeremy sits at a distance from them, relaxed, front paws crossed, showing complete disinterest. I am the one who resorts to flapping motions and shoo-ing noises. The chickens amble off in the direction of home, sounding a few clucks of dissent, but I know they will return whenever my back is turned. A few months earlier, I would have been apoplectic. Looking back, I recognise that both chickens and visitors became synonymous with St John's Row where so much of my life is coloured more by incident than chronology. The connection between folk and fowl began early in my tenancy, when mother hens and their yellow, fluffy offspring provided much visitor delight and many photo-opportunities in the front garden, which they visited on a daily basis. At first, I thought it was charming, too, but the novelty wore off when I discovered that as the chickens grew, they used their vice-like claws to systematically lift and destroy every new plant I was misguided enough to introduce.

I am pathologically incapable of passing the roadside produce and plant stall at nearby Winston without stopping to buy something. The subsequent planting was tantamount to declaring 'open house' for hens. Day after disappointed day, I would throw the remnants of yet more lacerated plant tops on to the compost heap. The roots were already beyond hope. As for the soil, this was now in perfect condition for more digging. And spreading. My hours and days of effort are flung across the lawn in an arc of dismissal. When enough earth has been removed to provide a hen-sized depression, activity ceases as the marauders settle in for a sun-bathing break. I learn one lesson and stop buying plants. But there is still the problem of the digging. After a few weeks of destruction, I summon up the courage to talk to Ben and Jo about the activities of their recidivist flock.

They look as perplexed as I feel and with good reason: they show me a well-constructed wire cage, eight feet tall and extending over a large part of their garden ground. It has a secure gate to give them access to feed, water, clean out and collect the occasional egg. As we tour the cage to check for weak points, we discover that chickens are more powerful diggers than we suspected. Tell-tale depressions at intervals around the base of the cage reveal where the birds are burrowing their way out and back in under the fence. This explains why eggs in the cage are so few: if only I'd known earlier, I would have hunted down my breakfast on a regular basis on my doorstep. The chickens had formed a highly effective escape committee but they'd been rumbled.

I've been rumbled, too. Any notion of a quiet life indulging in nothing but research is dashed early on in my tenancy and lasts for months until winter puts a stop to it. Word travels rapidly along the grapevine. I am living in a stunning rural location and visitors arrive in a steady stream to see for themselves. Most, once they have toured the tenant's domain, want to see where the landlord lives, so the party moves on to visit Helmingham Hall Gardens. Trips conclude, inevitably, in the Coach House Tea Rooms. I lead guests into the rear room on their first visit, and after that, they choose it for themselves. Once settled with coffee and cake or tea and scones, their eyes begin to roam the walls. Displayed all around the room are beautiful photographs, portraits of people. No, these are not generations of the Tollemache family but a gallery of their Estate staff. All are pictured doing what they do best.

When my visitors begin to comment on the stunning quality of the portraits and ask who these people are, I am delighted to tell them, because I have met many of them. Jane smiles out from her desk in the Estate Office. She is back at work now after the birth of her baby. There's Rob, laughing broadly, surrounded by the Estate building and maintenance team. You have to have a sense of humour in his job, given the proclivities of tenants and the vagaries of Victorian building construction. There's Ray, Head Gardener, wearing the broad smile that he always wears. Who would not smile in these beautiful surroundings? But then the surroundings are beautiful because he has given almost sixty years of dedicated professional service to two generations of the family. Whenever Lady Tollemache leads garden tours, she never fails to pay tribute to Ray as her garden mentor at Helmingham. And there's Chris, who has contributed more than his gardening skills. The most recent Helmingham guide-book, which I urge everyone to buy, is filled with his stunning photographs of flora and fauna under the by-line 'Wild about Helmingham'. We all are, Chris, we all are.

My visitors are visibly impressed when I tell them that Chris occupied the cottage before me. They clamour for cuttings before they go home. They are even more impressed if Chris and I spot one another in the Gardens and have an affectionate hug and a chat about growing conditions. Then there is the Forester who, like Chris, is more than that. Armed with his unique working knowledge, he leads visitors on long walks through the Estate. Then there are the professional estate management and household teams, smiling and hospitable, pictured as though perfectly at home in the setting of the Tudor house and its environs – which they are. By this time, cake and scones demolished, my visitors are on their feet, examining in detail what I can only describe as the Estate Family portraits. They leave my cottage clutching their cuttings, and with a greater understanding of what life on the Estate means to me.

One of the best things about living in the Row is that I have such good neighbours. Gill welcomes me days after my arrival, comes to visit and, with her husband Brian, offers continued friendship and practical support that I value enormously. In the early weeks of my tenancy, other neighbours come and introduce themselves one by one, tell me their stories over the garden gate. Most offer practical information unasked: names and numbers: who, where, how much; someone to clear and brush-cut the field and remove rubbish; a reliable source of fruit trees if I want to get an orchard going; someone to clean the upstairs windows; someone to supply solid fuel for the stove come winter. 'No, don't wait till winter – order it now so it's at summer prices.' Their advice is always sound. They know the score. Most of them have lived here for decades and have an instinctive understanding of what I will need to know. We are family in a curious sort of way because we are individuals sheltered under the same protective umbrella held aloft by the Estate. I'm sure I can hear my late father muttering 'Ah, them buggers…'

On occasion, our Estate is visited by Her Majesty the Queen and other members of the Royal Family. Local people, Estate tenants or not, take these occasions in their stride. The landlady at The Dobermann Inn puts it in a nutshell: 'You'll be out there one day cutting that grass of yours and you'll look up just as someone drives past. You'll think to yourself "Where have I seen that face before?" Then, next time you look at a postage stamp, you'll remember'.

Despite the fact that we all know we are tenants, I detect more than a hint of possessive pride along the Row. One of my neighbours tells me: 'You'll hear people call this the Showcase Row because it's what everybody sees as they drive to the Hall from this direction, so somehow we stand for what Helmingham is.' And what *is* Helmingham? Each tenant has his or her own experience. The first thing that strikes me as I listen (I never ask but somehow I attract life stories) is that each of us is treated as an individual. The installation of my cat (and cat-flap) is a good example and I perceive others when I look more closely. The miracle of it is that the Estate maintains us and our idiosyncrasies with its small but hard-working and impeccably polite team, headed by Rob. On one occasion, I make some comment about this and am taken aback when I hear: 'Oh yes, they're very good but you do have to keep pushing. I have been ringing Rob for a week now because he hasn't been to fix a loose floor tile on the bathroom floor.' Words fail me and I have an even greater respect for the long-suffering Rob. St John's Row consists of seven pairs of cottages. We are fourteen among more than one hundred Estate properties extending over a radius of many square miles; some are large, detached, five- or six-bedroomed farmhouses, some of them much older than our Victorian cottages. All are complex in construction and time-consuming to maintain expertly, let alone upgrade and renovate or refurbish. As they'd say in France, '*Chapeau Rob!*'

Speaking of hats, I am surprised and delighted when Pamela and Michael, old friends living in the next village, invite me to a pre-lunch drinks party one Sunday. As I sift through my abundant stock of unfashionable gardening clothes, I confess to some apprehension about my wardrobe, but I need not have worried. Pamela and Michael were concerned only to introduce me to a wider community. I was not there to be judged. They are wonderful and generous hosts. Today was designed for circulating, meeting and greeting in convivial surroundings. I hear anecdotes about local life, am teased gently about living in the 'Showcase Row', and return home contentedly afterwards and find, to my eternal shame, that my own lunch guest, Jennifer, has arrived ahead of me. She lives not far from my Attleborough cottage and has the most wonderful and productive garden imaginable. Needless to say, her priority is not lunch but plants. By the time she leaves, she has more than a few roots and shoots tucked into her car boot. One of them Jennifer describes as clary sage. Jo pointed it out to me soon after I moved in, telling me it was planted by Chris to attract wildlife, which it does supremely well.

'That's SO rare!', enthuses Jennifer.

'It grows like a weed here', I say nonchalantly, tugging a couple of plants out of the driveway. Jennifer never visits empty-handed. Today she brings little punnets of fruit and vegetables that she has nurtured in her garden and extensive polytunnels. Before she leaves, she says: 'I can quite understand why you like living here. It is just gorgeous. But I think you're going to find the garden a challenge, and winter-time might not be much fun.'

I wave her off and don't think any more about her comment, choosing to think instead about the occasion at Pamela and Michael's house this morning. There, I have a clear picture of what it is to build, create and sustain a rural community by contributing to it actively. In the space of an hour, I met people who are rebuilding a valued mosaic village sign painstakingly; others who are volunteering in myriad ways, from Meals on Wheels to the Citizens' Advice Bureau; one who observes and reports as a Village Recorder, laying the foundations for tomorrow's historians; many who work tirelessly for their local church. It is a sharp reminder that I will belong here only if I make an effort. That might well be the biggest challenge facing me. Jennifer's perception of the challenge facing me, on the other hand, proved to be prophetic, and much sooner than any of us might have expected.

It is early November and time to augment the rapidly diminishing stock of solid fuel. I am prompted by Chris, who calls in to see me one day, recommends that I don't rely solely on coal to see me through the winter but that I should buy some logs from the Estate. Days later, the Estate Forester delivers my first half-ton load. He occupies a picture-perfect Regency cottage designed to herald one of the entrances to the Park, the archetypal 'trumpet at a distant gate'. His bulky, fat-wheeled quad bike contrasts sharply with the slender Gothic details of his elegant home. He knows the Park intimately and reveals its wildlife and ecology on seven-mile guided walks for the curious. I am assured by Chris that I will be able to rely on supplies of properly seasoned logs cut from the Park, and I don't doubt it for a moment. I am impressed by the sight of this man of wood as he and his vehicle take my bumpy drive at a lick, the load of logs bouncing in their wake. With equal speed and efficiency, Dave opens his trailer and deposits a few centuries of history on to my driveway, neatly split and chopped. 'Oak and ash', he confirms, 'well-seasoned, nothing green, just right for your stove. Some of that oak is nigh on as old as the Hall.' I am even more impressed when I find an acorn nestling in the heap. I have it still. It reminds me of William Brereton and his letter about planting acorns in January: I pocket the acorn and think cheerful thoughts.

I need all this optimism and more to counteract the cold that I will face for months from that day. If I knew then that we were about to face one of the earliest, longest and most cruel winters for decades, I might well have given up. But as I open the door of the stove to feed it with one of the logs, I reflect that in temporarily losing access to my

Norfolk cottage I have burned my boats, closed off my escape route to a dual existence. There was no going back, not yet. Later, as the temperature plummets and the first flakes of snow fall, my muscles are screaming with the effort of moving all these logs into neat, weatherproof piles. The Forester couldn't offload any closer to the cottage and currently his delivery is partially blocking my driveway. In any case, I need a supply indoors so that I can fill and refill the log basket without having to freeze in the attempt. It is hard work but I find treasure and hope in handling these offcuts of ancient origin.

Later that evening, still tingling from my exertions, I will relax, finding warmth, laughter and companionship at the Village Feast. I have been visited and vetted by a member of the committee. Surprised to find a telephone message from a complete stranger asking to buy a ticket for the Feast and claiming to live in St John's Row, Colette calls to introduce herself and look me over. Finding me to be who I say I am, and reassured when she learns that my neighbour Gill told me about the Feast and will accompany me, Colette extends her own welcome and sells me that ticket. We talk for some time, she stays for coffee, and I learn that she and her husband, who works in Ipswich, bought a derelict farmhouse a few miles away and spent years restoring it. During that time, they began to grow their family. They love it here. They are settled. I envy them. We part as acquaintances, and I know that if I were to stay here, I would enjoy the company of Colette who works hard for the community, commits herself to it, belongs here, like Gill.

Snow is falling very lightly by the time Gill arrives in her car at the appointed hour. She is collecting another friend in Framsden Street en route to the Village Hall. Each of us clutches our one-third bottle of good cheer. The Feast is run entirely by volunteers who struggle into the tiny Village Hall kitchen under the weight of massive cooking dishes and pans, ready to re-heat and serve to the long tables of hungry Framsden residents. Even the children are roped into service, performing their task with good grace and good humour. We play games. If asked, I will say I hate playing games. I have to confess that I enjoy playing games with the people who fill this diminutive, corrugated iron-clad building.

Hot news over the supper table is that there are plans to raise funds to 'improve' this Village Hall. Version one is that repairs will be very costly. Version two is worse: the building will be demolished and its activities and activists will be forced to decamp to a building on the Village School site which – heaven forfend – is just over the parish boundary in Helmingham. It is unthinkable! Conversation ebbs and flows. I realise I have committed an almighty social solecism when the topic turns to 'what are you reading at the moment?' The question does the rounds of four of us, Gill is into another Penelope Lively, her two friends expound on their novel of note and moment. Then it's my turn: '*The Country House Kitchen Garden from 1600 to 1950*', I say brightly, not noticing the drop in enthusiasm until it is too late. Like an over-enthusiastic puppy, I bound on: 'It's fascinating! It's actually an edited collection of papers submitted to the Leeds Food Symposium in…' Light dawns and the words die on my lips as I finally recognise the exchange of pitying looks around me. I have so much still to learn, clearly.

For all that, the evening is a delight. My one-third bottle of red wine seems to have miracle properties. It is shared with a lady who forgot to bring hers to this unlicensed event and there still seems more than enough to satisfy and warm both of us. Gill sticks to non-alcoholic ginger beer, but it has that real kick of authenticity when she pours a little for me to try. 'You can buy it at Neave's, darling', she advises, 'it's one of the best shops in Debenham.' Evidence of Neaves' quality is all around: their delicatessen has provided the first course this evening with a choice of salt beef or pork terrine. Because they both look good, Gill has the salt beef, I have the terrine and we make it a shared buffet. The beef is like pastrami, paper-thin, deep brick-red, meltingly tender and flavoursome. The terrine is pleasantly coarse in texture and deeply satisfying in flavour; both options are served with home-made pickles, locally-baked bread and fresh butter. The bread is baked in Debenham, too. Inevitably, the conversation turns to the myriad excuses each of us finds to have a pastry or a cake when we visit the bakery. I don't admit to Gill that I have already savoured the delights of Neaves' butchery and delicatessen a few weeks earlier when I wanted to lay on a spread for a contingent of the many visitors who find their way to my cottage door. I came out with a battered wallet, just too tempted by the range of delights on offer and too weak to say no to any of them. Next time when I go to Debenham, I am head down and blinkered, marching past Neave's en route to the Co-Op supermarket, which is all I can afford on a regular basis. But at this place and time of feast it is so good to talk about food with the people around this convivial table. For the majority of people here, food is their living.

Gill gives me a running commentary as her eyes travel around the room, putting names to the faces of our neighbours, many of whom are farmers. Proximity to the farm and the farming community strengthens my growing awareness of familiarity here at Framsden. I feel at home. It takes me by surprise. There's this overwhelming sense of having lived somewhere like this before, a place in which I was briefly content. It all seems a very long time ago, this contentment. I drift momentarily and lose the thread of the conversation around me at the Village Feast: this buzz, these people, this place… even the fact that I am reading the wrong books. All are compass points to my distant past. I find the allegory unnerving for reasons I cannot quite grasp. I sway slightly in my seat, anxious for clarity. 'Are you alright, dear?' says the lady next to me, 'I expect it's the wine'. No, it's not the wine. It's not that at all. It's a memory, dug up, exposed. A sensation buried under sixty years of time and more than twenty house moves. It's more than a memory. It is a realisation: I never thought to find myself so at home in a place that reminds me so vividly of my past.

When the Feast ends, we revellers face a shock. In the few hours since we arrived, Framsden has undergone transformation. The snow has continued to fall, albeit gently, but then the temperature plummeted. All is quiet, still and icy, icy beyond belief. The chill is so intense that it strips us of speech momentarily. We advance, three of us and a walking stick struggling and waddling like ducks on a skating rink, to cover the few yards to Gill's car. Her car bonnet is coated with frozen snow, her windscreen concealed beneath a blanket of ice, thick and impenetrable. Mercifully, the car engine turns over without complaint and Gill raises the heat to maximum. We sit and shiver, our breath visible in steamy clouds as we wait for the heater to clear a patch on the windscreen so that Gill can see to drive. Eventually, we set off at a crawl. The short journey to drop off her other passenger, and then on to St John's Row, takes an age. My drive is impassable. I walk it. Gill sits patiently on the road, positioning her car so that her headlights can give me some help as I inch and slither my way along what feels like a ploughed field surfaced with ice. I give Gill a wave of confirmatory thanks. She sounds her horn briefly to acknowledge and inches homewards. Mercifully, she has a much shorter driveway to face than mine, with a more regular surface. I close the door.

The cat gives me a warmer welcome than the stove. I stroke him distractedly, go to the stove, give it air, let it burn brightly. Little do I know that today's delivery of logs will not see me through this winter; nor that my one ton of coal in the workshop will need replenishing three times. It will be tomorrow, and for weeks of sub-zero temperatures afterwards, that I will berate myself for overlooking a childhood lesson. In the Cotswolds, over half a century ago, I met the Romans. What I learned then convinced me that I should pursue a life of study, underpinned by warm feet and hot baths.

❀ ❀ ❀

I was eight years old before I enjoyed the pleasures of hot running water, a fixed bath in a bathroom, and, joy of joys, an indoor lavatory. To make space for these luxuries, our tied cottage diminished from three to two bedrooms but this was a small price to pay. My mother was grumblingly suspicious of the new arrangements; I was ecstatic. I had long been hungry for this change: many of my neighbours and school-friends took such things for granted. More perplexing, to my mind, was that the Romans had perfected indoor plumbing ages ago. I never could work out why we spent centuries regressing into questionable habits of hygiene and comfort, then centuries more rediscovering them. Perched in the middle of one of my hallowed patchwork quilt scenes, atop a green but windy hill in remote rural Gloucestershire, I found the question of the gap in lifestyle between us and the Romans indescribably taxing. I cast an appraising eye around the village, whose houses I knew intimately. Most were like ours, sturdy, 19th-century, purpose-built workers' cottages; but even then, in the early 1950s, the handful of larger, privately-owned, detached properties in Hampnett became desirable, attracting people from London, people who worked in the city all week and repaired to their country bolt-holes from Friday through to Monday. My mother cleaned one of these houses (them buggers had their uses, I noted) allowing me the opportunity to examine it in detail.

In The Old School House I encountered unimaginable luxury. I took it all in, processed it, thought how nice it would be to live like that. Nothing escaped my attention: the luxuriant thickness of the cream rugs laid on the floors, the surface patina of the heavy oak refectory table and the simple solidity of the rush-seated dining chairs ranged around it; the plumpness of the upholstered chairs in the drawing room, the sleek lines of the modern kitchen and the discreet, lingering fragrance that hung in the air of the bedrooms and bathroom. Best of all, one room was given over entirely to dressing. Imagine that! I did, frequently, sitting on the stairs responding to 'Just keep out of the way while I work' signals emanating from my mother. I saw myself in elegantly tailored suits, hats and gloves, *haute couture* evening gowns. I was always tall, slim, carefully coiffured and enhanced by understated cosmetics. There was never a trace of grime under my manicured nails, whose shapely profiles were emphasised ever so slightly by transparent, barely pink polish. My collars never had a tide mark because I changed my clothes daily in that room dedicated to their care, storage and selection. And anyway, laundry was easy when there was hot water on tap and a special machine to do the hard work.

Dressed and delicately fragranced, I drifted from room to room in my dream world, not soiling my hands in the kitchen but encouraging 'Mrs Keen' to place the canapés with a touch more panache before they were served to my guests in the drawing room. Dinner would be served shortly in the dining room, candle-lit, with the generous flames of the open fire reflected in the crystal drinking glasses. Gentle laughter and fascinating conversation would abound. My dream was based on observation. Mr Easton was a barrister, infinitely interesting to talk to, as were all of his guests. Everyone was courteous to the small, grubby, smiling child who sometimes 'did' out in the kitchen with her mother. The child was precocious and never failed to answer when spoken to, frequently holding forth on some arcane topic. Her listeners were generous, both in spirit and otherwise. Conversations were often brought to an end by the pressing of coin into small, clammy hand. One day, not even coin, but paper money: a whole, reddish-brown ten-shilling note at which I gasped with gratitude. That would keep me in books for weeks and I said so. Why did they all chuckle, I wondered, and why had my mother blushed and scowled at me so harshly? Perhaps it was because I was determined to hang on to that ten shilling note and use it for its purpose. Then I could tell all those nice people what I'd bought next time I saw them.

But even these lifestyle dreams paled into insignificance beside what I discovered at Chedworth Roman Villa. Life after that visit would never be the same again. Children who live cheek-by-jowl with the Romans are blasé about the achievements of their ancestral invaders: we took their civil engineering prowess in road-building for granted, dismissing the Fosse Way (pronounced to rhyme with 'loss', not 'bossy') as nothing more than a bit of straight road between two points. We travelled it daily in the school bus, passing fields lumpen with Neolithic burial mounds about which we knew little and cared less. After all, what good are people who just leave great lumps in awkward places in perfectly good fields?

By the age of eight, we could all draw and describe the cross-section of a Roman road, some of us with more skill than others, it has to be said. Even if words such as 'communications' and 'logistics' were well into our future, we understood the strategy well enough: Romans meant soldiers. Soldiers needed camps. Camps were linked by roads, the straighter the better because they were easier and quicker to travel than winding worm trails. Our bit of road was on the route that linked Cirencester and Stow-on-the-Wold. This was pretty much the compass of my world. Until I discovered the delights of maps and road atlases, I had no concept that the Fosse Way extended much further in both directions. Without a family car in which to explore the highways and by-ways, the school bus was the only means of knowing what existed beyond the front doors of home and school. It was from school that we piled on to the coach (not a bus, apparently, because it was hired for a special outing, although the vehicle looked exactly the same to my critical eye) and travelled the handful of miles to Chedworth.

We had been well prepared. A Roman Villa was the home of a Roman of high status. He chose his site strategically. He needed to be able to see clearly all around, just in case marauders approached and had to be seen off. I was a well-grown adult before I discovered that versions of history endure only until new evidence comes to light. Chedworth Roman Villa was not built by a Roman, but by a fashion-conscious British citizen who had an eye for what the Romans did best. It was just as well I didn't know that when I was eight years old because it would have added fuel to my fire of indignation. It was evidence that one person, at least, had the sense to see the benefits of warm feet and hot baths long after the Romans had abandoned our benighted, chilly isle. At some distance from the villa, we were informed, there was a temple to visit. This caused a bit of head-scratching: our school was affiliated to the local church, so we were steeped in religion: I even won a prize at the tender age of six for writing a piece of flat prose about Jesus picking a lily of the fields and giving it to his mother. My English teacher loved it because it was completely devoid of emotion or imagination, both undesirable traits that he spent years beating out of me with flourishing swipes of his red pen all over my essays, or compositions, as we called them. My effort was published in the school magazine. I read it years later and marvelled that I ever rediscovered the ability to write facts with feeling, let alone dig out and dust off my bruised powers of creativity.

Anyway, we intrepid explorers preparing for Chedworth struggled somewhat with the idea of depositing gifts at the feet of some stone statue that had a name and, allegedly, responded in kind with miracles. On the other hand, when I thought about it long and hard in my chilly bedroom that night, restless with excitement before the outing, it all made perfect sense. We do it now, I thought, every September when we have Harvest Festival in the church. For me, this happened twice: once at school, where I struggled under the weight of a box half my weight and twice my width, filled to overflowing with a selection of my father's carefully-chosen garden produce and my mother's prize preserves. We might be poor but never let it be said that we didn't know how to impress. Then it happened again in the village when the same performance was repeated in the tiny, squat, Norman church next to the manor house and opposite the tithe barn. After all, we were doing no more than the Romans, really, were we? Saying thank you to some indeterminate being or deity for the sun and the rain and the good harvest and simultaneously saying please will do you it again next year and here's a bit of our fruit and veg to say thank you. Even so, we didn't waste all this good food by leaving it to rot at the feet of some statue. We knew that every bit of ours ended up at the local hospital or went to help Old People or Orphans, or whoever was hungry, it seemed. The facts were vague but it was the sentiment that mattered.

The temple and giant snail shells found in the woods around Chedworth were intriguing enough; but it was the interior of the villa that turned my world on its head. Not only did these people have baths, they had whole rooms dedicated to them. This was like Mr and Mr Easton's dressing room with knobs on. Not only that, each room was designed for a bath of a particular temperature. None of that boiling like a lobster because Mum had neglected to add enough cold water to the detested tin bath, nor shivering with cold because she was being mean with the hot water or the fire was sulking, or both. My mind was in turmoil, and I hadn't yet seen the hypocaust. This unfamiliar word, which put me in mind of sotto voce comments about ailments, muttered feverishly between my mother and her women friends, turned out to be an underfloor heating system. I almost fainted on hearing this, but then, apparently, this happened a lot to women who had problems with their hypocausts. I got down on hands and knees, the better to examine this magical device. Exploration was made easy because the sub-structure of some of the floors was exposed. Disappointingly, the mysterious-sounding hypocaust turned out to be a bit of clay pipe, much like the ones my father found throughout the steep-sided fields when he was ploughing (some of those turned out to be Roman, too, evidence of a highly-developed skill in land drainage). But the Chedworth pipes carried water heated by a furnace elsewhere on the site, which meant not only did they serve the baths, they also warmed the floors en route. For someone who regularly suffered from 'hot-aches', painful chilblains, causing me to sob with agony when discharged from the tedious school-bus journey into our warm school, and who traced the crystalline beauty of ice on the inside of her bedroom window regularly, the idea of ever-warm feet was unimaginably glorious.

I thought there could be no more sophistication but then we were led into the villa's Dining Room. I knew enough from The Old School House and Mr and Mrs Easton's dinner parties to understand that you had to have a bit of style here. I'd noticed, when loitering between courses, that people liked something to admire whenever there was a bit of a lull in the conversation, or perhaps when they were struggling to conceal a bout of indigestion. You could always tell but then they did eat a lot compared with us, so I wasn't surprised. My limited experience of interior design left me totally unprepared for my first sight of the mosaic floor. The bathhouse floors had mosaics, but they were nothing in comparison with this. A country child did not need to have the symbolism explained. I drew pictures to represent the four seasons all the time. It's what you did when you lived on a farm. You lived by the seasons. These pictures were a bit battered, it's true to say, but it didn't matter. They were all there, instantly recognisable, especially winter. Like me, he wore a coat with a hood and it looked as though he had a scarf. It was blowing away from him in the cold winds that we get here. He's holding a stick in one hand and dangling a hare from the other. Off home to cook it, I shouldn't wonder. I hope he wasn't poaching or else he'll be for the high jump with 'them buggers' if he gets caught.

We were not allowed to step on the pavement but I was down on all fours again, as close as permissible, the better to look and marvel at the thousands upon thousands of tiny pieces of coloured glass and the ingenuity of whoever put them together. How could you see such a pattern emerging at close quarters, I wondered? And how could anyone afford to pay people to do all these hours of work? Beyond that, why on earth was all this skill lost? Why, now, did we seem so far behind this way of life? Even the Eastons didn't have such luxury. What had happened between the 2nd century and the 20th and would we ever catch up?

The equally vexing problem for me was that I had seen the art of the possible, liked what I saw but had no idea how to attain it for myself. The rot had set in with my quiet peregrinations of the Eastons and their lovely home. I could remember the days before they arrived, when the neglected Old School House was vacated and sold by its owner, a solitary spinster struggling to cope after the death of her caring sister. The siblings lived in the house and provided Sunday School in the separate, single-storey building which stood at one end of the garden. One gable supported a tiny bell which the sisters tolled to call the grubby faithful together for an hour or so of moral instruction, thinly disguised as religion with not a little interrogation on the side as to our social and moral habits at home. We weren't daft, despite appearances. We told the old girls what they wanted to hear, then giggled our way home, proud of our treachery. I did have a moment of panic one day when one of them turned up at our door and got an earful from my mother who refused to confirm what my father really earned… Epithets went well beyond 'them buggers' that day. If nothing else, it put a stop to my fibbing but my expressive vocabulary was expanded enormously. Why on earth do adults say these things and then get in a tizzy when you repeat them?

Characteristically, the Old School site was enclosed by dry-stone walls and set plumb centre in the middle of a field. Our cottages stood about 100 yards away on top of the hill in one direction, and similar ones were equidistant on the other side. By any standards, it was highly desirable as a property. When the surviving Miss Bowman had to give up and move out, it was as though she had simply risen from her chair and left. Village tongues wagged for weeks over the fact that when the removal van arrived, uneaten breakfast still littered the table, the bed was unmade and the chamber pot beneath it full to capacity.

The Old School House underwent what would be described now as 'a significant programme of repair and restoration'. It emerged as a comfortable and stylish country retreat. This was an important lesson for me: houses could be improved and standards of living with them; and you could live in two houses at once. Initially, the puzzle was why some of us could live that way and some of us couldn't but I found the answer eventually. It was simple and elegant. The answer was education. People, grown-ups, who had good jobs seemed to get them because they did well at school, or university, or both. All I had to do was succeed. I did, but not then and not without a struggle. As with much else in my life, I took several wrong turnings before recognising the importance of having a strategy. Strategy is about making winning choices. So why do I chose to sit here in my sixties in the chill of a rented rural cottage?

✦ ✦ ✦

The cold persists for weeks. Keeping the home fires burning is very hard work, and it is beginning to tell. Everything aches, and I seem to spend half my time pulling up my trousers as they slip inexorably over my hips. Any thought of research goes by the board. Whenever I visit John at the office, which is infrequently if the local roads are bad, he and Sue say 'you're looking thin. Are you sure you're getting enough to eat?' Even the cat seems to be paying me more attention. Either that or he is as cold as I am. Instead of sleeping at the foot of the bed, he ventures further up so that eventually he is on the bed cover right behind me, apparently changing sides if I turn over, because I always wake to find his back pressed against mine. I give in and move his blanket from the bottom to the top of the bed. He deserves some comfort: at least I don't have to struggle out of the cat-flap into six inches of frozen snow and brave the icy blast to perform my ablutions. I marvel at the pattern of paw-prints in the snow, revealing the route of his dogged, daily persistence in maintaining the hygienic status quo.

By the end of November I am convinced I have damaged my ribs somehow and I make a rare visit to my Norfolk GP practice. In the three years since I last had reason to see a doctor at Attleborough, all has changed. The new doctor fixes her eyes on the computer screen, barely glances at me, does not examine me, prescribes painkillers. But as the weeks pass the discomfort grows and so does a lump. I can't sleep because it hurts more when I lie flat, so I am eternally tired and down in the dumps as a result. Blood tests are reassuring, but the doctor is clueless: 'It's probably depression. You need counselling. I will organise it.' I am speechless but find words to decline the offer.

A few weeks later, by which time I am at the end of my tether, the doctor tries another tack: 'Your cholesterol levels are too high. Go and see the nurse who will advise you on diet.' The nurse says: 'Rubbish! There is nothing wrong with your cholesterol levels. You are underweight. You need to eat more.' I wonder, in passing, whether they ever talk to one another. My chest continues to hurt and the painkillers have little or no effect. I remember that I had rib problems some years ago. I am convinced that I am essentially healthy, just a bit damaged, so I turn uncertainly to an osteopath who specialises in sports injuries. With a bit of imagination, my energetic lifestyle could seen as sport.

The consultation is reassuringly detailed and lengthy. Philip asks me many questions about my health and recent treatment, examines me carefully, asks me to stand, stretch, touch my toes, bend in all directions, rotate my arms. 'I'm not surprised you are in discomfort', he says, 'because you have pulled one of your ribs out of place. That's what the lump is. Not to worry: sit there, wrap your arms right round yourself with this blanket held in front of your chest, then lean into me'.

Click.

'There. Does that feel better?'

It does indeed.

'Has the lump gone?'

I run an unbelieving hand down my front. The lump most certainly has gone. 'By the way', he tells me, 'you are underweight. You must eat more. You need to build yourself up, especially with your lifestyle, otherwise this will keep happening'.

It couldn't have been all bad: he tells me that I am supple, mobile and in very good shape, especially for my age, then he advises me carefully on diet. After such a boost to my self-esteem, how could I not take his advice? Philip knows how to win over a convert: his flattery pays dividends. I start eating porridge for breakfast every day.

Some time between the ribs and Christmas there is a break in the weather. Fortified by my daily porridge, I feel up to some more research.

Above: Rare breed Jacob sheep grazing in frost and mist at Framsden.

Below: Memorial to Catherine Tollemache, who died in 1620, on the south wall of the chancel in St Mary's church, Helmingham.

Author's images

7: Where there's a will…

On a foggy morning, I leave Jeremy prepared for a day without my company. I remind him sternly of his responsibilities under the clause inserted for his benefit in my cottage lease. He sits forlornly in the front window watching me as I turn away from the cottage to drive the 10-mile journey south-west to Ipswich and the Suffolk Record Office. Property is on my mind on this grey and gloomy day. Delayed by events and winter, but movitated by a desire to know more about Catherine Tollemache, writer of the 16th-century manuscript, I am anxious to found out more about the lady. Her memorial in the church says she died in Ipswich. Ipswich? Ten miles away from Helmingham? Why? Like all research work, it's going to be a process of one step at a time. Initially, my aim is to find out where she might have lived as soon as she became a widow. That would be the moment when her days at Helmingham Hall were numbered because the old order had to give way to the new, to her son and heir, the 2nd Sir Lionel Tollemache and his wife. The widowed Lady Catherine, now known courteously as Dame Catherine, would have been provided for by her husband. Property would have been earmarked for her exclusive use. So where was her 'dower house', and was it in Ipswich? To find the answers, I need to lay hands on Sir Lionel Tollemache's will which is not listed in the catalogue of family archives.

The drive to Ipswich is difficult: the density of the fog capricious. My headlights and fog-lights go up and down, on and off. By the time I have come nose-to-tail with several cars lumbering through limited visibility, I wish I had stayed at home with the cat but it seems wasteful to turn back now. Idling at the traffic lights on the outskirts of Ipswich, I wonder what the cat does all day; where he goes; what he sees, who he encounters; whether he is settled into this adoption. I am enjoying the routine of caring for him and it is good to have something else in the house that lives, breathes and enjoys the occasional bit of affection. Red, amber, green break the reverie and we're off. At least the suburban sprawl serves to break up the swirling fog.

I reach the Record Office this Saturday morning to find the car park deserted. For once, I have not reserved any documents. I am hunting for clues to the whereabouts of a missing will, but uncertain that I will find any. After an hour or so of desultory note-taking, I have a break and make use of the coffee machine in the entrance foyer. Sometimes it helps to step back physically from a search. In kinder weather, I pack a picnic, find somewhere interesting to explore en route, make an outing of it; but hoar-frost and fog make picnics doubly unappealing. Looking out through the expanse of glass I notice that the fog appears to be lifting and the sky is marginally less grey. It is a good sign; I might even be able to get out into the garden to to some much-needed tidying up later. But not until I have made more progress in what I came here to do.

Refreshed, I return to my favoured work table, one nearest to natural light, which is in relatively short supply in this converted Victorian school building. You contend either with gloom or traffic noise. On balance, I prefer the traffic noise. My spot is occupied by a busy researcher who has spread documents and books liberally all over the space. My notebook and pencils, left there deliberately to show that work is in progress, sit islanded, forlorn, in the midst of it all. I decamp to new territory. Beside me, I notice that the adjacent shelves hold books that list references for the wills of Suffolk people who died between 1444 and 1700. This is exactly what I need: Sir Lionel Tollemache died in 1612. I look carefully at every potential variant spelling of his surname but he is not listed. Time to seek help.

The lifting fog has brought a flurry of people into the Search Room and the duty archivists are busy. Still, there are plenty of self-help guides on the shelves. In a concise paragraph, which is a lot easier to assimilate than the book's oddly-indexed contents, *The Local Historian's Encyclopedia* offers a clear route to finding a will. First, when did the person die? 1612. For any will before 1858, probate was not a civil matter but an ecclesiastical one. In other words, a 1612 will would be proved in an ecclesiastical court usually in the county of death. Fine. He died in Suffolk but I already know his will was not proved in that county because I have just checked. Well then, says the Encyclopedia in the next breath, if the testator held land falling under the jurisdiction of more than one ecclesiastical probate court, even if they were in the same county, then the will would have to go to a higher court. How will I know? Knowing your local geography helps, says the LHE: we're becoming like old friends now so I feel I can afford to be familiar.

I view a map of Suffolk to confirm what I think I know already: Sir Lionel's lands were in Bentley and Helmingham, less than twenty miles apart, but in distinctly different areas of Suffolk. Armed with another informative map, I can see that these areas come under the jurisdiction of two, if not three, archdeaconries. Now what? Consider the facts further, advises LHE: even if the property is in two archdeaconries but within one diocese, then the Diocesan Court would deal with probate. This is becoming more demanding by the minute. I re-check my maps: ah! the lands were in *two* diocesan areas. Now what? Two likely options, says my old friend: the higher courts relate to Provinces, provincial areas governed by Archbishops. These were the Prerogative Court of Canterbury and the Prerogative Court of York. If in doubt, start with the Prerogative Court of Canterbury, known as PCC, because if land was held in both provinces, it was Canterbury that had overriding authority. Suitably informed and a good hour or so after I began this immersion into ecclesiastical jurisdiction, I am more optimistic. I had seen, and by-passed, a series of PCC Probate Record volumes on the shelf near my new working spot. It is time to take a closer look.

It takes less than a minute to find him. Lionel Tollemache, knight and baronet, died in Helmingham, Suffolk, 1612. And there is the all-important reference for the probate copy of his will. I am euphoric. The will exists. That means I will be able to see it, refer to it, learn from it. I note down everything, check and double-check what I have written against what it says in the PCC volume. Better still, I take a photocopy of the page just in case I mis-read my own notes later (it has been known). There is no point in staying any longer. I can go home, log on to my computer and find out how to order a copy of the will. Where there's a will, there's a way, I think cheerily as I make my way back to the car park and head for home. About three miles out of Ipswich, I run into a bank of fog. With a brave attempt at renewed optimism, I tell myself that I am bound to drive out of it. But my remaining seven miles are driven at snail's pace with headlights, foglights and wipers all on the go. I have never been so glad to reach home, nor has it ever taken me so long. Finding the entrance to my driveway is nothing short of a miracle. So much for the gardening, but never mind, I can occupy myself indoors once I have sorted out a copy of Sir Lionel's will. Famous last words.

The fire sulks. The cat whines. The day is so grey and dim that I have to put on all the lights. At least the broadband connection seems stable. One out of four is something to be thankful for. I give the fire more air and encourage it with a couple of tinder-dry sticks to coax it into something approaching a flame. I feed the cat far more than he is due. Having satisfied these two demanding appetites, I remember that I haven't eaten all day. Not to worry, I tell myself: get the will ordered and then relax into your cooking ritual. Two hours later, I am still hunched over the computer, close to gnashing my teeth and tearing my hair. I have searched and re-searched The National Archives on-line catalogue using the reference from the PCC volume. It dawns on me, eventually, that this may well be an archaic reference dating from a time when wills were housed elsewhere. But every other combination of search parameters fails to unearth My Lord's will. How frustrating! I know it is there. Do I need more information? Is there some other variable that is eluding me?

Temporarily stumped, I leave the computer and go to my bookshelves in the tiny and now very chilly east-facing study/dressing room. It never ceases to amaze me how far the temperature can drop, proximity of the multifuel stove notwithstanding, in the space of a few feet. I shiver and ask myself rhetorically why I came in here, what magical solution did I think would emerge from my bookshelves. And there, wedged between a book on the Cotswolds and two volumes of the Suffolk Domesday Survey, I find the answer: my own copy of my newly-made old friend, *The Local Historian's Encyclopedia*. I lift him, finger his spine and notice that it shows the sign of frequent use, and wonder how I could possibly have forgotten how often I used to refer to him. But over time, his generality was usurped by august volumes claiming specialisms that I couldn't live without: *Land, Law and Lordship in Anglo-Norman England*; *The English Manor*; *Medieval Suffolk 1200-1500*; and the eminently learned *Revised Medieval Latin Word-List with Supplement*.

Poor old LHE, abandoned in favour of erudition and yet, for an amateur like me, still one of the most valuable quick-reference guides on the shelf. I dust him off and carry him tenderly to the warmth of the Living Room. It is barely 2.30 pm but the outside world is starkly grey. I close the curtains, draw my chair closer to the fire and go back to this morning's starting point. In the event, LHE doesn't have much to tell me. Time had marched on since the book was first published in 1974, at which time 'The Wills proved in the PCC from 1383 to 1858 are in the Department of Literary Enquiry at Somerset House'. Not any more, my friend. Now they are part of The National Archives (TNA), housed in the magnificent building at Kew, a researcher's paradise if ever there was. I spent many happy hours there in its early days, marvelling at the opportunity to type notes directly on to my ancient word-processor which pre-dated even Windows Operating Systems. I was the queen of DOS in those days. So why was I failing now to manipulate a straightforward online search of The National Archives? I abandon LHE and return to the computer; eschewing LHE for TNA and, hopefully, solutions.

I am getting nowhere. The chill of the day is intense. Despite storage heaters, loft insulation and secondary window glazing, no amount of heat pumped into this relatively small cottage seems to have much impact on the ambient temperature. Forgetting the simple lessons learned from a basic study of 19th-century architecture was as unforgiveable as forgetting I had a copy of LHE. The walls of the cottage are relatively thin by modern standards. Model it might have been in terms of the underlying philosophy of its day – which was to raise the living standard of agricultural workers and enable them to be self-sufficient in food, but the house predated the thorough understanding and adoption of cavity-wall construction. This simple but clever process involved building two walls, and leaving an all-important air gap between the two to buffer the chill. Let's face it: I lack a buffer. I am a weak product of 21st-century sybaritism living in an upgraded but demanding 19th-century cottage on a penny-pinching budget. I know the method of keeping warm but lack the means. I try not to think about my non-tenants and the instruction I gave them when they moved in, lessons on re-programming the regular delivery of heating and hot-water… followed by advice to 'press the button if you want an extra hour of either…'

It is a relief, all in all, to return to the computer, none the wiser, where I persevere until around 4.30 pm. I accept that I have reached the limit of my options in this search. I call the TNA helpline. I don't really expect an answer at this stage on a Saturday afternoon but am pleasantly surprised by the response. Inured by years of unwanted and unwelcome cold calls at the receiving end and even more years of stultifying hanging on during endless merry-go-rounds when trying to get a simple question to a simple answer from overweening utility providers, the last thing I expect to hear is a real voice asking me politely how he can help.

Temporarily inarticulate, I struggle out an explanation about my failure to find the will by reference, deciding that the reference was out-of-date and abandoning that in favour of a search by name, place and date of death, and still failing to get a result. Unfazed, my helper (I am ashamed I was so far away in my thoughts when he answered the phone that I missed his name) begins by asking for the facts as I know them. Name, modern spelling, date of death, place of death. We discuss variant spellings of Tollemache, of which there are many. 'OK', says TNA man, 'go to Advanced Search – I'll do it too – and we'll try some different combinations'. Step by step we replace the 'o' with 'a' and vice versa. We try including and excluding the final e, and then permutations of all the above. Nothing.

'Hmm… have you tried a wildcard search?' he asks.
I look at my reams of notes on failed attempts: 'I did try T asterisk L asterisk M', I reply.

'Let's do something simpler', he suggests. 'Let's keep the known date and place of death but use only T asterisk L.' I had my phone set to hands-free and could hear him tapping away, selecting the parameters on the keyboard as I did the same. As the search results reeled into view, two excited voices, separated by one hundred miles, collide:

'Is he a baronet?' from the TNA.

'Gottim!' from me.

'Is that him? Lionel Talmage, knight and baronet, of – what it is it – Helling…'

'Yes it is!' I laugh, 'And it's Helmingham – I'm sitting a stone's throw from where he lived and died! His descendants still live there'.

'No! Really? And the family name is Tollemache?'

'Yes, that's right. And I would not in a million years have thought of trying the wildcard search you suggested'. I can't thank you enough! The family's archivist will be thrilled if I come up with a copy of this will. Can I order one?'

'You certainly can. And it's available in digital format which can be sent as an e-mail attachment if you pay by card. Alternatively, there is always snail-mail if you'd prefer to send a cheque..'

'No! no! I'd love it in digital format. I'll go to your ordering details now that I have the reference.'

'No need. I can do that for you myself. If you'd like to pay now by debit or credit card, I can transmit the digital image this afternoon.'
I thought I'd misheard him.

'Really? You can e-mail it today if I give you my card details?'

'Certainly. It will be processed within minutes of the payment being taken.'

'Can you hang on while I get my card?'

'Yes, indeed.'
There are times when I remember why I love technology. I give my payment details and the deed is done.

'That's fine, thank you. The document image should be with you within the hour.'

'That's amazing! Thank you so much for all your help.'

'I've enjoyed it, too. He's my first baronet!'
Sir Lionel is not only your first baronet, I think, he is the very first one in the Tollemache family. This will is important for that reason alone.

Not wanting to sit watching the computer, I begin the usual round of early-evening tasks: drawing curtains in other rooms, thinking about plans for supper, pouring a glass of red wine, finding Jeremy's brush ready for his early evening ritual… but the cat is nowhere in sight. Never mind: I will leave the cat-flap unlocked so that he can get back in whenever he likes. He was probably miffed about the lack of attention and went off to find adventure in the misty murk of the great outdoors. I abandon thoughts of food and return to the computer: the confirmatory e-mail is in. I download and save the file in a new folder made for the purpose 'SirL1Will'. I am impatient to read the document and, most especially, discover what he left to his widow, Catherine, whose scholarly activities and succinct writing have captured and hold my interest.

When I see the document on-screen, I am taken aback, firstly by the handwriting and secondly by the fact that someone else's will seems to be on the same page. It takes a moment before I grasp that this, the probate copy, was entered into a register, where the text of one will is copied by a scribe and follows straight after another. Sure enough, half way down the first page, I find the start of Sir Lionel Tollemache's last will and testament. Despite the fact that this is the most modern of the wills I have tackled recently, the writing is more challenging than that of the earlier ones. Known as 'secretary hand' this is a dense, rounded script with not much definition between different vowels or consonants. As ever, it is all a question of getting my eye in, but I decide to enlarge and print a version so that I can transcribe directly on to the paper. It will be easy enough to type a rough running version, leaving gaps for queries that I can resolve later.

That is the theory: in practice, there are more gaps and queries than there is transcription. After a couple of hours of work, I have barely got past the first few general statements and I begin to think I have bitten off more than I can chew; but on the other hand I am beginning to recognise words and how they are constructed. It would be silly to give up now, I tell myself. Perhaps the best thing would be to stop the word-by-word attempt and look for Catherine's name, or some mention of the word 'widow'. Then when I have satisfied my curiosity on that, I can go back and fill in the blanks. Things move a little faster. I find Catherine but I also find a phrase that disturbs me. Did her husband really say that if she wasn't satisfied with her settlement she would have to put up with what the law gave her? I find this compelling and make a note to ask Bill about it.

I am on the point of discovering what provision Sir Lionel made for his widow when all hell breaks loose. The absence of the cat has not concerned me until I hear that unmistakeable howl and snarl that signifies battle with one of his own kind – or, more likely, a bellicose tom who sees a small neutered male as fair game. I look at my watch and am horrified to see that I have been working non-stop for more than four hours. No wonder the cat went off in a huff. As the noise increases outside, I know I will have to intervene. Forgetting how foul the weather had been earlier, I open the door to a pitch-black pea-souper. The light over the front door does nothing except emphasise a ghostly swirl, and the fog is confusing. I am no longer sure where the sound is coming from. I realise, too, that the night is icy cold. I try calling the cat sternly, but to no avail. The sound stops briefly and then begins again with more intensity than before. I need to arm myself for this excursion, so run back indoors for coverings and a good torch. Even so, negotiating the garden with the fog swirling around the torch beam causes me to stumble and curse.

Growing more frustrated by the moment, I see a glimmer of something in the torchlight. A cat's eye! But which cat? The creature cowers and snarls, attempting to push itself into a bush out of sight. Another rushes past me, going in the opposite direction. 'Jeremy!' I shout 'get indoors this minute! Go on!' and then, turning on my heel, I make what I hope are fiercely dismissive noises in the opposite direction. The caterwauling has ceased, so at least I have separated the sparring pair, and thinking that is probably that, I head back to the house the way I had come, just in time to see the wrong cat making a beeline for the front door, which I had left ajar. Moments later, I hear the sound of the cat-flap at the rear of the cottage. But which cat is where?

The answer comes when I hear the two cats swearing at one another in that bloodcurdling, spine-chilling way they have when they are sizing one another up for Round Two. In these situations, water is always a good weapon so I run to the kitchen, fill the largest jug I can find with cold water, and follow the sound, prepared to hurl water at whichever cat moves first. There is a fleeting howl of disgust, a flurry of fur, then silence.

I am relieved to find Jeremy sitting beside his food bowl, ruffled spikily but apparently unbloodied and clearly peckish after seeing off the opposition. I stoke up the fire. Jeremy eats greedily and then comes to join me, nervous and twitching at every sound but eventually, after a good wash and brush-up, he settles down to sleep. At last I can get back to work.

It is approaching midnight when I make the discovery. Catherine's bequest from her husband was the Manor of Framsden. This is at once exciting and familiar: the Manor of Framsden was used to fund the family debt and to provide income for Catherine's mother-in-law. Framsden, where I am living and sitting at this very moment! I feel a tingle of excitement and frisson of anticipation as I read on. The manor was extensive, with lands not just in Framsden itself, but in four other parishes. Then I come across the word 'except…' followed by a long list of exclusions. In the margins of the will I write the names of each piece of land mentioned. There's more – something about timber – or not being allowed to take timber. So much for what she couldn't do and couldn't enjoy. But where on earth did she live?

I am exhausted by now, un-fed but past eating, and weary after a long day and two bouts of being a cat-fight referee. This isn't the time to think clearly. It is almost 2 am. At the end of this demanding day I accept finally that it is time to give in. I drag my protesting bones up to bed. Half-way up the stairs I remember something: I have not yet explored the surrounding villages but I know that less than a mile from here stands Framsden Hall, a significant house that was built well before Catherine Tollemache's time. I knew where I will be going tomorrow, whatever the weather. The dreamless sleep does not last long. In the middle of the night I sit bolt upright in bed, much to the disgust of the cat. 'No!' I say. 'Something's not right. Her memorial in the church says she died in Ipswich. What on earth was she doing living in Ipswich if she had a house in Framsden?' The search has not ended; it has only just begun.

I do, indeed, brave the bitter weather and drive to find Framsden Hall next morning. The house is barely visible from the road and I do not plan to trespass. In any case, it can tell me nothing but it is like an itch that I must scratch. The most impressive thing about this site is the magnificent, brick-built and thatch-roofed tithe barn that stands in front of the house. Until the middle of the 19th century, this would have housed the tithes, or tenths, of the crops due to the incumbent of the parish church. After that, as with so many other customs, cash replaced kind. I take a photo but achieve little else. I stand forlornly studying Framsden Hall and its Tithe Barn as though willing them to give up their secrets. Even though it is only about 11 o'clock in the morning, the light levels are low because fog is descending again. Worse still, this is freezing fog. I have with me a map showing a public footpath at the rear of Framsden Hall. I venture a few yards along its supposed route but the gated entrance is calf-deep in frozen water and mud, and the field beyond looks to offer a similar quagmire. I don't have the energy or the spirit. It was a long day and an even longer night yesterday and I will learn no more, not from here. I make the most of the outing, discovering and following a road that is new to me. If it were not for the weather conditions, this would be enjoyable, but as it is I catch only fleeting glimpses of signposts showing me how close I am to the boundaries of Catherine Tollemache's bequest.

The fog seems to be a metaphor for my state of mind since reading the will. It is time to give in and ask for help. I rejoin the road that leads me back through the familiar village street of Framsden, past the Rectory, the Church, the Dobermann Inn and up the short hill to the Y-junction where St John's Row, and my somewhat battle-weary cat, are there, solid and reliable, to welcome me home. Renewed by the warmth of the fire, a hot drink and the unusually lavish attentions of Jeremy, I send an e-mail to Bill. I think he's going to like this. 'Dear Bill', I write. 'Thanks to some professional help from TNA, I tracked down the probate copy of the first Sir L's Will yesterday and received a digital image by e-mail. I've done a rough first transcript but am surprised by what I find. Can we talk? Let me know a good time to phone. By the way, would you like a print-out for the archives?' I don't tell him it took all night, that my grasp of it is poor, nor that it was interrupted by a cat fight of the first order, nor that I am in a state of high dudgeon regarding the wording. I am surprised by the speed of Bill's response. 'Dear Moira', he says, 'this is excellent news! Yes please, a print-out would be admirable. I'll put it in the archive with a note to explain how it got here. Do phone any time after 4 pm today', he adds.

By approximately 4.15 pm, I have learned much about 16th-century marital relationships and why it was essential for the legal terminology to confirm what would happen if Catherine Tollemache chose to challenge her husband's will. In his inimitable way, Bill cools the heat of my fire on this last point by saying 'I wouldn't worry about the wording. It doesn't say anything unexpected. Remember a will is a legal document so everything has to be spelt out. The two of them probably rubbed along together quite nicely. I'll tell you what, would you like me to do a transcript for you? Then you can compare it with your own and we can talk again if you have any other queries.' It is typical of him to make such a generous offer without denting my confidence any further, and I accept with gratitude. 'Oh, by the way', he says as we are about to break the connection, 'I must say it is quite exciting for you that the bequest to Catherine was the Manor of Framsden'. I couldn't have put it better myself.

I feel doubly privileged to be able to call upon someone whose knowledge and experience are encyclopaedic. Now it's up to me to make the most of it. With Framsden uppermost in my mind, I do a bit more armchair sleuthing, entering 'Framsden' as the keyword. The results are promising, showing a lengthy list of deeds relating to Framsden that are held in the Suffolk Record Office. Was it really only yesterday morning that I was there? As I scroll down the page, something important comes into view. I can scarcely believe what I am seeing: '1613: Lease: Dame Catherine Tollemache to her son: her dower lands at Framsden for £324 a year, *all except the Manor of Framsden Hall.*' This is dated less than a year after her husband died. Why was she renting her land to her son? And did the exception mean that she did occupy Framsden Hall? And if so, why did she die in Ipswich less than seven years later? Another trip to the Record Office at Ipswich is on the cards.

When I call at the reception desk next day to collect what I imagine will be a single document, I am surprised to be handed a heavy box. 'Your reference was the last of 19 documents and the box contains all of them', the duty archivist explains. I remove the lid from the box. There is document 19, neatly folded, on the top. Content, for the moment, to take a series of photographs as carefully as I can so that I can work on the transcription at home, I do not investigate the rest of the box. In fact I do it almost as an after-thought just as I am preparing to pack up and go home. It proves to be one of those moments I wish I could bottle. As I lift out each of the other eighteen documents and place them side by side on not one but two tables, I notice that each is carefully marked with a lightly pencilled regnal date. I head for the trusty *Local Historian's Encyclopedia.* I make a note of each date. By the time I reach the earliest of the eighteen documents, I have worked my way back through eighteen monarchs who, between them, span more than four hundred years.

Here, recorded on documents large and small, some bearing elaborate seals, others no more than narrow scraps of parchment and vellum, is a complete picture of the tenure of the Manor of Framsden from the early 1200s to 1613. I have to sit down. It seems barely possible that these documents have survived intact through periods of war, pestilence and social upheaval, let alone many changes of Lord of the Manor. I pick up the earliest document, barely daring to breathe. I cannot even begin to transcribe it. The feeling of euphoria is dispelled by one of complete inadequacy. Here is a story that I cannot read, let alone tell. This is the legal evidence of every person who had held the Manor of Framsden over those four centuries and more, for how long and under what conditions, and who held it next and next and next. This is a story of four centuries of control. Control of land and property, and control of the people who lived and made their living from the land. This record stretches from feudal England to Early Modern England: this *was* England. I replace the documents one by one, and carefully, into their archive box. I return them gently to the duty archivist as though transporting the most precious treasure. In a way, I am.

But after all that, and even armed with Bill's careful transcripton of Sir Lionel's will, I still have no idea whether Dame Catherine lived in Framsden or Ipswich or both. I turn again to Bill, ask him if there is any way of finding out. He encourages me to take another step into the past. It may or may not answer my specific question but it will reveal much more detail about Sir Lionel's estate than his last will and testament. The document is the grandly-named *Inquisitiones post mortem*, or IPM, enquiries after death. This is all about death and taxes: that enduring partnership. Bill explains that anyone of Sir Lionel's status was likely to possess land and property in several places and the lordship of several manors, at least some of which were held principally by the Crown. As with the red rose discovery, I am about to enter a new phase of learning. This time, it is all about the value of a deceased person's land, property and manorial holdings. Unlike the wills I have read so far, the IPM is not concerned with the distribution of bequests but with the calcuation and recording of fees, ancient rights or services, in short, anything that might be due to the Crown.

The value of an IPM to a local historian is obvious: the document will identify all of the deceased's manors and land by name, often describe its physical area, status or current use, and will assign a value to it for tax purposes, or declare what is due to the Crown by way of services. The National Archives can provide me with a digital image. It thuds into my in-box. There is a problem. It is written in Latin. Bill is going to be away from home for some considerable time. I don't blame him. I'm on my own with this one.

As with all those eager 'Who do you think you are?' subjects, I tell myself this is not a question of what I know but who I know. Who can help? Although I visit the Suffolk Record Office at Ipswich regularly, I am more familiar with staff at the Norfolk Record Office in Norwich, which is within reach of my Attleborough cottage. I make contact with the archivist by e-mail, asking her if anyone would be willing to either transcribe the IPM for payment or, alternatively, give me a tutorial and send me on my way. If an e-mail response could groan, this one would.

'Don't even think about paying for transcription. It will cost you a small fortune…'

But Susan goes on to tell me much that will help. IPMs follow a format, a template. The legal framework will be common to all. The format begins with the name of the deceased, date of death, date of will, then the names of the jurors commissioned on behalf of the Crown, and how many of them there are (because that can vary). The whole of the will may be recited, or parts of it, and things like the heir and the widow, if there is one, will be identified, as will their bequests.

I perk up at this. Susan guides me to concentrate only on what I need to know:

'The bits you are interested in, I suspect, are to do with local place names, manors and values – although values have to treated with some suspicion because the jurors are likely to be people of the same ilk as the deceased and possibly even friends of his heir and family, so values can be on the low side. If you want to follow that up it will be a long job even if the records exist, because you would need to have hard evidence of what was actually received by way of rents for each piece of land in question'.

I swallow hard and read on.

'Because you are familiar with the county of Suffolk, and bearing in mind that you are trying to answer one particular question, I would advise you to spend less time on the overall framework and more on the local, recognisable details of manors, land and property. You will need some Latin but you should be able to cope with the help of some cribs. Although it is Victorian in origin, one of the best guides is still Trice-Martin's *The Record Interpreter* because it offers translations of words to and from Latin, Norman French and archaic English. All or any of these might crop up in an IPM. We've got a copy of *The Record Interpreter* here in the Search Room'.

'However, I would recommend strongly that you follow the link below. It is part of the Shakespeare Oxford Society's site and will provide you with the ultimate crib, which is a side by side, word for word transcription of the 16th-century IPM for the Earl of Oxford. This was prepared by Nina Green and is an invaluable piece of work:

http://shakespeareoxfordsociety.wordpress.com/2009/12/10/nina-green-translates-16th-earls-inquisition-post-mortem/

PS: If you haven't already, visit this site, too: http://archive.org

Good luck!'

Who do you think you are? An extremely fortunate amateur to have the benefit of such sterling professional support in two counties.

Aided by Nina Green's truly brilliant notes and transcription, and supported by Trice-Martin, whose *Record Interpreter* I can view on the archive.org site (operated by Cornell University Archive), I take my tentative first steps into the world of post-mortem enquiries. Will this one answer my question?

In brief, no, it cannot tell me whether or not Catherine Tollemache occupied Framsden Hall, but it does reveal exactly what her dower bequest, the Manor of Framsden, comprised. With a large-scale Ordnance Survey map spread before me, and a list of the local names identified in the IPM, I have, at last, a view of the extent of the Manor of Framsden in the 16th century. Better still, a view of Catherine Tollemache's widowhood is emerging with it.

Put simply, the Manor comprised 1200 acres of prime High Suffolk dispersed in an area stretching from Framsden to Debenham, but in diverse holdings sometimes miles apart. The IPM and Sir Lionel's will confirm that Catherine has no right to take timber from any part of the land bequeathed to her. There it is again – the importance of timber. Another piece of information slots into place: the exclusions in Sir Lionel's will referred to timber. I dig out my transcription: now all becomes clear. Timber was for the benefit of the heir, not for the relict. The widow was not being robbed. Timber was an investment in the future, valuable because it ensured a source of income. Income ensured survival; survival ensured continuity. The evidence of that became very clear in the 1708 sale of timber when, a few heirs down the line, the family received a great deal of money in return for its very long-term investment. Some of that timber might well have stood, have been growing, on the land that was bequeathed to Catherine Tollemache. Certainly, when I take a closer look at her husband's will, which he prepared in 1605, seven years before his death, I find that Sir Lionel had 'recently purchased' some of these timber-bearing lands with his successor's future in mind.

Through the detail of the IPM, the Manor of Framsden comes to life: the people who will become the tenants of the widowed Dame Catherine rent pightles (small pieces of land, probably enclosed), arable and grazing land. Some of them live in the 'messuages' (buildings and outbuildings, broadly speaking) within their 'curtilages' (areas of land surrounding buildings, some of which could be gardens or space for the pig and chickens). According to the IPM, the Manor of Framsden Hall, which is part of the Manor of Framsden, was in the tenancy of a man called Ellis. I know I have to tread carefully here: Ellis may have cultivated the land: he did not necessarily occupy the house that stood on it. Whichever way I look at it, the Manor of Framsden is a thriving, productive entity. Dame Catherine should do well out of it.

The information slots into one gap in the jigsaw puzzle but immediately reveals another: why, with all this at her disposal, did the widow choose to let most of her dower land to her son? I know from the agreement I saw recently that she retained only 'the Manor of Framsden Hall'. I need to revisit that document to see whether I have missed anything.

I had missed something, something significant, too. Tucked into the wording of the agreement between mother and son there is evidence of some other, earlier agreement under which a line is now being drawn, about which no further action will be taken. What's this? Whether by design or accident, it seems that Catherine's son, the 2nd baronet, assumed her land to be his from the moment his father died. He had already let this land, or part of it, to others. That arrangement had to be cancelled, a new one made, enshrined in this same document. Catherine Tollemache may never have occupied Framsden Hall, but she made very sure that she retained the income from a good part of the land that surrounded it. Under the terms of the new agreement, her son would earn the income from 800 acres of the 1200 but pay out of that income a market rent to her. The income from the 400-acre Manor of Framsden Hall, occupied by Mr Ellis, came directly to her.

The proportions sound familiar... I look through my references again. And there it is: when the father of Catherine's husband was on his deathbed, (before her marriage to his son), he, too, had let 800 acres of the Manor of Framsden to cover a debt. The same debt followed Catherine and her young husband into their marriage until 1597.

1597: that rings a significant bell. Her portrait was painted that year. More to the point, the Household Inventory for Helmingham Hall was compiled that year, too. 1597 marked a watershed in Lionel and Catherine Tollemache's lives.

Whatever the complex arrangements surrounding dower land (was it flexible collateral, useful when there was no widow to support?), I begin to feel myself slipping into one of those tempting by-ways. I do pinpoint evidence to show that she was living in the vicinity of Ipswich by 1613; but I may never know whether Catherine Tollemache lived at Framsden Hall briefly, nor identify exactly where she lived in Ipswich at the time of her death. Another day, someone else might.

This has been an absorbing and fascinating interlude. However, it is time to concentrate not on death but on life, including my own.

Memorial to John, 1st Baron Tollemache.

Author's image

8: Shaping the future

Concentrated research interludes such as the recent will-chase are motivational but mentally exhausting. I find it best to follow them with something undemanding and, yet again, opt to consolidate my notes, tidy the study, bring my filing up to date. At least, that is the intention. Moving aside a box of papers, I discover a 35mm slide wedged lengthways at the back of the pile, lift it to allow light from the window to illuminate it from behind. I laugh out loud with surprise. Almost thirty years ago, in freezing fog, I stood here in St John's Row, outside this very cottage, and took a photograph. I do not believe in fate; inspired choice is another matter.

There is something different about the front garden. I sharpen the image. There, planted for all to see in the showcase front garden, are cabbages. They are one of the sturdiest of winter vegetables and essential for feeding hungry mouths through the dark months. The texture of the snow-covered surface suggests that both sides of the front garden were under cultivation. There is a pair of trees close to the front hedge, now gone, although their stumps are still concealed near the buddleia bed. This is how I imagine the garden would have looked when the cottages were first built in the 1870s. Their purpose, after all, was to encourage self-sufficiency. And that included growing a good supply of greens to keep the family going over the winter.

Once I have got over the shock of living in one of my own historic records, I concentrate on the changes revealed by the image. Whoever lived in this cottage less than 30 years ago would be surprised, possibly appalled, at the evidence of good growing ground going to waste. Where they grew cabbages, the area is covered with grass that is not much better than field-grass. I find myself wondering whether the tenant had a patch of grass at the rear of the cottage, and, if so, how he cut it. It is unlikely that the original tenants had the luxury of lawn. When these cottages were erected, lawn-mowers would have been something of a novelty. I am off on another trail, browsing my bookshelves for a copy of *The Victorian Album* and then going online to find out more about the origins of this indispensable piece of garden machinery.

I learn that the first version of lawn-mower was developed in England in 1827 by the appropriately-named Mr Edwin Budding, who was a cloth-worker in Gloucestershire. His novel application of revolving shears, an idea he adapted from his own experience of cutting cloth, was patented in 1830. The canny Mr B sold the design under licence before it was patented, and his revolving shears spread all over the world. Even then, early machines were often horse-drawn, particularly over extensive areas of greensward. I have a picture somewhere of the lawns being cut this way at Shrubland Hall, a once great Suffolk house nearby. There, the horse is wearing special leather boots to prevent hoof damage to the grass. Push-mowers and later motorised mowers were adapted for the smaller domestic garden over successive decades, but the lawn was a luxury that the Helmingham Estate workers were unlikely to have enjoyed, let alone a lawn-mower, for decades more.

Even when I was living in the rural Cotswolds, my parents considered grass to be a waste of space for us and fit only for the gardens of 'posh folks'. I remember visiting the Sunday School teacher who replaced the Bowman sisters. Our morning instruction was enlivened by the sight and sound of the antique grandfather clock in Miss Bellamy's dining room. On the hour, its dulcet chime was accompanied by the animated scene of a shepherdess coaxing her flock across a rural scene depicted in miniature. Everything about Miss Bellamy and her garden was in miniature, neat, and well-ordered. She had a tiny patch of grass to one side of her front path and someone to cut it for her. The lawn was edged, in spring, with a soldier-straight border of grape hyacinths. We didn't grow those, either, but they have become one of my favourite flowers. Returning from this haven one Sunday, I announced that we ought to grow 'grey pie-a-cinths', have a lawn and eat brown bread, just like Miss Bellamy did. My parents said nothing but eyed me with suspicion. Perhaps, even then, I was a lost cause, my head turned by yet another of 'them buggers'. Now, I grow grape hyacinths and eat brown bread, so in my parents' eyes, I must be two-thirds of the way there. I haven't quite managed the animated grandfather clock but there is still time.

Meanwhile, this fascinating image of my Framsden cottage dominates my thoughts for the next few days and soon enough I give in to it. I decide to set aside the multiple challenges presented by 16th-century history. If I am honest, it will be a relief to be on more familiar ground. I need to remind myself how important these cottages were when they were built. This begins with a second look at the person behind the plan. Once again, instead of immersing myself immediately in the documentary evidence, I make a return visit to St Mary's church, Helmingham. Here, in the muted light of the stained glass windows, I am surrounded by people who left their mark on Helmingham. I glance up at the now-familiar memorial to Catherine Tollemache with a respectful nod. To its left stand the memorials I have come to re-visit. High on the south wall of the chancel there is a marble bust within a pedimented surround. Below is a discreet brass plaque. Both commemorate the life and death of John, 1st Lord Tollemache. I pay my respects to him in silence, then return to the cottage to learn more about this far-sighted man, his achievements, and their context.

❋ ❋ ❋

By the late 19th century the standard of housing for the working classes in England came under increased scrutiny, particularly by forward-thinking people concerned with public health. Reports were filled with innumerable examples of insanitary, undrained and overcrowded development, identified as breeding grounds for disease, let alone all manner of social ills. However, there were good examples, those that would serve as models. Mostly, better housing standards had been achieved through philanthropy, or in some cases paternalism. Enlightened employer-landlords recognised that improvement, costly though it might be, brought tangible benefits to them as well as to their employees. The phrase 'five per cent philanthropy' described the measurable financial return on their investment.

The big names of 19th-century industry included men who were also religious non-conformists. Non-conformism was a barrier to full participation in public life, and the energy that might have been contributed to an active role in national politics, for example, was poured instead into exemplary housing schemes. The roll-call of men behind the models includes some enduring household names: George Cadbury (Bournville), Joseph Rowntree (New Earswick), Josiah Wedgewood (Barlaston) and William Hesketh Lever (Port Sunlight). History loves idiosyncracies: the Quaker George Cadbury is probably as well remembered for instructing his employees to sleep with their mouths open as he is for his farsightedness. His forethought led to provision at the chocolate factory of a cheap, nutritious hot meal every lunchtime and drying rooms where his employees could leave their wet outdoor clothes. His village on the outskirts of Birmingham is familiar to me. I learned shorthand there in the Bournville Institute on the village green. His philosophy surrounded me, in more ways than one. Bournville, from the outset, was not confined to employee housing. Cadbury saw the sense of creating a mixed community of tenants, providing for those who worked for him and welcoming those who did not. The Village Green is remarkable for housing two medieval timber-framed buildings, Selly Manor and Minworth Grieves, dismantled and brought here at Cadbury's behest to prevent their demolition and destruction. This was a man who understood the value of protecting the past, a man who strove to share the benefits of heritage long before the concept was packaged and presented against a soundtrack of music in a minor key.

Other model villages have endured, too. Collectively, their houses did contribute standing examples to which early statutory housing (council housing, as it became known) aspired, 'models' in every sense of the word. The early garden cities like Letchworth and Welwyn are on a larger scale altogether and were driven by an enlightened approach not just to planning but to the management of resources and, crucially, the social ownership of land. Ebezener Howard, who proposed both cities, was neither architect nor town-planner: he was a stenographer in the Houses of Parliament, galvanised into action by the disturbing litany of living conditions that he was called upon to record. Nonetheless, Letchworth, the first Garden City, absorbed examples of design and planning from the industrial settlements that predate it. Outward appearance is a powerful driver in what we have come to know as 'heritage'. People do not need to know the history of a building or a place to like what they see. Just as St John's Row is undoubtedly admired today more for its appearance than for its concept, so a number of model housing schemes from the same era have become part of 'heritage'. In the case of Saltaire, built to house the alpaca-wool-processing employees of the entrepreneurial Titus Salt beside the River Aire, the entire village, mill sites and all, is now a UNESCO World Heritage Site.

The vast majority of rural housing for the working classes remained sub-standard well into the mid-twentieth century, so any scheme dedicated to agricultural workers was notable. In Suffolk, the most remarkable of these was the significant building programme embarked upon by the Helmingham Estate between 1870 and 1890. This is not congregated into one village but extends across five parishes. The housing is based on three sets of model plans providing over one hundred cottages. The scheme was commissioned by John Tollemache for occupation by his Estate workers. According to his grandson, writing in 1949, the cost amounted to some £280,000 – about £13.5m today.

Eager to see what else I can learn, I abandon my source materials and turn to the Internet. There I discover that word of the newly-created Lord Tollemache's methods spread surprisingly far and wide. A sharp-eyed American editor gleaned an article from a London-based periodical called *Truth,* and quoted it in *The New York Times* on 13 January 1887:

LORD TOLLEMACHE AS A LANDLORD
From the London Truth
Lord Tollemache, who has long been famous as a model landlord, has just given another proof of his desire to do his utmost for his tenantry by presenting each tenant who won a prize for cheese at the recent dairy shows with £50 worth of bone manure, while to those whose exhibits were recommended he gives £25 worth of the same article. If there were a few more landlords like Lord Tollemache we should hear less about agrarian agitation and the ruin of farmers.

The *Truth* was probably reporting on county dairy shows that were a forerunner of the Suffolk Show, the annual, two-day, modern agricultural extravaganza which can trace its pedigree back to 1831. 'Bone manure' was fertiliser, and in 1887, this was a highly valued commodity, thought particularly useful for promoting good growth in turnips, which in turn were the principal source of winter food for cattle. Lord Tollemache was canny, his prize well-chosen: his winning tenant would enrich his land with bone manure; lift a bumper crop of turnips; feed the turnips to the overwintering cows; keep the cows in calf and enjoy the milk; use the surplus milk to make cheese; enter the cheese at the county dairy show; gain a 'Recommendation' or more and win next year's supply of fertiliser: and what a supply it must have been. In modern terms, £50 sterling in 1890 is the equivalent of almost £3,000. No wonder The *New York Times* thought it worth a mention, nor that the 1st Lord Tollemache was applauded for his prescience.

The Victorian Estate at Helmingham was as close to self-sufficient as it was possible to be, involving much of what still sustains it: horticulture, forestry, arable cultivation and stock-rearing. Helmingham eventually had a school (still there) and a post-office (closed now). Cottages, similar in external design, varied in size and offered between two and four bedrooms. Most were built in pairs by the Estate's own construction team and all were supplied with detached lavatory facilities, earth closets then, upgraded to water later, also built in pairs at the rear. Every cottage had access to a bakehouse, usually sharing the massive, brick-built oven with its neighbour: I have seen one of these survivors, although no longer in use. The outstanding feature of the Helmingham Estate housing was the provision of enough land for each tenant to keep a cow, pigs and chickens, as well as ample space for growing fruit and vegetables. Behind my large workshop the solid base of the pig-sty survives, even if my field is no longer put to its intended use.

Model leases were issued to every tenant. Over a century on, respect for the nature of the cottage is built into my lease in remarkably similar ways. Every cottage garden began life with a fruit tree, usually an apple, and keeping this tree in good condition, or replacing it if necessary, was a condition of early tenancies. It is a condition of my own, too, that any fruit trees on site when I arrived must be sustained in good condition or replaced before I leave if the tree has expired on my watch. The original occupants' agreements stipulated that windows had to be cleaned regularly, any broken glass replaced without delay: mine contains the same conditions. In fact, I had a moment of panic when I discovered a cracked pane of glass in the workshop window only after Pauline and I had completed the Schedule of Condition. I spent a sleepless night with thoughts oscillating between the cost of replacing something I had not broken and eviction because I had not conformed to the conditions of my lease.

Victorian model leases stipulated that the model tenants of the Helmingham Estate kept their model gardens neat and tidy, as well as exploiting them for food production. One major distinction between their leases and mine is that the original tenants were expressly forbidden to sell any surplus produce. Their gardens and fruit trees were not designed for entrepreneurial activity. Discovering this gives me pause for thought and I scour the small print in my Lease to see whether I have put my tenancy at risk with all those apples and bunches of flowers gathered for the boot sale… I'm safe, it seems, as long as I don't set up shop blatantly on site. Using the cottage for the purpose of running a business, or, indeed, as a second home, is not permitted. I am perspiring by now, concerned that I could be seen to be here under false pretences as I maintain two properties. But then I relax: there is nothing in the arrangement of which the Estate Office is unaware. They, like me, would be considerably happier if the 'Sold' sign appeared in Attleborough. At least now with the non-tenants in place there, I can shelter under only one roof.

Despite the energy invested by the 1st Lord Tollemache in the late nineteenth century, the Hall was in dire need of attention some fifty years later. And it's not just the Hall, but the tenant farms and the model cottages, too. By the 1950s, the Helmingham Estate properties, although by no means unusual for working-class people in rural England, were sub-standard in a number of ways, principally that most still relied on their outdoor lavatories. There are some telling reports about standards of living in the UK's Census. This is more than a national head-count, it is a searching enquiry into people's lives. I looked closely at one of the reports revealing the reality of rural housing in Suffolk in 1951. The enquiry reveals unremittingly low standards not much advanced since the 19th century, but similar conditions were reported throughout rural England.

A government response came through the provision of housing improvement grants. Theoretically, this was a good solution but, as ever, the devil is in the detail.

To qualify for grant funding, properties had to meet certain eligibility criteria, including minimum ceiling heights. Many thousands of rural cottages failed to meet this condition, and it strikes me that some of the Helmingham cottages might well have been among them. Mine is an example where, with the first-floor bedrooms tucked into steep-sided eaves, headroom is restricted. What happened on many rural estates in the 1950s and 1960s was that cottages ineligible for funding and not required for employees were sold off because the cost of improvement was beyond many landowners. Some re-invested the proceeds of sale into modernisation of the tied housing they retained. This could so easily have been the case at Framsden, where there would doubtless have been a ready-made and willing market among the upwardly-mobile young professionals working in Ipswich and yearning for a taste of 'the good life'. With a pleasant yet direct 10-mile trip from Framsden into the centre of this thrusting county town, it is not difficult to see how the entire stock of Estate cottages had the potential to be sold off to eager commuters. It never happened but it could so easily have been otherwise.

Estate employees, past and present, continue to live here as tenants of these cottages. This ensures that local people are not ousted or disadvantaged in favour of applications from 'incomers' like me, although I meet such tenants who share my appreciation of this location and its protected seclusion. Some of them are ex home-owners, people who have made the commitment that I am considering. Through the framework of its tenancy agreements and approach to maintenance, the Estate strategy ensures that the cottages retain their special character and environment, their 'heritage'. Practically, the large gardens are still able to sustain those people who are up to exploiting them. I think of Ben and Jo with their chickens, the people down the road with their geese, almost all of us with fruit and vegetables.

On the Helmingham Hall website, Lord Tollemache touches on heritage when he writes with candour about his home as it was in 1953. 'There was no electric light, no bathrooms and no running water - in fact, until this time, drinking water had come from the moat. There were many holes in the roof, and wall tiles and bricks were lying everywhere. Without the vigour and enthusiasm of my father and mother, Helmingham and the heritage which it brings with it would have joined the ranks of so many other family homes which have been pulled down and have disappeared forever.'

As luck would have it, a neighbour in the Row has allowed me to borrow her cherished copy of *The Return to Helmingham 1953* written by Lord Tollemache's late mother, Dinah, Lady Tollemache, and published in 1991. With emotion and humanity, the writer describes the struggle to restore the Hall, the tenant farms and the Estate cottages to a state where each of them is viable. The task is enormous. The legal work and building work, the business of breaking up family collections in order to finance repairs, all are laid bare. The expenses of repairing the Hall are mind-boggling, let alone the tasks themselves. Budgets are set but go through the roof: the final cost of installing electricity was double the estimate. Advice is given but found, too late, to be inaccurate and, eventually costly because the level of understanding about centuries-old building materials and techniques is by no means as fully understood as it is today.

Despite all this, what emerges vividly is that John and Dinah Tollemache were committed to resurrecting the Estate long before they inherited the title and its responsibilities. It is apparent that they were thinking laterally as they faced the enormity of the task ahead of them. They planned strategically, set things in motion and, importantly, followed them through when the time came. Bound up with the story is the parallel one of raising a young family, including Timothy, their eldest son who inherited the title of Lord Tollemache from his father in 1975. It is little wonder that he continues to display their passion and enthusiasm for Helmingham: it is in the genes. Forward thinking governed everything: Dinah, Lady Tollemache, speaks of painful decisions made as early as 1948 about which paintings would have to be sold in order to cover the cost of essential works and, simultaneously, clear debts that would arise under the complex Family Agreement. The sales do not take place until 1952.

Amidst the painstaking plans for the Hall, attention turns to the lot of the tenants, both of the farmhouses attached to tenant farms and of the cottages. The list of essential works was growing inexorably, but this did not deter the Estate from making a major decision in 1952. Street Farm, Framsden, became vacant when its 92-year old tenant died. The Tollemache family sought the Trustees' permission to take it over themselves, even though Helmingham had not been handed over legally to the 4th Lord Tollemache at the time. This was a major undertaking, as Dinah, Lady Tollemacher explains: 'Most of the fields were so dirty they were left fallow that year and the men spent their time hedging and ditching and getting the drains running again and the farm buildings cleaned up... a large capital outlay had to be found by an overdraft at the Bank for buying machinery, seed, fertilisers, etc. However... farming during and just after the war had been a profitable business. How lucky it was that we couldn't see into the financial future of our farm or we should have been very depressed.'

I read this and think how lucky it was that the view did not extend even further into our present dire economic conditions.

Street Farm was added to twenty-five existing tenanted farms. Their new landlord and his wife visited them all, making appointments to visit two or three at a time, even before they moved to live at Helmingham Hall. 'One thing we learnt very quickly', says Dinah Tollemache, 'and that was what a lot there was to do to get the farms improved and modernised. They were in a bad state of disrepair and neglect and inexperienced as we were, it was easy to see that a lot had got to be done if they were to be able to compete with modern farming methods. John was determined to get all these farms, - and cottages too, painted and repaired and a plan of improvements made out... It has of course cost a vast sum of money to accomplish, but John had to pay for fifty years or more of neglect.'

John, 4th Baron Tollemache, died on 27th May 1975. His widow, Dinah, survived him by a long 23 years until 10 January 1998. Their legacy endures to this day. The beneficiaries include people like me, who recognise and value the Estate environment as it is today, and are prepared to put effort into keeping it that way, even if that is limited to keeping the garden tidy and making best use of it. If I didn't understand it fully before, I see now that heritage is more than history. It is bound up in the activities of generations of people who look beyond the here and now and envision life for their successors. As I have found on every immersion into Helmingham's history, distant or recent, the business of looking to the future whilst retaining respect for the past is the key to survival.

❦ ❦ ❦

The present Lady Tollemache has an international reputation for garden design, practising professionally as Xa Tollemache, Landscape and Garden Designer. Helmingham is often her test-bed for design ideas. The rise in poplarity of the Helmingham Hall Gardens as a destination venue is entirely due to her efforts. The gardens are of national importance, reflected in a Grade I listing by English Heritage, even though some areas were created as recently as the 1980s. These were designed to be 'historically sympathetic' and include the knot, herb and rose gardens to the east of the Hall, all lying outside the moat on a site that was uncultivated previously. Visitors could be forgiven for thinking that 'twas ever thus; or that evolution of the gardens was a foregone conclusion.

Nothing could be further from the reality, and Lady Tollemache explains to visitors who join her garden tours at Helmingham that she was fearful on her first acquaintance with the garden. She recalls the unease with which she contemplated making changes. She was aware that the garden had been brought back from the brink, like much else on the Estate, by her mother-in-law. It was Roy Balaam, already Head Gardener at the Hall then, who gave her courage when she asked how to begin if she wanted to change something. 'Look', he said, 'just go and get a fork and start digging.' With a smile that belies the reputation she has earned for her expertise, Lady Tollemache says: 'I haven't stopped digging ever since!' In a recent 'Country Life' article, I discover this extends to completion of a digger-driving course.

❦ ❦ ❦

Drawing my thoughts together, from the 19th century to the 21st, I recognise that the Helmingham Hall Garden Events team represents the face of the future. Expertly, they look at what draws people to Helmingham and build on that foundation. When I think about it, I have been spending my money willingly on events for years because they are too appealing to refuse. That is the art of good marketing. And it was, of course, that simple act of booking to attend the Roy Lancaster event that encouraged me to browse the website a bit more, a chance encounter that led to my becoming a tenant. That was the result of good marketing, too.

My thoughts turn back to that day, to the way in which the event made the best of everything that Helmingham has to offer: hospitality in the Hall, a rare privilege because this is a private house, a family home. On the chimney breast in the Great Hall, above the expansive fireplace, there is an oil painting that looks to be Elizabethan. It shows a neat row of children, looking curiously adult in the manner of the time. There is a baby, lying swaddled in a cradle. A visitor explains that the portrait was to celebrate a visit by

Elizabeth I to Helmingham to act as the baby's godmother, but by then, the baby was already dead. They dressed it up and went ahead in the hope that the Queen would not notice. I think about the persistence of the myth, cited albeit doubted. Heritage exerts a curious power.

It becomes obvious, the more I think about it, that attending such events, with their unique mix of heritage and expertise, makes me feel special because they are designed to do just that. I can pay my £6 at any time between May and September as a visitor. But if I want to meet some of the world's great gardeners and designers and enjoy Helmingham's gardens through their eyes, I must pay the price of exclusivity. In fact, I have paid for this exclusive historical consumerism on two occasions. Both were unforgettable.

❈ ❈ ❈

Roy Lancaster stands as one of the most respected plantsmen of this century but he wears his honour lightly. There was a buzz in the packed Coach House as we waited for his presentation to begin. We broke into spontaneous applause at the sight of him with his ruddy cheeks, ready smile and shock of grey hair. He emanates the vigour of confidence because he knows his subject inside out. He takes us back to his beginnings; shares with us his lifelong love of plants, whether these were wild and growing alongside railway embankments or cultivated and cherished. We follow him from his English childhood through his introduction to the famous Hillier Nursery and then out into the wider and wilder world of plant-collecting, even to the Himalayas. We are in awe but he makes us laugh, makes light of his knowledge, encourages us to talk to him, ask him questions.

Roy shows his own skill at employing the third degree over lunch when I am thrilled to find that he is seated at our table. There are knowledgeable people here, including a couple who run the excellent Walnut Tree Garden Nursery at Rocklands, not far from my Norfolk cottage. We nod in recognition and lift a glass to toast Roy, give him a bit of peace so that he can enjoy his own well-deserved lunch. Between courses, though, it is he who encourages us to tell him why we are here, where we garden, how we garden. His eyes light up when he learns that he has nurserymen at the table and the rest of us eavesdrop on a detailed exchange about rain-forest plants. Roy is genuinely interested in the people as much as their expertise. He draws them out with a sequence of quietly-worded prompts. 'So how did you get into the business? And what did you do before that? You were a scientist? What was your field?'

There is a florist from Felixstowe, a lady with a large garden just a few miles from here, and a couple who are avid attenders of anything to do with Helmingham. Roy turns his attention to them and asks about their interests in gardening. 'Oh, we like to go plant-hunting', says the wife. I am about to discover what not to say to a professional plantsman. Roy, expressing strong interest, asks: 'Where do you go?' The answer is the one I would have given. 'Oh, we just get in the car and potter about. We have a couple of favourite stalls we visit regularly, but we don't mind.' There is a pause. Roy puts down his cutlery with measured care. 'Do you know', he says, not giving any hint of what is to come, and addressing his remarks to all of us around the table, 'I've heard that so many times from people I meet. And I'm disappointed that I keep hearing it'. You could have heard the proverbial pin drop. He goes on, kindly enough, but indicates the couple who run the nursery to make his point needle-sharp: 'These people are professionals. They make their living from running a nursery. They might not be far from where you live – I don't know – but even if they are too far distant, there will be somebody within reach of where you live. They are knowledgeable. They will know all about your local growing conditions, they'll be able to advise you, answer your questions, recommend plants. Many of them, like our friends here, will have travelled to see where those plants grow in their native surroundings. You can have confidence in them. But if you don't go and buy from them, if you don't support them, they will go out of business. Really, they will. You should support your local nurserymen. Really, you should.'

Silence descends. I feel a twinge of guilt about enjoying my regular local roadside plant-hunting expeditions, both here and in Norfolk. My guilt is assuaged, marginally, by the knowledge that I do shop regularly at Walnut Tree Garden Nursery, that I do rely on their expertise and value it enormously. I go to them for unusual plants, for special treasures; but I cannot afford to go as often as I would wish. I am thankful for the roadside stalls when it comes to filling my Norfolk garden with familiar perennials, grown on local ground and in the same conditions as my own. They never fail to thrive. They are ordinary but essential. I take his point but I don't let it pierce me. I dread to think what it would cost me to stock the Framsden cottage garden fully. The moment passes. Xa Tollemache, perhaps equipped with a sixth sense, strides over to the table and whips away Roy's plate. 'Pudding!' she announces, and reels off the delights on offer. 'I'll have a bit of each', says Roy. 'You're worth it!' responds Xa, doing a half-decent interpereration of the teasing 'L'Oreal' advertisement. It breaks the ice. Roy tucks into his trio of puds and we ease our way into coffee and light conversation between ourselves as he and the nurserymen return to a more serious discussion from which local plant-hunters are excluded.

Then it's the walk. Now I would see a side of Helmingham that I never expected to see and never would have in any other circumstances. We leave the Coach House but stop to admire a magnificent catalpa, an Indian Bean Tree. Roy gathers us and points to it. 'I'll bet you can't tell me where you can find the oldest specimens of these in England, can you?' Now this I do know. It is probably the only thing I will admit to knowing today. 'Yes, I can!', I venture, and then, cheekily, 'Is there a prize for the correct answer?' 'Yes! I'll give you a hug!' says Roy.
'The Palace of Westminster or Houses of Parliament', I say, and step forward to claim my prize to the collective amusement of the group and my eternal delight.

After this lighthearted exchange, we divert from the public route and I wonder why we are heading down the drive towards the park. Xa Tollemache opens a gate, unobtrusively set to one side of the drive, and all becomes clear. She is taking us into the family's personal gardens, the ones they can enjoy in peace, gardens that are not designed for public access. There are trees and shrubs galore, an extensive pond edged with a profusion of marginal plants. Then there are roses and much laughter as Roy hears, and shares, hairy stories about advancing on thugs such as *Rosa Kiftsgate*, clad in protection that is little short of body armour, ready to do battle. We skirt the swimming pool, see and admire an elegant statue that Xa brought home from one of her RHS Chelsea gardens where she won the coveted Gold medal. Roy continues to stride ahead, delighted with the plants he sees. He is calling out to Xa to give him the lowdown on how, where and when she found them, and soon a little knot of professionals gathers around them. This is how the walk continues. It takes us a couple of hours, little groups surging forward and dropping back to be closer to Roy, the better to hear his encyclopaedic commentary, so freely and willingly given.

It is when we are almost at the end of our walk, replete with stories of species and hybrids, anecdotes demonstrating horticultural disasters and triumphs, that Roy stops suddenly and says: 'Look – there's the flower that started it all for me.' It is an insignificant-looking wildflower on the edge of the grassy bank of the moat. I can't even recall its name. But what I do recognise is that years of travel, discovery and professional acclaim have not robbed Roy Lancaster of that first moment when he recognised his passion and responded to it.

It is my good fortune that shortly before I move into St John's Row, the Roy Lancaster event is followed up with another. I can't possibly afford any more, I tell myself, especially now. But my barricade is breached when the Events Team contact me one day to say there are a couple of spaces unexpectedly available due to unavoidable cancellations. They knew I hadn't booked but... well... as I had attended the Roy Lancaster event, they just wondered... would I like to come at half price? Indeed I would. The presenter is the legendary Helen Dillon, whose ever-changing Dublin garden speaks volumes about her approach to professional garden design. Another day in the company of a world-famous designer, plantswoman, writer, broadcaster. And what a revelation the day proved to be. Helen Dillon sweeps in like a breath of fresh air, recounting lively stories about herself, her life, her acquaintances but, most of all, her garden. She has us laughing with her and hanging on to her every word.

I sat in an awkward position during Helen's first presentation so moved myself to somewhere more comfortable, from where I could see her better and enjoy her illustrations fully. Later, after lunch, when we took our walk around the gardens, she said to me: 'I'm very glad you moved seats. You looked so interested. I could see you smiling and nodding and it really helped.' Helen Dillon is inspirational: as a gardener, as a garden designer, as a raconteur, but I recognised that accomplished as she was, the response of an audience was the measure by which she judged her own achievement.

I was to remember that moment when I stood in the Coach House at Helmingham to face an audience a few years later, but in the meantime, I have a few more to face.

Above: Interior of Stranger's Hall Museum, Norwich

Below: Spring flowers emerging in the 'roundabout bed', Framsden.

Author's images

9: Steeped in history

Living in Suffolk and working in Norfolk means that I have a foot in both camps and a growing list of new and renewed contacts. Unexpectedly, I find myself in demand in both counties with requests to give talks, presentations and day-schools. I prevaricate for as long as I dare, but these days people are forced to think not months ahead (unless they are trying to fill a last-minute cancellation) but a year or more. Requests are often vague 'something about recipes; something about roses; something about history…' The obvious thing is that I should try to combine my old and new research to create stories that can be tailored to fit the the brief. All these events, whether they last an hour or a day, are equally demanding because they need a lot of preparation. I find the preparation rewarding because stories emerge as I rediscover half-forgotten facts that I will add to more recent work. I find myself setting aside any thought of new Helmingham research as I commit time and energy to events that are not going to happen, in most cases, for another year. Nonetheless, forward-thinking is essential and 'blurb' is demanded with sharp reminders from anxious programme organisers working to printers' deadlines.

Christmas has come and gone. My non-tenants are still in place in Attleborough. I spend Christmas Eve and Christmas Day enjoying the kindness of friends in Suffolk and Norfolk. On Boxing Day, in the glow of the modest Framsden cottage Christmas tree and a well-tended fire, I share a roast duck with the cat. His previous keeper has given me a stocking full of little gifts for him (guilt-inspired, I suspect). Jeremy ignores the lot and pounces on the piece of string that secured the parcel, gloriously happy to chase, pounce and chew to his heart's content. Later, discreetly, I recycle the assortment of unwanted toys at a boot sale.

Now, duck carcass in the soup pot, enriched by giblet stock and livened up with a spoonful of marmalade to prolong the memory, decorations down and resolutions made, the pressure is really on, some of it originating from me. I retain many contacts in the WEA and still contribute a little to support their volunteer effort in Norfolk. The Norfolk Federation of WEA Branches has established a well-deserved reputation for the scope and quality of its Summer School Programme. As the New Year dawns, I am sending my own sharp reminders to presenters saying that we need their blurb now, please. It is with not a little shame that as I work my way down the list, I find myself to be one of the culprits. Apart from chasing contributors and producing the fair copy of the 2009

Norfolk WEA Summer School programme on my computer, I am committed to 'doing something' at the end of June 2009. 'Something' is an understatement. It is to be a day school offered jointly with the John Innes Centre and the Institute of Food Research in Norwich.

❋ ❋ ❋

The John Innes Centre (JIC) and the Institute of Food Research (IFR) share extensive resources. They work side by side on the purpose-designed Colney Research Park on the outskirts of Norwich. The Norfolk and Norwich University Hospital, better known as the N & N, shares the same site. It is no accident that some of the most important work on food-related bioscence is undertaken here. Between them, JIC and IFR make a significant contribution to ensuring food safety. JIC concentrates on the technology of growing and sustaining food crops, IFR investigates what our food does for us, and to us. At the other end of the spectrum, deadly food toxins are identified and investigated here. As for John Innes, forget compost: the man never made a penny out of giving his name to the product. John Innes, the man, was a London property developer whose bequest of the Manor Hosue at Merton Park in Surrey, his former home, paved the way for ground-breaking research at the John Innes Horticultural Institution. Much that we take for granted now, including genetics, emanated from the beneficiaries of his far-sighted gift. The word 'genetics' was coined in 1905 by William Bateson, who was appointed first Director of the John Innes Horticultural Institution. The well-known composts that bear the John Innes name were developed in the 1930s in response to a need for a new growing medium. After hundreds of trials, William Lawrence and John Newell arrived at two basic composts and published the formulae through a series of leaflets designed to support the war effort.

My initial reason for contacting JIC was simple. The outcome was anything but.

'Come and meet us at IFR', says Catherine Reynolds, then the Head of Communications for the two academic organisations.

Catherine introduces me to Dr Sarah Wilmot, who is a science historian with the enviable task of curating the John Innes Foundation collection of rare books. I have come today to ask if the proposed day school could be built around books from the collection, whose catalogue I have browsed online. It is formidable: not one but two original copies of John Gerard's 16th-century *Herball or Generall Historie of Plants*, and others equally rare, some of them hand-coloured. My opening gambit is that we track the progress of botanical knowledge, and its dissemination, through the rare books. We relate that to the plants used in Catherine Tollemache's recipes under the title 'From Plant to Plate'. I am hoping, for the WEA's sake, that we may benefit from a reduced fee if we hire the impressive facilities of the John Innes Conference Centre for the event. It's asking a lot. I tread softly, begin by asking Sarah about the rare books and access to them.

'We house them on the John Innes site under controlled conditions within the Library. Scholars can refer to them at any time – you could if you like'.

I would like and we arrange a date.

'Is there any chance that you could make some of the books accessible for the day school?'

'Well, as things stand, we could not admit more than a few people at a time to the room. How many do you expect?'

'Probably not less than 20 and probably closer to 40'.

'What did you have in mind?'

I tell Sarah and Catherine about Helmingham Hall and the Tollemache Family Archive, show them a few examples of the recipe transcriptions, talk them through the techniques, tell them a little about Catherine Tollemache and her manuscript, outline the way the day school will tell the story. Catherine Reynolds is first to spot the opportunity.

'This is mind-blowing stuff! How much more of it have you got?'

'There are 42 recipes in all, many of them use fruit and a lot of them use sugar. In fact, I was also going to ask if I could pick IFR brains about the history of things like sugar. Oh – and the exotic imports, too, like gums, resins and perfumes…'

A broad smile spreads across Catherine's face. 'I think we can do better than that', she says. 'I'd like to pull a team of our bioscientists together, let them loose on this – and include Sarah for books and history of science input.'

'Bioscientists?', I ask. 'Would they be interested?'

Catherine doesn't pause for breath.

'Would they! You've just mentioned sugar, yes? Well, Dave Hart, one of the IFR research chemists, has a background in the stuff and he is an absolutely BRILLIANT communicator. Then we've got Vic, Professor Vic Morris, the world's leading authority on pectin – your Catherine wouldn't have known it by that word but there's no doubt she knew its effect – you've just confirmed it with that recipe of hers using whole apples. And I think we should pull in Mike, don't you, Sarah? Mike Ambrose has responsibility for the JIC Seed Bank. I reckon he would love to get his teeth into Catherine Tollemache's bread!'

She laughs at her own pun, and I am caught up in her enthusiasm, intoxicated by the excitement of it all. And then I imagine the hard-working WEA Federation Committee and their aim always to make these events self-financing, and the smile leaves my face.

'I… well, I am thrilled that you are so positive… the trouble is that there is nothing to fund this… in fact, I am here with begging bowl in hand to see whether we could use your Conference Centre at an advantageous rate… the WEA is a charity…'

Catherine laughs. My strategy is all out in the open now.

'Look. Leave it with me. Go and visit the Library with Sarah as soon as you can. I think there is a way that we could protect the books for a limited period of time and that they could form part of your day school. Take that as read and leave the logistics up to us.'

Sarah looks more than a little worried at this, but Catherine is in full flood now.

'Are you prepared to let me photocopy the recipe transcripts you have brought with you so that I can share them with the team, see what they think? If they play ball, and I feel sure they will, the next step would be to get you back here to meet with all of them and to thrash out the detail of the day school. It's alright: we will contribute our professional time so it is not going to cost the WEA anything. As for the use of the Conference Centre, we'll see what we can do '.

Communications flow back and forth for the next few weeks. Keen to find ways of increasing public understanding of their research programme, the John Innes Centre confirm their generous offer to host the day school at their impressive conference facility on the Colney Research Park on 26th June. The WEA Norfolk Federation Summer School Committee is overjoyed. They believe this could be a winner of an event.

They are right. Catherine Reynolds was right. 'From Plant to Plate' is fully booked within a week of the Summer School Programme being circulated in January 2009.

The responsibility for the planning and delivery of the day is mine. All I have to do now is make it happen.

❋ ❋ ❋

It is one thing to read a stark line of catalogue information but quite another to see and handle two original copies of John Gerard's 1597 *Herball,* and more. The light levels are kept very low in the rare book room, and hands need to be suitably gloved to prevent acid from the skin damaging the fragile pages. I leave shivering, partly because I am in awe of what I have seen and partly from the bone-chilling cold of the books' repository. Needless to say, I make several return visits, suitably prepared with layers of thermal protection.

Preparation is everything, but I was not prepared for the galvanic impact of Catherine Tollemache's recipes upon the group of bioscientists I meet next time I visit the Colney Research Park.

We agree a programme for the day. Each of us outlines the contribution we would like to make and the resources we will need. One by one, the bioscientists explain to me and to each other what it is in the handful of recipes that has sparked their interest. If the day school is anything like the discussion meeting, delegates are in for a treat. By the time I leave, I have a long list of additional information requested by the participating team members.

I learn also that I am not the only person to be impressed by the clarity of the recipe book's language, which is remarkable for its day in comparison with its contemporaries. One of the team remarks that the langue is that of a scientist, someone who is used to observing and recording events systematically, interpreting them logically. Someone else points out that there is clear evidence of experimentation: 'You can't explain to someone what may go wrong, and how to avoid it, unless you have seen for yourself why, how and when it goes wrong. Finding a solution relies on trial and error. She was a scientist. I think we should call her "Catherine Tollemache, early empirical scientist" – what about it?' His suggestion meets with unanimous agreement, but it is more than a lighthearted acceptance. The awe in which these professionals treat the science behind the recipes has its effect on me, too. I realise that I am going to have to reassess the recipes – and their writer.

❈ ❈ ❈

As I make the long journey home to Framsden, this plays on my mind and adds a new level of responsibility. The scientists will explain their theory about Catherine Tollemache as an 'early empirical scientist' through their presentations at the day school. But if I am ever to produce anything in publication, I will need to do justice to this lady and her achievements.

These thoughts prompt me to look outside the recipes, to explore them more broadly in their context. The postman beats a path to my door over the next few weeks. I no longer fall at his feet or sign in blood, but my bookshelves begin to fill with facsimile copies of 16th- and 17th-century household manuals and, broadly, cookery books. I haunt the Internet in the small hours of insomnia, searching the academic databases of organisations who have collections of original household manuscripts. I bury myself in the output of modern writers on the same topics and find there to be many. I run out of bookshelf space. Not least I return frequently to my copy of *Two East Anglian Picture Books,* which includes a partial transcript of the 1597 Household Inventory for Helmingham Hall. Fascinating though it is, I would like to see the original in its entirety. Bill arranges for the archive to be transported to Ipswich. I visit the Record Office several times, photograph the pages describing the contents of rooms likely to be concerned with processing raw materials, preparing and cooking food. Then, at home in Framsden, I begin the slow process of transcription.

Jeremy is getting used to my frequent disappearances to foreign parts and has taken to sitting in the front window of the cottage to watch as I drive away. If I am absent for a whole day, he goes into paroxysms of delight on my return. He waits until I am inside the door, sits a few feet away from me, then bends his head until it touches the floor in the manner of a sweeping bow. Holding this position, he looks up at me to make sure I am paying attention, waits until I make some noise of greeting, then springs himself upright and does a little dance of delight. It is almost worth going out for the day to have such a rapturous welcome home. Now I am at home for several weeks in a row, busy with transcription, he strives to keep me within sight – in case I try to escape, I imagine. He seems settled here and perhaps he staked his claim on his garden territory during that noisy cat-fight a few months ago. It would be a shame to have to take him away from all this. I put the thought from my mind and buckle down to encouraging the 400-year old Household Inventory to release its story.

❈ ❈ ❈

Throughout the weeks filled with research and transcription, excoriating winter loses its grip and submits to the rejuvenating and nourishing balm of spring. But the weather remains capricious: after a night of particularly heavy rain in February, I awake to see the fields opposite under water. News on the radio gives a litany of local road closures due to flood. The floodwater persists and presents me with a 'February Filldyke' scene of ethereal, silvered beauty. Days are short and predominantly grey until a weak sun breaks through, often in mid-afternoon. By the time I close the curtains, evenings bruise the sky with blues and purples shot through with blood red. Just as the water begins to recede, February throws a tantrum. In a vicious attack of Arctic weather, the lingering layer of floodwater freezes, and the fields are covered for days with a mirror of ice.

❖ ❖ ❖

News breaks in March: my non-tenants are on the list for a government-supported scheme to purchase their own home. I am delighted for them. But I know in my heart of hearts that when they move out, I must move back in and restore my cottage to a state fit for sale. We have no idea when their application will be determined.

I want to make the most of my remaining time at Framsden. As spring breathes softly in the wings and threatens to bombard the garden with life and me with demands for attention, I throw myself into preparing for a day school that will take place when the garden may no longer be mine to enjoy.

❖ ❖ ❖

The balance between mental and physical endeavour tips in favour of the garden, inevitably. I have to dust off the Flymo and cut the grass for the first time on 1ˢᵗ March, 2009. Despite the onslaught of cold weather, I see the promise of spring everywhere, shouldering its way through the stony clay soil, some of it still partially frozen. A few daffodils brave it, looking lost in a garden of this size; but there are fat buds on the apple tree and even fatter ones of hellebore in the borders. One morning, I am rewarded with the sight of dark purple hellebore flowers and, as if by magic, I investigate a fuzz of green and pale yellow under my hedge to find a promise of primroses.

Further into March, a ray of hope emerges. I am still weighing up my long-term property options, would still love to live in Suffolk, preferably in or around Debenham. I don't give up hope readily. I continue to browse 'Rightmove' on a weekly basis. And one day, as if in reward for my persistence, I find a house for sale in Framsden Street. The Estate Agent is based in Debenham. I call him, explain my odd position. He has no doubt that the Framsden house will sell quickly because it is priced realistically but says come and view it anyway. Why not?

The semi-detached property, probably built in the 1950s, stands on the north side of Framsden Street on rising land. As a result, there is a precipitous slope up to the house from the road. This gives me cause for concern when I think about access during winters like the recent one, still reluctant to withdraw its claws completely. However, that same slope endows the house with wonderful views along the Street from its front rooms and glorious ones of arable farmland from the rear. Better still, there is an extensive range of outbuildings and a very long garden. Inside, the layout has been modified on the ground floor and gives an unusually spacious feel to this otherwise charmless fifties building. Fittings and décor are dated but these are a matter of taste and can be changed over time. The roof, walls, windows and doors look sound. There is a central-heating system, albeit oil-fired and therefore expensive to run, but there are plenty of ways to improve insulation and keep running costs down. All in all, this is exactly the sort of project I would enjoy. The setting is stunning and the possibility of living in Framsden makes my spirits soar. Is it achievable?

The Estate Agent phones two days later. An offer has been made and accepted but the buyer has not yet signed a contract. Any news of my outgoing tenants yet? No? Well, let's see what happens, shall we? He phones a fortnight later. The buyer has signed the contract, has the finance in place and completion will take place within the month. But do keep in touch.

❈ ❈ ❈

Many months later, I check Land Registry data, curious to see what the Framsden Street property achieved. I am not surprised to learn that the sale price was well above the asking price but a second discovery makes my blood run cold: the difference between the estimated value of my Norfolk property and the sale price of the Framsden house is in excess of £40,000. When I first moved to Framsden, values were no more than £2 - £3,000 apart. Based on past experience, I would have expected confidently to complete the purchase of the Framsden Street property with funds in hand to finance improvements. This is the shape of things to come.

❈ ❈ ❈

Spring moves from gentle kindness to outright generosity. I set up a field kitchen most days, cooking and eating my evening meal outdoors. Jeremy joins me, content to stretch out at my feet and soak up whatever the sun has to offer. He does not beg or attempt to steal food. All he wants, it seems, is company. Occasionally, he will make a spirited attack on a dandelion, eyes wide and ears flattened. Then he will abandon his victim temporarily, charge up and down the garden, returning to base at high speed, making a bee-line for the offending weed and pouncing on it anew. I can't help but think that he would make a formidable hunter. But if he does hunt, he never brings the evidence home which is unusual for a cat. As baby birds increase in number, and a few adults are brave enough to hop about in the garden to hunt for food, he continues to show no sign of wanting to give chase or otherwise disturb them. Bird and beast eye one another from a safe distance, untroubled. This cat, adopted under pressure, is growing into a very rewarding little companion. It is a happy thought: wherever I go next, this pernickity ball of grey fur, completely lacking in social graces, will come with me. I can't help thinking that we are well suited.

If I felt a tug before, I am hooked and landed when the cowslips appear in my rear garden. They are prolific and I gather bunches of them, burying my nose in their flowers to inhale their fresh, soft fragrance. Memories of my Cotswold childhood flood in. I used to haunt the hedges for primroses and the meadows for cowslips. Other Framsden flowers, both wild and cultivated, emerge in profusion. With them comes gradual, soothing warmth, outdoors and in. For the first time in months, I let the stove out overnight, light it later and later in the day, and eventually not at all.

All it takes is the sight of another Jacob ewe giving birth, or the antics of her lively progeny, and I am transported back to my childhood yet again. I bottle-fed orphaned lambs regularly, then waved them off as their fat little bodies disappeared into the throng of the flock. I am not familiar with rare breeds, and I am fascinated by the Jacob sheep. The adults are spotted, but their lambs are born black and have a curious habit of nodding their heads up and down. With the head-nodding and the vertical take-offs for which all lambs are renowned, they give me hours of amusement. I can watch them from my bedroom window as the days lengthen generously, but more often than not I walk over to the field and lean on the gate to watch the action at close quarters.

In the cottage garden, my efforts last autumn in the 'roundabout bed' are paying dividends. Bluebells emerge, as yet a forest of green centurions holding aloft spears bearing the promise of a bright blue carpet to come. Healthy new shoots of perennial shrubs are everywhere to be seen. Soon, the roundabout bed will be head-high in fuchsia, tamarisk, tree peony and the rest. And overseeing it all will be that magnificent old cooking apple tree. I won't be here to see it bear fruit this year, though.

As the sap rises, I have the urge to gather up anything I can against the day when I must leave. Uprooting half the garden is clearly impractical, let alone contrary to the spirit of any half-decent tenancy agreement, but I find an alternative. Opting to take a different route to Debenham one day, I discover a garden nursery with an exceptional collection of fruit trees in all shapes and sizes. I cannot resist the towering greengage, despite the fact that it will not fit into my tiny car. No matter, says the man at the nursery, he will deliver it. I add red and white currants and a fig tree to his load. I explain that they are going to move on with me, ask if they will survive in pots for a few months.

'Where do I deliver?'

'St John's Row, Framsden'.

'And where's that?'

I describe the route from Framsden windmill.

'Oh, there! How lovely. Why are you leaving?'

I wish I had the words.

❋ ❋ ❋

Words keep me going, principally the words that I will deliver at the June day school. When I am not dashing across the road to welcome successive black lambs, I am concentrating my attention on the 1597 Household Inventory. Initially, I focus only on rooms and their contents that can help to illustrate the recipes. It strikes me that the day school would be much livelier if I could show illustrations of 16th-century household goods and culinary equipment. The more I ponder this, the more the Inventory entices me with its 'posnets', 'potion peeces', 'perfuming pannes' and more. Then again, there are numerous items that have the same names today: mortars and pestles, preserving pans and pastry boards among them. I browse the Internet but am loathe to steal images, whether they claim to be 'copyright free' or not, because I want to use them in presentation. I contact Catherine Reynolds to ask if she knows of any academic sources that I could approach; which is how I find myself on the doorstep of one of the oldest buildings in the city of Norwich.

* * *

Strangers' Hall Museum is part of the Norfolk Museums and Archaeology Service (NMAS). The building is one of the most historic in Norwich, a gem within striking distance of the busy central market (the site of which is medieval), a stone's throw from the Norman cathedral, and next door but one to a sex shop. Such is city life. Medieval life was probably not that different. The street, known as Charing Cross, is unprepossessing and dominated by multi-lane traffic. Modern infill has robbed it of its medieval character, although there are hints in roof lines, jettied frontages and, in the case of the Museum, an enormous arched entrance gate, large enough to admit horses and carriages, into which a smaller pedestrian door is cut.

The gate opens on to a paved courtyard with buildings around four sides. One of these forms a range with the entrance archway and is, in effect, a shop-front. Viewed from Charing Cross, this large glazed area, shallow in depth, offers enticing displays of what can be found inside Strangers' Hall.

A flight of steep stone steps leads from the courtyard to the front door of what was originally a 13th-century merchant's house. Over successive centuries, citizens of status and wealth have extended the original building, both outwards and upwards. Now, the interior is arranged to offer a series of rooms designed as self-contained set pieces. Each tells the story of a different historical period. In this way, seven centuries or more are on view in a spacious, lively and accessible layout. Nothing feels contrived. I enter at the 16th-century, appropriately, to be faced with an elegant dining scene that could have come straight out of Helmingham's household in Catherine Tollemache's time. I can see that a return visit is going to be essential.

The reason for today's visit is to explain the purpose of the John Innes day school and to ask whether the Museum has any domestic or culinary equipment from the 16th century that I could look at and photograph. Helen, the Museum's curator, asks: 'Is there anything particular that you have in mind?'

'Well, yes', I reply, 'I am intrigued by the recipes for things like artificial walnuts made with a mixture of sugar, cinnamon and gum arabic, then pressed into a walnut-shaped mould. Do you have any moulds like that?'

Helen consults her computer, calls up a database of the Museum's collection. 'Yes, we do. There is a walnut mould in our Reserve Collection, although it is Victorian. I don't think we have anything earlier.'

'Reserve Collection?'

'Yes, thousands of items held by NMAS but not on display. I can e-mail you a link to the database. Then you can select what you'd like to see and I'll do my best to have items brought here for you. You'll probably want to come back anyway because of our collection of historic recipe books. None of them is anywhere near as old as the ones you've been working on, and most of them are printed, not manuscripts, but even so...'

I am smiling ear to ear by this time but realise I can't accept all this help without making some contribution. 'Is there anything you think might be useful to you from my research?', I ask innocently. Cathy has joined us by now, and she leaps at the opportunity: 'I'd love to know what you find out from that 1597 Household Inventory you mentioned' she ventures, and encouraged by my nod she continues: 'because I specialise in the history of textiles. It is my passion but it is also really important here because Norwich was at the centre of the textile industry. Anything you can share about 16th-century textiles would really interest me.'

By the time I return to Framsden, Helen has e-mailed me with the promised link to the Reserve Collections database. If I pick out what I'd like to see, she says, and can suggest some dates for my next visit, she will do her best to have everything there waiting for me. In a separate message, Cathy says it would be wonderful to have any information I can provide on textiles and, by the way, I must meet Bethan next time I come. Bethan is one of those brave historians known as an interpreter. Her speciality is food of the Tudor period.

Over the next few weeks I produce transcripts of other rooms mentioned in the Inventory and, much to Cathy's delight, these cover not only bedrooms but the Wardrobe. We e-mail one another frequently, Cathy swooping on my descriptions of embroidered cushions, coverlets (for the beds), carpets (not for the floors, but for tables) and, not least, clothes. Further links to other experts, other works of reference, fly between us. Cathy is stumped by some of the words and phrases I find in the Inventory. More work ensues but, as ever, some gaps remain unfilled. In turn, I travel several times to Norwich to view everything from replica linen to original and massive cast iron mortars. One is dated 1597. It matches Catherine Tollemache's specification in one of her perfume-making recipes. She pre-heats the mortar before filling it with exotic gums and resins, pounding them as they melt to form the material for her pomander beads.

As if there is not enough on my plate, I am unable to resist the temptation of yet more historic recipe manuscripts. I select from the database of the Reserve Collection, and spend more days than I should in viewing and photographing instructions dating from the 17th-century through to the 20th. Inevitably, there are tempting byways, but I resist. Yes, I may explore the UK's World War II strategy for producing and cooking food, look at the legislation and nutritional advice – but not now.

On one of my trips to Stranger's Hall, I meet Bethan, who is young, full of life and good humour, and looks marvellous in her Tudor costume. She tells me that she spends several weeks a year involved in re-enactments, an activity that is growing in popularity. This goes way beyond 'living history' days for groups of schoolchildren and visitors. Bethan works regularly with people who have developed professional expertise in a wide range of techniques. The appetite for recreating the food of the past is strong. The delivery of authentic examples by dedicated professionals is more extensive and more organised into specialisms than I had realised.

Over mugs of coffee in a back room of the Museum, Bethan and Cathy initiate me into the delights of 'Sodde Eggs' and 'subtleties'. Wide-eyed, I learn that 'Sodde Eggs' are hard-boiled eggs drowned in a sauce made with butter, wholegrain mustard and a generous dash of vinegar, either cider or white wine. It sounds like a good way to cheer up a hard-boiled egg. 'Oh, it is', says Cathy, 'I'm taking a batch to a party tomorrow night'. 'Subtleties' are sugar-based confections, usually highly decorative. It will not be long before I see one for myself, made by Bethan, but not this side of the 'From Plant to Plate' day school, which is now only weeks away.

❧ ❦ ❧

One Sunday morning, I leave Framsden early with the aim of indulging in a bit of rare retail therapy at the Stratford St Andrew boot sale. I like this site: it is one at which I set up shop some months ago when funds were low. The cross-country route takes me from Framsden to Saxtead, where I admire the windmill, then to Framlingham, where I admire the castle. From Framlingham, I follow narrow by-roads that lead me past Glemham House, with its fascinating gardens and surviving glasshouses, which I was lucky enough to visit in my WEA research days, and from there to Stratford St Andrew.

The boot sale occupies a large, grassy area beside the Village Hall and within sight of the church. A stream runs through the site, adding to the pleasant atmosphere. There is ample parking and a spacious L-shaped layout of stalls covering two fields. Anxious to find anything that I can add to the garden, whichever one it happens to be, I pounce on sweet peas. At 50p per pot, and advice from the couple who grew them, this makes the journey worthwhile without taking another step. I put Roy Lancaster out of my mind. I move on to find a colourfully decorated outdoor table, circular, on a pedestal and about the size of a wine table, a long, loose jacket, embroidered around the edges, which looks Indian, and some freshly-baked rolls and scones.

This is as a good as a holiday for me. I go home, join Jeremy in the garden, introduce him to the new table, which he sniffs suspiciously but approves ultimately, and enjoy my rolls and scones in the spring sunshine after transplanting the sweet peas into larger pots, as instructed.

The following weekend, a friend from Attleborough comes to visit and we travel the few miles to Stonham Barns where we do nothing very much except potter around the bric-a-brac shop where I buy two decorative plates.

The weather is so beautiful (for the second week in April) that we go back to Framsden and I cook a three-course meal out in the garden.

Looking back, these interludes mark the lull before the storm.

❧ ❦ ❧

On 27th April, I learn from John that my non-tenants will be vacating my Attleborough cottage on 1st May. They will need help to move out and to recover their various supplies of stored furniture from at least two other addresses. They will then need help to move it all into their new home. We all pull together, do our duty, move them out and in.

I aim to spend a day as soon as possible at my Attleborough cottage making a list of what needs to be done, facing my own music. What I don't expect is a full-scale opera.

❋ ❋ ❋

My neighbours drift in, one by one. Relief is palpable when they see me there, cleaning cloths at the ready, my windows and doors open all over again.

Their overture of complaint opens softly, but rises steadily to a crescendo. I am left little short of horrified at what they tell me they have had to endure. Even allowing for magnification and multiplication in the re-telling, what they say makes me sit back on my heels. In the months that I have been away, I have received only one complaint by e-mail. The dog had been howling when it was left alone. I spoke to Annie who said petulantly 'He never cries.' I point out that if she isn't there, she cannot possibly know. I respond to the neighbour, apologise on behalf of my young, dog-adoring tenant, say that I have addressed the issue but please to let me know if it happens again.

I ask why none of them has contacted me, why they let things drag on, why they didn't report all the other issues to me.

'We didn't like to bother you.'

'We knew it was only a temporary arrangement, so…'

I act the mediator, express concern that people have been upset; defend the inexperienced, youthful but well-meaning couple I have just spent two days cursing. I could almost be a parent.

But in truth I am shriven by the news. I lose all my energy and enthusiasm for the task I came to do. In any case, the more I look at the state of my house, the more obvious it is that I will have to commit myself to a bigger programme than I expected. What I thought would be a quick spruce-up is looking ominously like a major piece of work. My neighbours will not be happy if the house stands empty, particularly in the state it and its garden are in now.

'From Plant to Plate' is now only six weeks away. There are several more visits to Norfolk in view. The decision seems clear. I am going to have to reverse the pattern of the past ten months. Attleborough must become home and Framsden must be relinquished. I abandon the pitiful attempt at cleaning. Instead, I spend time speaking to my closest neighbours, the ones most affected, and assure them that I will be back within the week and in occupation as soon as possible thereafter. I remind them of my contact details.

As I am about to lock up and leave, the telephone rings. It is Annie. If I thought I had problems already, they are about to get considerably worse.

'I meant to tell you before we left', she says, 'the dishwasher went a bit funny'.

I'm not laughing as I ask 'Funny how?'

'Well it just kept running and running'.

What? I leave silence for her to fill.

'It didn't matter which programme you selected, it just ran for about three hours, then it stopped'

'Has this just happened?' I ask, dreading the answer.

'Oh no, it's been like it for ages'.

'Why didn't you tell me sooner?', I ask, trying not to sound like an agent of the Spanish Inquisiton as I recognise yet another reason for the worryingly high electricity bills.

'Well I didn't think it mattered that much because it still worked, it just took longer.'

I am silent.

'Anyway, we knew we were leaving, so...'

In a weak moment I wish I could curtail sentences and responsibilities with 'so...' and just walk away from it all. But if you aspire to be one of 'them buggers', you have to learn to accept responsibility. I'd hate to waste the lesson.

Above: Debenham Guildhall, with High Street beyond.
Below: one of the last views of the front garden at Framsden.

Author's images

10: Speaking of the Past

The dishwasher has to be replaced; and the stair carpet; and other fittings. Whichever way I look at the situation, the responsibility is mine. I am disappointed, stung, because I had expected more. I had expected the house to be left exactly as it was found. It was a ridiculous expectation; I should have known better. Toby and Annie were not maliciously neglectful nor uncaring about their surroundings: but that was the point, these were not their surroundings. And dogs and small children, it seems, are the answer to everything that 'can't be helped'. So…

❈ ❈ ❈

My priority is to speak to openly to my landlord, Helmingham Estate Office. They are a beacon of light in a grim period. They suggest that if I am actively vacating, they could re-offer the cottage for letting, subject to my being willing to move out at short notice when they have a suitable tenant in view. If a tenant materialises sooner rather than later, they will formally terminate my lease and refund any unused rent and, of course, the large deposit that I paid initially, subject to there being no call on it to cover damage. I think ruefully of my Attleborough cottage and of the lessons I have learned the hard way. Equally, the Estate Office reassures me, if there is no tenant in view, then the cottage is mine to occupy as long as I continue paying my rent to the end of the lease.

What more could you ask of a landlord?

❈ ❈ ❈

Property issues and day school plans notwithstanding, I am determined not to waste my last few weeks at Framsden. In particular, I want to make the most of my proximity to the Suffolk Record Office at Ipswich. I go online to see if there is anything else I would like to request. So it is, with absolutely no expectation of finding anything, that I browse the catalogue. I cannot pinpoint now what it is that I do differently, but somehow I must have used search parameters that I have not used before. Because now I see something potentially valuable and something that I will, without doubt, want to see without delay. I fire off an e-mail request to the Record Office and cite the reference number, together with a few others. I might as well make the most of my visit. 'Is it too short notice to request these documents for tomorrow, Saturday?' I ask. 'No, that's fine, your request has arrived just in time', comes the welcome reply.

Once I move back to Norfolk, my ten-mile, pleasant, rural journey to the Record Office will become a fifty-mile, hair-raising trek on the traffic-filled main arterial roads linking the two counties. This is reason enough to relish my hastily-arranged visit. The blanket of cloud breaks en route to Ipswich to reveal ribbons of palest blue. Hope is on the horizon. A tempting pile of documents awaits me on the Search Room reception counter.

'I'll take HD1538/265 first, please.'

The manila folder looks worryingly slim. The duty archivist opens it, glances at the single piece of paper inside, then up at me.

'Sorry', she says, 'but that's marked "Too Fragile for Production"'. These are the four words no researcher wants to hear. It stands to reason that by dint of their inaccessibility the documents are bound to be more desirable. In this case, they are desirable by any standards. They are the two years of household accounts for Helmingham Hall dating from Janaury 1587 to January 1589.

1588 was the year in which Lionel Tollemache's mother wrote to him at Tilbury Camp as he stood and listened to his Queen and cheered at the news of the departing Armada-borne Spaniards. These are two out of Catherine Tollemache's 32 years as the Hall. With access to the household accounts, I can make the link between her recipes and her resources. I don't believe in fate, kismet, destiny and all the rest; but for a moment I do believe in Sod's Law. Why, when I am facing all sorts of other challenges, does this happen? I dismiss the thought, take a breath, persist.

'Does that mean permanently too fragile for production?' I venture.

'Well no, probably not.'

'Probably not?' My interest is piqued.

'It means that the document can't be handled now but it might be suitable for conservation.'

'And how does that work – I mean, what would be the next step?'

'There are hundreds of documents waiting for conservation in the Record Offices at any one time because, as you know, we have three Offices in Suffolk, not just one.' I nod, encouraging more. 'But if a document is suitable for conservation, then it joins the queue.' And? 'Once it reaches the head of the queue, work is undertaken and hopefully the document put into a condition that enables it to handled again.'

There are a number of provisos here, so I pounce on the first one.

'What determines a document's position in the queue?'

'Importance: its significance in the County's history – maybe the need to produce it to coincide with some anniversary or event – that sort of thing.'

'And how would I make that importance known?'

'Well, if you are really asking how to bump it up the queue, then there are two ways: the first is to offer to pay for its conservation, or at least contribute significantly to the cost; and the second is to lobby the County Archivist, setting out the argument to justify the request for priority'.

I thank her; use my visit to make use of the other records requested. They pale into insignificance beside the chance to look into the very heart of the household through its accounts. I go home on a mission.

The next few days are spent plotting the campaign. As it happens, there is a significant anniversary in view. Works to build the tower of Helmingham church were commissioned by John Tollemache, the Hall's builder, in 1488. A fund-raising effort to repair the bell-tower is ongoing. I played a small part in some background research for this recently to help the committee charged with preparing an application for funds. A number of events are planned for 2010 to bolster the funds. We're already in 2009. Can I argue for the conservation be done in time, I wonder? I e-mail Bill, who will know better than anyone what his archivist colleagues face..

'How do you think I should approach this, Bill?'

'You should point out Helmingham Hall is one of the most important houses in Suffolk and that your studies relate to the period around the creation of the first baronetcy – that is VERY important. And these records are the only ones that tell us anything about the household in the years immediately before he was elevated to that title. Add anything you can about dates of significant local fund-raising events.'

I draft, re-draft, share my proposal with Bill and others. It goes forward. The Record Office responds to say they will give this consideration.

❁ ❁ ❁

Between early and late May, I repeat the moving-in strategy I adopted when I came to Framsden less than a year ago; I am lacking the poetry but possessed of rather more furniture.

The move out of small items is gradual. A car-load at a time, and then gradually I disperse and sell furniture and other items at Framsden that are surplus to requirement in Attleborough. One of my neighbours has the chest freezer, whose lid I have never opened, other than to dream how I might fill it.

I go through the motions: organise someone to cut the field for me because it needs doing and I don't have the heart to leave it as I found it; the same man to be on standby if I need the lawns cut; and so on.

On 18th May, John drives a small lorry to Framsden to bring home all the furniture that he had to move out when his family occupied, in every sense of the word, my Attleborough cottage.

I have a nightmare journey taking Jeremy to his new home. It is best forgotten, although he gives me short shrift for at least twenty-four hours afterwards then surprises me by making friends immediately with the elderly cat who lives next door to us at Attleborough.

Peace reigns, temporarily. 'From Plant to Plate' is creeping inexorably closer.

The Framsden cottage empty, the chimney sweep attends, followed a few days later by the carpet cleaner, the one stipulated by the Estate. I duly accept his receipt as evidence that I have, in this respect at least, acted in accordance with the terms and conditions of my tenancy agreement.

By this time, a trickle of prospective tenants has begun to visit the Framsden cottage. Some of them see the cottage furnished, others see it half-empty. So far, I understand, no-one has made an application for the tenancy. I divide my time between reinstating Attleborough, finalising 'From Plant to Plate' and vacating Framsden.

On 2nd June, I spend six hours in searing heat at Framsden cutting the grass. On 20th June, I return to tidy the garden plants. The choice of a Saturday is deliberate. I want to stop mourning. I have a treat in mind. This is what I call my exit strategy.

❖ ❖ ❖

Today, I want to re-live the pleasures of Debenham so that I have happy memories to carry away with me when I finally hand in my keys at Framsden.

At a convenient and pleasant six minutes from Framsden, Debenham became my shopping destination of choice. It offered me all I needed and more. Today, I begin my memorial tour at Websters, the newspaper shop. This used to be one of my frequent ports of call, not necessarily to buy newspapers but because the shop stocks a good range of essentials. In addition, there is usually a small selection of local history books, and an excellent and ever-changing box of secondhand books to dip into, with the proceeds going to a local good cause. Today, I am donating several boxes of books and, inevitably, browsing the ones they have on offer, old or new.

Next stop is the fish and chip shop. It stands in a row of architectural delights: there are medieval and Victorian cottages and medieval cottages hidden behind Georgian and Victorian frontages The juxtaposition of past and present is a delight, particularly since the shop stands immediately opposite the church. I stand in the queue, mouth watering, anticipating what will probably be last my portion of Debenham's fish and chips. I feel only a minor twinge of passing guilt that I am not going to share this treat with Jeremy, who loves a morsel of fresh fish. I don't know what I plan to enjoy more: the succulent, crisp and delicious picnic, or the memory of the first time I came here.

❖ ❖ ❖

There are two wooden benches in the churchyard opposite. They are visible as I queue on my first outing to sample Debenham's fish and chips. Supplied with my lunch, I cross the road to the churchyard and ask the elderly lady seated on one of the benches if I may join her. She is enjoying her own helping of fish and chips and makes me welcome, smiling in recognition at my reason for asking.

Ellie tells me that she used to live in the next village. Then she married and moved the mile or so to Debenham. It was unheard of for the chapel-goers of Rishangles (Rish*angles*, I notice, not *Rish*angles) to go to church in Debenham. Parties of expatriated Rish-*anglers* used to walk the three miles to their chapel every Sunday to keep the faith, and three miles back, spiritually invigorated. Ellie's husband died some years ago. She wanted to keep her independence but was forced to admit defeat when she found herself spilling hot water over herself and burning her food. She was moved into sheltered accommodation just down the road in Debenham. I know where it is: I have passed it many times on my travels. It stands on the edge of the cemetery. You have to wonder at town planning decisions sometimes. Anyway, much as Ellie likes to eat in the communal dining room, she treats herself to fish and chips once in a while. Because she can't walk back home before her treat becomes cold and congealed, she has taken to sitting on the bench here in the churchyard. The staff in the fish and chip shop give her an extra carrier bag which contains a deodorised cloth for hand-cleaning and a small towel for hand-drying. That way, even though Ellie uses one of those silly little forks, she can tuck in as nature intended, with 'fingers before forks'. Still, it would not be nice to walk around town afterwards with sticky fingers, particularly since she usually fits in a bit of shopping at the Co-Op, so she is grateful to the shop for their thoughtfulness. Oh, and then there's the waste. Well there is a basket over at the fish and chip shop but she thought it would be a good idea if there was one somewhere near the benches in the churchyard, so she mentioned it to a few people. And it was done.

We talk for a while longer and because Ellie finishes eating before I do, she asks me would I mind returning the towel to the fish and chip shop? It would save her crossing that road, since today all her shopping is on this side, as is her destination. It makes me feel useful, and it also makes me happy to think that people have bothered to take notice of someone else's needs. For that reason alone, although the positively incomparable cooking helps, I frequent Debenham's fish and chip shop more often than I might have done.

❋ ❋ ❋

Today, I will not sit on the seat in the churchyard because I have long since discovered another very pleasant spot in Debenham, which is where I am heading next. I plan to enjoy my farewell feast in style. I have with me my own little bag of handwipes, towel, and, to make my outing feel extra special, a squeeze of lemon in its little gizmo and a big linen napkin to spread across my knees.

The spot is less in the public eye than the churchyard. I discovered its virtues soon after I met Ellie. Parking can be difficult in Debenham because it is a popular place; so I get into the habit of using the small and well-concealed public car park on the edge of the cemetery. Here I discover not only the dearly departed of Debenham, but a playground, a lovely walk into some gardens, and a delightful view of the rear elevations of some of Debenham's oldest houses. Ellie's sheltered housing complex lies to one side. Perhaps the town planning wasn't so ill-considered, after all.

Lunch over, I take my shopping bag for a final spree in the Co-Op. Throughout my time at Framsden this has been another regular destination, with good reason.

❋ ❋ ❋

Lack of choice worries me far less than too much choice, so when I first arrive to live in Framsden I am relieved to find that the Co-Op is the only supermarket in Debenham, but pleasantly surprised by what it offers.

I never fail to be tempted by the 'local and seasonal' display which appears only when there is anything local and seasonal worth having. And there is plenty worth having, as I discover. This branch of the Co-Op has an especially good buyer for fruit and vegetables.

The display is well-planned and positioned: into the shop and sharp left. Much of the produce is British, which I applaud, and it is always fresh and in good condition. But the cunningly-positioned local stall is opposite the main one, facing the entrance door. I find it impossible to ignore. That is the art of good marketing. During my time at Framsden, 'local and seasonal' provides me with the joys of freshly-picked asparagus, spinach, strawberries, raspberries, beetroot, new potatoes and more. Then the Co-Op surprises me even more one day and takes the bottom right out of my budget. A newly-erected sign points the way to products from the Orford Smokehouse, which is legendary for its range of high-quality, locally-caught fish smoked over oak. Kippers, smoked haddock and more find their way to Framsden. Resistance is useless.

❂ ❂ ❂

Today, I buy extra-large eggs, locally cured bacon and a treat for Jeremy, return them to the car and set off for the next leg of my exploration.

Dining and shopping opportunities apart, Debenham holds other attractions for me. Gracechurch Street and the hilly main thoroughfare of High Street are lined with buildings that reflect centuries of history and gradual change. In the early medieval period, Debenham's wealth came from involvement with the cloth industry. The town's site gave it a valuable resource: the fast-flowing River Deben. Although barely more than a stream today, there is no doubting the power of nature when the tidal Deben is in full flood. A trickle becomes a torrent in the steep-sided gulley which contains the river in the centre of Debenham, and at times the water exceeds these limits and spills out on to the road at its lowest point. Debenham's role in the medieval wool industry was to finish and dye cloth made elsewhere. The water was essential for both processes and Debenham's inhabitants developed skills and the means to organise them.

At the junction of Gracechurch Street and High Street, at the head of a broad green, stands a jettied building known as the Guildhall. This was a market hall, erected in the first half of the 17th century on the site of an earlier market cross. Later, in 1668, an upper room was adapted for use as a school. The building has been put to other uses latterly, including shops and offices.

The Guildhall and many surviving houses in Debenham speak volumes about the town's history. Some are medieval in origin, impressively large, with ornately carved archways under which their horses, carts and carriages would have passed. Others are smaller, and around these there is later infill, a sign of the times. When the cloth industry began to develop rapidly in the north of England, Suffolk's position declined. However, Debenham appears to have diversified. My trusty Victorian gazetteer volume 'CHAR-GRAS', now on its way back to Attleborough with me, identifies no industry for Debenham but does note that it has a market and that the property is 'much subdivided'. Ironically, this sub-division might be the key to its survival throughout the centuries. In towns with a dominant industry, there tended to be few masters and many workers. Those masters tended to continue to control the fortunes of a town, whether through employment or through the restrictive ownership of the property and land.

Debenham's 19th-century history shows that it was strong in dairying and engineering, and, notably, in retailing. The ancestral founder of Henry Abbott, without whose hardware and houseware stores I could not have survived at Framsden, moved to Debenham in 1650. This was around the time when the Countess of Dysart was sharpening her wits and her quill pen to write letters in code to counter Oliver Cromwell. Thomas Abbott supported the independent church; he would have flourished rather than withered as battles raged between the polarised religious interests of the day. By 1707, the family expanded their interests, bought up more property and established the forerunner of the hardware and houseware stores that survive to this day. Subsequent family members were equally entrepreneurial: in 1747, William Abbott was a tailor and draper; his son, John, set up a grocery business and the two businesses shared premises for 50 years.

Retailing must have been in the blood because by the 19th and even into the early 20th century, the Debenham Abbotts ran stores in other Suffolk villages. Eventually, in 2001, the Debenham store was dispersed and part of the premises bought by the Co-Op, who took over the grocery business. This explains why there is a single entrance door leading into the Co-Op on the left and Henry Abbott's Hardware on the right.

The sophisticated Henry Abbotts Houseware store is on the opposite side of the road. It is a great temptation, particularly for a keen cook. I can't resist going in there now. I broke my cafetière last week and will buy a new one to take with me to Attleborough.

Debenham has two Estate Agents. This may not be the best time to look in their windows, but I do. By now, prices are well out of my reach. I can understand why this place is sought-after. The town's visible history is appealing enough but it has other attractions for potential residents, especially those who share my appreciation for the life of a self-contained rural community. Debenham's geographical position naturally restricts its opportunities for growth, and this is recognised by the local planning authority. New housing is limited to small amounts of infill and modest estates.

Perhaps it is Debenham's long history of independence and its instinct for survival through diversification that I find so compelling and attractive. Co-Op apart, there are no chain-stores here. There is pretty much one of everything anyone could need, and all offered by independent retailers. The Co-Op is outward-looking. Every Saturday, in the car park at its rear, the Swiss Farm mobile butcher sells from his refrigerated display van. I realised quickly that this was popular and after my first visit I make a point of arriving as early as possible before he sells out. Succulent lamb, tender stewing beef and plump chickens all found their way from Swiss Farm to St John's Row. Today, I have left it a bit too late.

Other businesses flourish alongside the Co-Op: a shop selling organic produce, some of it fresh, some of it imported, another selling fruit and veg, a dispensing chemist and pharmacy, antique shops, florists, a pub and places to eat, hairdressers and more. The bakery is a delight, always happy to sell me croissant dough whenever I arrived too late to snap up the fresh morning bake, or to produce a freshly-cooked bacon roll if I have skipped breakfast. Neave's butchery and delicatessen are not to be missed.

If all this were not enough, Debenham's tree-lined hilly street includes David Shacklock Books who announces his part-time presence with a quirky obelisk on the pavement. His shop is the quintessential book-lover's bolt-hole. I spend a long time rootling through his shelves and piles of books on his floor. Here I find a copy of 'The English Housewife in the 17th Century' by Christina Hole, published in 1953.

Under the circumstances, this seems the most appropriate volume to carry away with me.

❊ ❊ ❊

I want to make a detour today before I return to Attleborough, and I head east, to Peasenhall.

Emmetts of Peasenhall is less a village store than a legend. In the unlikely surroundings of Peasenhall's elongated village street skirting the busy A1120, the Royal Warrant is carried with pride above the shop door.

The door opens to the unmistakeable aroma of good food. Emmetts hold the Royal Warrant for their black hams, home-cured to their own recipe. The appetising, smoky smell of this collides with others: in a toothsome display of fresh produce, heads of elephant garlic take pride of place. Then there are cheeses chasing the aroma of freshly-ground coffee beans. The place is a riot of mouth-watering delights.

Today, I am here to buy something for the day school. I leave Emmetts bearing two shallow wooden boxes.

All will be revealed, soon enough.

❊ ❊ ❊

Six days later, 'From Plant to Plate' exceeds expectations. The success of the day school is testament to six months of input from everyone involved.

I lead with the first session and act as co-ordinator for the remainder of the event. I stick to what I do best, which is to provide a context for the recipes. People see and hear about Helmingham Hall, Catherine Tollemache's role there, and, thanks to the generous spirit of Stranger's Hall, Cathy not only contributes to my session with her expertise, but brings with her the massive 1597 bell-metal mortar, the Victorian wooden walnut mould, examples of replica linen and tableware, and, best of all, a replica sugar loaf.

Then we negotiate the step from 16th century raw materials to 21st century bioscience.

We hear first from Dr Lesley Boyd who holds the room spellbound as she describes 'St Anthony's Fire', a limb-robbing, life-taking disease common in the medieval period. Despite popular belief at the time, this was caused not by the wrath of God but by the toxic effects resulting from the use of mouldy wheat. But is it over, dead and buried in the distant past? No, it is not. Ergot, to give it its modern name, killed off a few thousand people in Eastern Europe less than a decade ago, and all because of some mould-ridden peanuts. The question and answer session is so prolonged and searching that we run late for Sarah's rare book session and even later for lunch.

Giving access to rare books outside the confines of the library took a great deal of organisation and care. Sarah has arranged the volumes skilfully so that she can lead people around the room, book by book (we can look but not touch). As well as displaying text and illustrations of the kind that Catherine Tollemache herself would have seen, the books chart the progression from manuscript illumination to the printing press, including volumes that had been printed and then hand-coloured in intricate detail. Some people linger in the rare book room to feed their souls. The feedback and the buzz in the Conference Centre foyer over lunch speaks volumes about their appreciation of the day so far.

Our next act is sugar, and it is theatrical. To add to the sense of occasion, I produce the two flat wooden boxes I bought from Emmetts of Peasenhall. They contain an assortment of crystallised fruits, enough to share with the group and all of the speakers. I've agreed this bit of subterfuge with Dave Hart, our next presenter, because they return us neatly to the topic that has led us all to this day, Catherine Tollemache's recipes, and most particularly her sugar-heavy sweetmeat recipes. It is all the opening he needs.

Dave leaves no stone unturned in his presentation about sugar, a commodity that Catherine Tollemache used in large quantities. We move from the growing and processing of sugar in her time to its use in her hands. With the help of an electrically-heated cooking ring, a pair of fireman's gloves and a bowl of ice, Dave shows what it takes to emulate the stages of cooking, heating, temperature recognition and testing long before there was such a thing as a thermometer. We watch, transfixed, as he draws out a thread of sugar 'the thickness of a hair', as Catherine Tollemache puts it, recreating her test of 'candy height'. We accept Dave's kind offer of ready-made 'artificial hazelnuts', and then spit them out discreetly as we discover the unpalatable reality of equal quantities of sugar and cinnamon.

Sugar is followed by pectin. The group is addressed by Professor Vic Morris, one of the world's leading experts on the subject. Pectin helps jam to set, as any jam-maker knows, but although the word would have been unknown in Catherine Tollemache's time, she was aware of the role played by whole fruit, which is high in pectin. She was unequivocal in her instructions, always stressing where the fruit should be used whole, particularly apple. And as though reading the mind of her skeptical followers, she says, more than once, 'Do not core. Do not pare.' She knows that the inclination will be to do both. Professor Morris describes the most up-to-date microscopy techniques that have led to new discoveries about pectin and its potential. Seeing is believing.

❋ ❋ ❋

Writing retrospectively, I am delighted to learn that in 2012, Professor Morris was awarded an MBE in the Queen's Birthday Honours List in recognition of his ground-breaking work at the Institute of Food Research.

❋ ❋ ❋

From gums and resins, and pectin, we move to grain. Mike Ambrose explains the important role of the extensive John Innes germplasm facility (seed bank), which he manages. Mike produces samples of grain, stalks and all, for us to handle and compare. He speculates on the type of grain that produced the flour used by Catherine Tollemache and reveals news of an archaeological find that brings one of her 'biskett' recipes to life vividly. A ship's biscuit, dating from the time of Elizabeth I, was collected intact from a shipwreck. It contained added protein in the form of dried peas. This leads to a discussion of what 'ship's biscuits' were, and, in turn, to a comparison with Catherine Tollemache's recipe. By allowing her flour and egg mixture to dry over a period of days, then coating it in sugar and only then baking it, she manages to produce something that will keep for long periods.

By now almost sated with information, the group is treated to a stunning display of modern chemistry with the recreation of one of Catherine Tollmemache's perfumes. Before our very eyes, and noses, Dave Hart rejoins us and creates perfumed pomander beads. And when we think we can't absorb any more, Dave ends the day by presenting the disbelieving group with a bouquet of artificially-coloured carnations – a final nod to the lady's recipe for 'How to make flowers grow of any colour'.

The room erupts. Hands are shaken, compliments shared. Catherine Reynolds is delighted: her aim of increasing public awareness of what happens at the John Innes Centre and the Institute of Food Research has been fulfilled.

As for me, I am elated. I return to Attleborough tired but happy. Jeremy greets me with his sweeping bow. Yes, it has been a long day, but a good day.

❈ ❈ ❈

Soon after the day school, invitations begin to come in for other events, many of them in Norfolk. My diary for 2010 is filling rapidly. Some but not all are related to the recipes. There are invitations for landscape and garden history, the history of roses and more. At this rate I will be occupied for the next year and beyond. However, there are two invitations to delve more deeply into the organisation and management of the 16th- and early 17th-century household. I had almost forgotten that I bought a book on my recent tour of Debenham. I settle down for an evening with Jeremy, Christina Hole and her 17th-century housewife. I have other, more recently-produced volumes on domestic history but this is a useful compendium, thoroughly researched and well written. I am reminded how much was expected of the lady of the house, how broad her range of skills had to be. The book encourages me to think hard about Helmingham. Catherine Tollemache was there from 1580 until 1612; had nine children, seven of whom survived into adulthood. Widowed in 1612, at the age of about 55, she had to leave the Hall but survived for another 8 years and never remarried. On the face of it, she represents the archetypal 'lady of the house'; but what did that entail?

I call up my transcriptions and look more closely at the original Household Inventory document. I dipped into it and skimmed textile details for Cathy and for the day school, but this is the first time I have looked at the detail of the house with a view to seeing how it was managed.

The first surprise is that despite having 64 rooms, only about four of them are for the personal use of Catherine Tollemache, her husband, Lionel, their four daughters and three sons. Catherine shares a bedroom with her husband and a bed striped in red and yellow and hung with bells. They could be upholstered bells, I tell myself. There is another bed in the room, and that has a blue coverlet. Altogether, there are 23 bedrooms, most of which are occupied by staff. The Inventory describes each room according to who uses it. There is no overcrowding or second-rate bedding here for the staff. At the most, two peoople share a room. There is only one 'flock' mattress, the lowest quality, in the whole house, but there are several feather ones described as 'new'. Every member of staff bar one has a feather bed. This is astonishing and shows a high regard for the care and comfort of residential staff. Nowhere does the Inventory use the word 'servants'. The staff are referred to as 'husbandmen'. The distinction is a measure of the respect the master and mistress have for their employees.

Another 32 rooms are given over to running the house like a hotel. Some are not really rooms but partially enclosed outdoor spaces, of which a few are attached to the house but do not share its roof. The house is as self-sufficient as it is possible to be. It grinds its own grain, has its own bakehouse, dairy and brewhouse. There are spaces dedicated to curing meat (and there is an on-site slaughterhouse, too), and others dedicated to storing cheese once it has been made in the dairy. My vision of the serene and now very quietly-run household is turned on its head. This place was a positive hive of activity. And speaking of hives, they kept their own bees, as well as chickens, ducks, quail, geese, sheep, pigs and cattle.

To meet the laundry needs of the master, mistress, their seven children and a resident team of between 20 and 30 staff, clothes had to be made, maintained, laundered (sometimes), and stored. This is when I discover that there was something of the peacock and peahen about Lionel and Catherine Tollemache. Lionel's wardrobe, described in exquisite detail, speaks of silk, satin and velvet clothes in colours described as 'ash', 'duck's meat' and, best of all, 'popinjay green'. His wardrobe contents fill pages of the Inventory. Catherine's barely fill a page and a bit. Her outer wear is modest, both in quantity and quality, mostly black and white in colour; but I am delighted to discover that she has a liking for peach-coloured petticoats and carnation-coloured silk stockings.

The essential business of running the house accounts for much of the Inventory; very few rooms are dedicated to family life, private or otherwise. Luxury goods are almost non-existent. The children have a 'goose-game' (a popular type of board game at the time), and there are some virginals (the precursor of the harpsichord) and a lute. Otherwise, Catherine's time is occupied in the blazing kitchen, the cooler 'pastery' (think modern-day confectionery and pastry chefs), in amongst the furnace and six stills in the 'Stilling Yard' (what Christina Hole describes as the Stillroom, which was anything but still and everything to do with distillation), or in the 'Soope House'. This stumps me, but only for as long as it takes to read what is in the room and realise that 'Soope' is soap.

The Soap House is where Catherine also makes perfumes. Her recipe book gives evocative instructions for 'washing balls' (perfumed soap, in other words, for personal washing), and 'a sweete muske to lay emongst clothes, that will not offend the head'. Her 'candle to burn in a chamber' sets me thinking. Which chamber? Theirs, maybe, with its red, yellow and blue upholstery? Possibly. But a much more likely candidate is the 'Best Chamber'. 'Best' implies 'guest', so I take a closer look at how the room is furnished. This is the joy of the Household Inventory: it describes not just furniture but textiles and colours. I am delighted to find that the Best Chamber is in restful matching tones of green and silver, with silk, satin and velvet upholstery and fringes on the chairs.

My thoughts move quickly from guests to hospitality, and from there to dining. The Inventory is revealing: there is a massive stock of linen stored in various trunks and chests throughout the house. The numbers are challenging, particularly when I think about the implications of laundering and drying linen. There are 524 table napkins, 110 table and 'board' cloths (used on serving tables or sideboards) and 35 towels. These towels, I learn from Strangers' Hall, were held, neatly folded, by staff waiting at table. In the days before forks (there were none at Helmingham in 1597), diners carried a personal knife with them, and were provided with a spoon at table. Foods served on large plates or dishes (chargers) could be speared with a knife or collected in a spoon, but it was unthinkable to transfer that knife or spoon to the mouth, particularly if the diner was going to return for another helping to the communal serving dish. As a result, much food was eaten with the fingers. Helmingham's inventory explains how this was catered for: there are descriptive pages of silver and silver-gilt items, including basins and ewers. Water was poured from the ewer into a basin so that the diner could refresh their fingers. The waiting servants, ever attentive, would step forward with a towel on which diners could dry their fingers.

The picture that emerges is one of frenetic activity on the one hand and elegant, high-status hospitality on the other. Holding the reins, ensuring that all runs smoothly, stands the lady of the house. But between Catherine Tollemache's own recipe book and Christina Hole's erudite description, and with the evidence of the Household Inventory staring me in the face, it becomes obvious to me that this lady doesn't do much standing. In addition, I discover another side of Catherine Tollemache. Her memorial in the church speaks of her 'singular skill' in surgery, and tells of the 'love and honour' in which she was held because she cared for the 'sick and sore wounded' with 'piety and charity'.

The lady has a 'Working Chamber'. I ask my contacts and scour not only Christina Hole's book but umpteen other sources in libraries and on the Internet, but I fail to find evidence of its equivalent. This room is positioned between the brightly-coloured marital bedroom and the children's nursery. In the next generation, who made their record of the house and its contents two years after Catherine's death (and ten years after she left to live out her widowhood elsewhere), this room has become what I would have expected it to be: 'My Lady's Chamber'. However, for Catherine Tollemache this room is not equipped with delicate silk and satin-upholstered furniture for her comfort and privacy, but with yet more equipment: here is the 'great coffer for spice', mortars, pestles, and much else. Conveniently situated on the first floor of the house, the Working Chamber allows her to labour at all hours. Here, she may mix her medicines, and perhaps write up her medical notes with the aid of candlelight. There are thirteen candlesticks in here. She also has the use of a close stool and a chamber pot, the 16th-century equivalent of en-suite facilities. The only concession to comfort is a chair with a cushioned back.

The Working Chamber and what it conveys is nothing to the impact of a reference I find by accident when I am browsing the Internet.

I find mention of a lady and her 16th-century library and marvel at what I read: the lady is Catherine Tollemache and at least one book she owned is sitting now in the Folger Shakespeare Library in Washington, DC. Catherine's ownership is confirmed by the presence of her signature, or what we would call now her *ex libris* on its flyleaf: 'Catheren Tallemach oweth this boocke'. The 'boocke' she 'oweth' was published in 1600, and it is known as Partridge's *Treasurie*, glorying in the full title of *The Treasurie of Commodious Conceites and Hidden Secrets, Commonly called, The good Huswife's Closet of Provision, for the health of her household. Meete and necessarie for the profitable use of all estates. Gathered out of sundry Experiments lately practised by men of great knowledge.* It is much more likely that the sundry experiments referred to by John Partridge were practised by the likes of Catherine Tollemache, then gleaned and collated for publication by men like him because it was considered unseemly for women to publish.

I go to bed full of ideas about how all this material could be brought together fruitfully.

Next morning, the Helmingham Estate Office contacts me to say that a new tenant will move in during the last week of July.

❀ ❀ ❀

I make my final visit to the cottage in St John's Row, Framsden, on 18th July. I give the cottage a thorough clean, the garden a brisk tidy-up and read the electricity meter. The telephone will be disconnected at midnight tonight. As I think the thought, the telephone rings. It is Suffolk Record Office. The household accounts, which I had all but forgotten in the flurry of recent activity, have been approved for conservation. They should be ready within the next four to six months, certainly in time for any celebration planned for the summer of 2010. Smiling, I tour the cottage one last time and lock up. I leave my keys in the appointed place. Outside, I pause. Despite everything, the Flymo has done a good job here. The garden looks loved, cared for. As indeed it was.

I open my car door, leave it open and walk slowly down the path to the garden gate.

I look across at the green and gold view and commit it to memory, just as I did on the day I arrived here a year ago.

This time there is no chicken in the footwell when I return to the car.

Above: disused swan pit at The Great Hospital, Norwich, April 2010.

Below: Oxburgh Hall from SW: site of what was once swan pens and water gardens.

Author's images

11: Losing my place

Received opinion has it that hindsight is the only exact science. Lacking a crystal ball, or perhaps peering into one that is distinctly clouded, I cannot possibly foretell what is going to happen next in the property market. In the event, the value of my Norfolk property is less at risk from the erection nearby of nine new houses than from collapse of the world's perilously financed debt. There is no doubt that my view is hampered by introversion when I do finally drive the car away from Framsden in July 2009. Regret is one thing but wallowing in it is quite another, and unacceptable. With the move back to Norfolk and 'From Plant to Plate' under my belt, now is the time to take stock of my property options.

I try to contact my trusted sales agent in Norfolk. He has seen me through several canny moves and has always given me dependable advice. He was a little uncertain about this up-sticks-and-off-down-a-goat-track-in-Suffolk sojourn of mine last year but was supportive. As I listen to the telephone ringing out in his office, I reflect.

❊ ❊ ❊

I was disappointed at the agent's valuation when he visited to prepare sale particulars in the late spring of 2008.

'Is that all?' I asked. 'I've spent thousands on the renovation, as you know.'

His response was unequivocal: property values were not holding; sales activity was sluggish and getting slower; a higher asking price for my cottage would be unreasonable in the current climate.

'You have three options', he explained. 'Sell now, if you can, before values reduce any further. If you don't, then you should stick it out while building development takes place next door. No-one finds property appealing while building work is under way on its doorstep. If you take that option, you'll have to be patient, wait until the landscaping of the new estate is done and people are beginning to move in. However, you then face another risk: people will compare your cottage with a brand-new, high-efficiency house just up the road with the benefit of its own parking and mains drainage. So your potential market, which is first-time buyers or young couples on the next step, are more likely to go for the new house. Third, don't sell at all...'

I begin to protest but he raises a hand to prevent my interruption: 'You are going to lose money whatever you do. Believe me, the way things are going at the moment, no-one in our industry expects any quick fixes. If property values continue to fall, and if the market stagnates or, worse, grinds to a halt, your end of the market will suffer most. None of us could have predicted this but you invested your life savings just at the wrong time. I don't believe you will recover your costs in the foreseeable future, let alone make a profit. That is why your third option is not to sell. Stick it out. No-one can take your lovely house and garden away from you, so live in it. Everything changes, but don't live over the fence worrying about what used to be.'

***

That conversation took place over a year ago. At the time I remember being taken aback by the agent's openness. Here was a man whose business was selling houses doing his utmost to persuade me not to sell mine.

I feel the need for his advice now. I hear a recorded message on his office answering machine telling me that no-one is there. Really? Mid-week and mid-morning? I leave a message. It is not returned by the end of that working day. It was to be the first of several unanswered messages, ceasing only when the agent's phone line is disconnected a few days later. The agency was one of the first local victims of the great property crash that was gathering pace in the UK.

While living the dream in rural Suffolk, I had tried to avert my eyes from the gloomy picture the agent had sketched for me twelve months ago. Property values were falling even more rapidly now; houses were being repossessed in previously unimaginable numbers. Purchasers are now limited to buy-to-let landlords or speculative investors with cash to spare. Agents were going out of business. Some read the portents, adapted, diversified, strengthened their letting portfolios, encouraged people to become landlords to accommodate the burgeoning numbers of ex-homeowners who were swelling the ranks of the letting market. There was a domino effect: solicitors were the next in line to put staff on short time, consolidate resources, maintain themselves at minimum strength.

I gleaned the story in bits and pieces when I went on the hunt for another agent. Home ownership, the holy grail of the English aspirational classes, whatever their starting point, is no longer a bedrock but a crumbling cliff, they told me. This was just the tip of the iceberg, they warned me.

The new agent I find is pragmatic. She understands the implications of the successful planning appeal next door but one, but holds out a ray of hope: 'In the current climate, they may not build. Other new houses, whether at the top or bottom of the market, are not shifting. Just last week we negotiated the sale of six houses on a new development of only eight. They had stood there, unsold, for over a year. In the end, we sold them to a housing association for less than the price it cost to build them. They're now being let. What the developers may do is sit on that site down the road in the hope that land and property values will recover'.

'Do you think they will recover?'

'Eventually, but it will take longer than anyone first thought. A few years, at least.' She pauses to let this sink in. Then goes on: 'I think what really matters is whether you want to stay here or not. Attleborough is earmarked for considerable growth over the next decade. If it doesn't happen here, in this road, it will happen somewhere else.'

'I did look at a house in Framsden. It would have suited me down to the ground but at the time this house was off the market. It was only recently that I discovered it wouldn't have made a scrap of difference. The difference between your estimated value of this house and the sale price of that was £40,000'.

She says nothing but gives me an appraising look.

'Only you can decide what you want to do. Give yourself a bit of time. And get this place cleaned up.'

✹ ✹ ✹

For the next few months I divide my time between preparing for a heavy programme of 2010 presentations and bringing my cottage back to its best. That puts off decision-making and keeps me fully occupied.

As winter approaches, I rediscover the delights of warm feet and on-demand central heating. I light my own multi-fuel stove. It is a miniature version of the workhorse at Framsden and does not provide hot water, but it does pump gentle background warmth into my clay-lump terraced cottage very effectively. The carrying of fuel in and ash out is a fraction of the task it was at Framsden.

Jeremy is settled, busy climbing trees and fraternising with Mary, his elderly feline neighbour and new playmate. She calls for him daily, sits outside patiently until he is ready to join her. His new target for ferocious attack is the bed of lavender in the rear garden. The bed develops a series of gaps where he pounces, clutches stems until they submit, after which he climbs in, curls up and sleeps. He comes back to the house wafting lavender in his wake. It's either that or rosemary, which he adores equally. I watch as he seeks out the shrub, rubs vigorously against it, then settles himself at its feet. He does suffer as the result of one battle royal with a neighbouring tom and later a bout of illness that lays him low. Both times I call on the dependable mobile vet, Rosie, who runs 'Paws Indoors'. The name makes me smile, and so does Rosie.

Rosie is familiar with all the tactics employed by hard-to-handle animals and, more to the point, their neurotic keepers. She is relaxed, down to earth and professional. She shows me how to pinion Jeremy effectively as she greets him with 'Hello, you' in a cadence that calms and reassures him for long enough to permit examination. On her second visit she can find nothing obviously wrong except a high temperature, and treats him with antibiotics.

'He is getting on in years', she says thoughtfully.

Afterwards, I ask John and Sue if they know Jeremy's age. I am astounded to learn that he is already at least twelve years old, a good age for a cat. He recovers quickly enough but I begin to look at him with all the respect due to someone of his advanced years. It would help if he looked or acted his age, but, like his keeper, he defies the standard expectation and refuses to oblige.

With some research needed on my doorstep, I rediscover the delights of the Norfolk

Record Office. This stunning, purpose-built facility becomes my regular Saturday morning destination. It is good to reacquaint myself with the duty archivists, and particularly to thank Susan in person for her valuable help while I was at Framsden.

'Are you going to write up your research?'

I am nudged by a feeling of guilt that I have not carried through my original intention to publish.

'Well… I'd like to, but I seem to be inundated with new things to do.'

'Don't waste it. Catherine Tollemache sounds fascinating. By the way, did you know we have some of her Cromwell family's 17th-century swan-keeping records here?'

As it happens, I am setting out on an exploration of swan-keeping today, so this is music to my ears. I put all thoughts of moving house behind me and settle down for a winter with the swans of Oxburgh Hall. I've been asked by the WEA to give a day school: 'something about Oxburgh', they said, and I have responded with 'The Lost Landscapes of Oxburgh Hall', which will centre on the story of swan pens, water gardens and swan keeping, now discernible only through archaeology and documentary archives. The date seems a long way off: May 2010, but research has to be undertaken in good time, visits made, photographs taken, routes of walks plotted; so there is much to be done.

❋ ❋ ❋

This Christmas I put the swans to one side, buy another duck to share with Jeremy and decide to celebrate with a real Christmas tree, a pot-grown one. Ever the optimist, I think it will be nice to take it with me wherever I go. I write cards to my friends and neighbours in Framsden, try not to think about the view they will be enjoying as snow settles on the fields opposite.

The New Year, 2010, finds me immersed in swans and visiting the Norfolk Record Office regularly. One Saturday, having taxed my transcription skills to the limit on a set of 16th-century records, I opt for a bit of light relief. I ask to see one of Norfolk's medieval swan rolls. It is not often that laughter is heard in the hallowed confines of a search room, but the sight of thousands of coloured images of swan's heads, the perspective flattened to produce a clear view of their beaks, is a surprise and a delight. Their heads and eyes are outlined in black, their beaks coloured brightly in orange. The all-important swan marks, incised into the membrane of the beak with a sharp blade before the birds reach adulthood, are clearly visible. Above these exaggerated, extended beaks the swan-roll artist added facial expressions. As a result, some swans had bags under their eyes, making them look for all the world as though they were hung over after a night on the tiles; others had smiling eyes, as though they were proud of the marks they bore; some looked out with eyes full of expectant surprise as though anticipating a particularly toothsome morsel of aquatic vegetation.

Swans, I learn from a book by the acknowledged expert on the subject, N.F. Ticehurst, do not eat fish. They eat plants that thrive in slow-flowing water, which is their habitat of choice, and are fed grain by swanherds. I roll the word around on my tongue… swan HERDS with the aitch sounded, or swannerds with the aitch silent, like shepherds? Tom, one of the duty archivists, comes over to see what has amused me. I half think he might threaten to throw me out of the search room for displaying excessive humour or making a noise, or both, but he joins in. We ponder and come to the conclusion that 'swannerds' sounds more natural. With the enviable natural ease of a professional, he begins to read from the set of 1558-65 swan-keeping accounts which I have just abandoned.

'Look at this', he says, 'they've let their flock of swans this year…'

I lean in, anxious to see how he fathomed this from what looks to be a scurry of squiggles across the page.

'And here', he indicates, 'they've sold some swans for meat'.

I am eager to learn. Tom indicates some key words, warns me that swan-keeping records are notoriously difficult to transcribe fully because of the archaic and specific terms used to describe the birds. There are barans, bluebills, staggs and cobs, names that relate to ages and stages of development.

'I see you've got Ticehurst to hand', he says, indicating the copy of *The Mute Swan in England: its history and the ancient custom of swan-keeping* open on the table, 'You can't do better. Some of his original notes are here, too.'

I go home that afternoon and stalk the Internet. Here we go again, I think to myself as I select the 'Buy now' option and a copy of Norman Ticehurst's invaluable tome wings its way to my Attleborough door.

On a trip to Strangers' Hall Museum one day to view a 17th-century recipe book, I mention something about swans to Cathy. She surprises me by saying: 'My dad used to work at the Great Hospital. You can visit the swan-pit there when the Great Hospital has its annual public open day, but I'll give you some contact details if you like because they'd probably be interested to know what you're doing. You might even be able to have a tour of the site.'

It comes to pass. I am entranced by the Great Hospital, with the church of St Helen at its heart. Tucked away not far from the soaring Norman cathedral in the centre of Norwich, the hospital, founded in 1249, is operated now as a charitable housing trust. To qualify for residency, applicants must be retired and limited in their housing options by low income, and, importantly, they must have lived and worked in Norwich. The scheme offers both sheltered and supported accommodation.

My guide, who tells me he is about to retire, leads me to a framed illustration: there they are, two swan heads shown in profile, looking slightly bad-tempered, and below them, a tabulated and illustrated profusion of orange beaks. In all, there are fifty different swan marks. 'The thing is that every swanherd had to learn to recognise these marks, not just those of the Hospital. When swan-upping was carried out, usually in July or August every year, every swan registered to an owner had to be accounted for.'

Norman Ticehurst's diligent research comes to life as we look at the fifty distinctive swan marks displayed before us. 'The Hospital, as you can see, had several swan marks to its name. Then there were those for the Bishop of Norwich, the Corporation of Norwich, and others for the various surviving religious institutions in the city. At the end of the list are some of those belonging to local families with seats along the main rivers.'

We walk into the grounds, approaching what looks to be a large, rectangular garden pond, devoid of water. 'This is the swan-pit. I'll show you how it was fed and then we'll come back and take a closer look.' We follow a path that leads, surprisingly, to a deep culvert in a steep-sided bank within full view of the industrial riverside of Norwich. 'This sluice was used to control the flow of water from the river. The water is piped underground and carried into the swan pit'.

At one end, the pit is straight-sided, but at the other there are ramps sloping at a shallow gradient from the pit's base up to ground level. 'Those ramps enabled the cygnets to climb in and out easily.'

'Cygnets?'

'Yes. That was the purpose of the swan-pit – to fatten cygnets for the table and then sell them. If we go back to my office, I'll show you some photographs'.

The black and white photographs are full of activity. Cygnets at various stages of development are congregated at one end of the pit, some flapping their wings, others stretching their necks with mouths open. At the edge of the pit stand two men: one holds what look like a drainpipe and a large funnel, positioned at its top. The other man is pouring grain from a bag into the funnel.

'The keepers fed grain through the pipe and it fell into the pit where the cygnets could feed on it. They weren't force-fed but they were well-fed.'

'When did the pit stop being used?', I ask.

'After the second world war.'

'As late as that?'

'Oh yes. It was a very ancient tradition to prepare and serve a swan on important feast days and because Norwich was at the centre of swan-keeping for centuries, it was a tradition that survived.'

'Why did it stop when it did?'

'The price of grain became too high because of the war. It wasn't tenable any more to keep and feed the cygnets. And I suspect the taste for swan-meat was well on the wane by then, anyway, so there was no commercial imperative to continue.'

The Great Hospital captures my imagination. When I return home, I visit the interactive website http://www.thegreathospital.co.uk/ created by the University of East Anglia, where the whole colourful history of this and other medieval hospitals is set out in an engaging way.

I also begin to compile a long list of additional documents I want to see on my next visit to the Norfolk Record Office, not least the swan-upping records of Catherine Tollemache's Cromwell successors in North Elmham.

As if by osmosis, Catherine Tollemache comes to the fore. In lightning succession, I am invited to lead a study-day on her recipes and household with Strangers' Hall, and then to do something similar at Oxburgh Hall for the National Trust. Best of all, I am invited to give a talk at Helmingham in 2010 as part of the ongoing fund-raising effort for repairing the church bell-tower. Only then do I wonder what has happened to the conservation of the household accounts for Helmingham Hall. Before I have time to follow this up, I hear more news of note.

Catherine Reynolds tells me that the John Innes Centre celebrates its centenary this year, 2010. There will be a major programme of events starting quite soon, including a public open day. But there's more: a new rose has been bred by Peter Beales Roses to mark the centenary. It is to be called *John Innes*. Catherine thinks it would be a great idea to celebrate at least part of the centenary at Helmingham Hall. She plans to offer Lady Tollemache a bed of *Rosa John Innes* for planting at Helmingham Hall. In response to Catherine, I mention that I have been invited by Helmingham Parochial Church Clouncil to give a talk in the village in the summer to help raise funds.

And like Topsy, it just grew.

Soon, the two aims are combined. What was to have been a fairly low-key presentation designed to raise modest funds for Helmingham PCC turns into a full-scale event organised by the Helmingham Events Office. Lady Tollemache will be delighted to accept a bed of roses from the John Innes team, and, better still, she will lead visitors on a walk around the gardens.

Lady Tollemache, Helmingham Hall Gardens and a presentation of a celebratory new rose on a summer evening. It is a winner before it leaves the page. With a talk from me on the recipes, followed by wine and nibbles, the whole idea comes together as a tribute to Catherine Tollemache.

The John Innes Centre and Institute of Food Research teams have long wanted to acknowledge the 16th-century lady and her recipes. Catherine Tollemache, early empirical scientist, is about to be revealed through her own words.

Something else is about to be revealed, too. Never content to take on one challenge at a time, I put my property on the market shortly before delivering the Oxburgh day school for the WEA in April 2010.

There is still no sign of building next-door-but-one. My decision to sell might just have something to do with my ribs.

❋ ❋ ❋

I return from a challenging session with the osteopath to find an anxious message from the agent selling my house. She prefers me to lead the viewings. I can't think why: so far there have been two, early on, neither of which results in a sale. In fact, having lived through this experience several times, I have a sneaking suspicion that agents line up a few viewers in the opening weeks of every sale to keep vendors quiet. She tells me that today they have had a request from 'a man with a tight deadline'.

He plans to cross several counties which he can only do on a certain day within a strict timeframe. Fine, I understand that, but it happens to be tomorrow, during the hours when I will be leading a group of people around Oxburgh's lost gardens.

'Oh' says the Agent.

'You have a set of keys, can't you do it for me?'

'We'd rather you did it. He's a cash buyer and very keen. What time can you get back?'

I groan. 'Not before 4 pm at the earliest.'

'OK, that just fits his brief. We'll tell him to arrive with you at 4.15 pm'.

The day dawns. The weather is beautiful. My muscles behave. I lead the talk, take questions, skip lunch while I answer yet more questions, then guide the walk to bring the historic site of swan-keeping to life. It is a good day, except that my nerves are getting to me as I think about the next task.

I leave Oxburgh hurriedly, counting the seconds as I clock up the miles driven at the edge of speed limits. I had switched off my mobile phone just before we began the walk and forgot to activate it again before I left for the journey home. When I unlock the door of the cottage, grateful to see no-one waiting, no unrecognisable car in the street, I see that my landline answering machine is flashing with messages. There are three, each more anxious than the last. Just as he was about to leave, the potential viewer with the tight deadline learned that his son had been involved in a serious accident. Clearly, he would not be coming today. The next message was an update: the potential viewer had found that things weren't half as bad as he'd been led to believe. Could he come on Sunday?

The third message says 'Someone else wants to view tonight. Can they come?'

Tonight turns out to be within the next twenty minutes. I throw down some food for the long-suffering cat, who, sensing trouble, eats quickly and does a bunk when the doorbell rings.

This young couple live in the busy city of Norwich, about 15 miles north of here. They have been looking for a house for about 18 months and want something – well – a bit out of the ordinary. They couldn't find what they sought in their preferred search area, so decided to extend it by a few miles. Listening to this, I don't hold out much hope but I do what I always do: give them a brief tour so that they can get their bearings, then let them explore without me, invite them to ask me any questions later. Strategically, I find it best to show them the ground-floor first, then take them out into the long, now lovingly restored rear garden, so that they can take it all in, then back indoors to view the first floor.

It works. By Monday morning, they have put in an offer. I grimace when I hear what it is, but the agent advises me to accept. The 'man with the tight deadline' did arrive on Sunday with his argumentative wife. They argued their way through the cottage, down the garden and back to Leicestershire, and all in the space of less than ten minutes, with their cash still firmly in their pockets.

I accept the young couple's offer. It is exactly what I paid for the cottage in 2006. I have spent over £30,000 on it since. Even the purchasers' surveyor shakes his head in disbelief, particularly when he sees the quality of what has been done, but adds that he is seeing, and hearing, similar stories everywhere he goes these days.

'So where are you going?', he asks, 'somewhere with a bit less garden, perhaps?'.

I laugh. He should have seen Framsden.

'Yes, a lot less garden, actually. Some good friends of mine live in the centre of town. They have created a separate dwelling out of what was the annexe to their house. I'm buying that.'

It is called downsizing.

I still can't quite believe I am doing it.

Completion is set for 1ˢᵗ August 2010, exactly two years after I began my silver gap adventure at Framsden.

❋ ❋ ❋

With so many Helmingham-related events in the offing, I enquire about those household accounts. There have been unavoidable delays, Suffolk Record Office tells me. So sorry, but conservation work should begin quite soon. I tell them about the planned centenary celebration involving the John Innes Centre, explain that it is now part of the fund-raising effort for the parish church. A few weeks later, an e-mail comes direct from the conservator working on the accounts. 'I'm sorry about the delay but I can let you have access to the pages that have been repaired on the strict understanding that you do not touch anything beyond the marker that I'll insert into the book.'

Next day I devour the miles between Attleborough and Ipswich, my digital camera at the ready.

I return home with gold.

Even while I am busy in the Record Office, my eye glued to the viewfinder of my camera, I discern a fascinating and detailed view of life at Helmingham Hall between 1587 and 1589. Staff are paid to run errands, they are well clothed and shod. Sugar, spices, wine and dried fruits are purchased twice in 1587, and for significantly large sums of money.

On the long journey back to Norfolk, I am miles and centuries away, a household steward plodding to Ipswich with the horse and cart and returning to Helmingham heavily laden with 'North Sea Kodd' and herring. It is the week before Christmas 1587. I buy a barrel of salt in the same week. As Christmas approaches, the household staff and I will be up to our elbows preserving and storing 100 cod and many more herring.

I have photographed a year's accounts for 1587. Despite decay that has robbed the pages of some of their detail, a clear picture emerges. I keep in contact with the conservator, thank him and tell him how valuable it is all turning out to be. He's pleased; he assures me it will be a matter of weeks before the rest of the work is complete.

It isn't. For reasons beyond his control, the conservation work grinds to a halt. I am kept informed. Time ticks on, drawing ever closer to the increasingly high-profile event at Helmingham Hall. The event aims to show the added value that accumulates when several lots of expertise are brought together. It is about saying thank you, from one great institution, John Innes, to another, the Tollemache family. The event is a chance for the scientists to explain their enthusiasm for a 16ᵗʰ-century lady already held in high regard by her 20ᵗʰ-century descendants. In the midst of all this, I want my contribution to be as good as it can be.

The months evaporate into weeks. The talk is almost upon us. And then the phone rings. The conservation work is complete. When can I go to Ipswich? I look in my diary.

It is going to be nigh on impossible to make the journey, let alone do the work, before delivering the talk. 'Look', says the conservator, 'I know you are up against it, so I am going to photocopy the last few pages and send them to you by post'.

A fat parcel lands on my doorstep a few days later. The night oil is burned all over again. I am almost cross-eyed with transcription. I select those facts I think will interest and amuse people: the fluctuations in the price of sugar between 1587 and the Armada year of 1588, the number of roses purchased for the distillation of rose-water (10,500 one year, 12,500 the next).

I'm ready, just about.

❋ ❋ ❋

The late June afternoon is bright and sunny. Early guests gather in the Rose Garden at Helmingham Hall wearing their sun-hats. They are full of anticipation and they are not disappointed. Lady Tollemache, already well-known to many of them, strides purposefully into the centre of the gathering. She smiles a welcome and people relax. It's just the presentation team that feels nervous, and me. Catherine Reynolds, then Head of Communications for the combined academic team, gives a spirited address. I wince as excitement gets the better of her when she proclaims to all and sundry, including the Rector of Helmingham church, 'The woman [Catherine Tollemache] was a goddam scientist!' Her colleagues and I laugh nervously to hide our embarrassment but we needn't have worried. The moment is over, a potted rose is picked up from the ground and pressed into the welcoming arms of Lady Tollemache, who expresses her delight and then invites the throng – is it growing or is it my imagination? – to follow her around the gardens. Everyone is in for a treat. But to my horror, what I thought to be about twenty people seems to be multiplying. I had hoped to join the garden tour - anything led by Lady Tollemache is not to be missed - but the Events Organiser beckons me anxiously to the Coach House, where my talk is set to follow the walk.

'We expected 20', she confides, 'but decided to cater for about 30-40, just in case'.
'And?'
'And there were 80 at the last count.'

It's all hands on deck. I help them carry in more chairs. The caterers stand there looking shell-shocked as they hear the news. I suspect they set to and halve the portions of 'nibbles' that they were in the process of plating up carefully on tables in a room designed to accommodate 20, 30 or 40 people, but not 80. Lord Tollemache arrives. He ignores the frenetic activity and asks me if I would like to see the original portrait of Catherine Tollemache. He understands that I have never seen the original, has a few moments to spare if I will come now. This is so unexpected that I stand, open-mouthed before saying that I would be delighted.

I follow Lord Tollemache across the moat, and he asks me if I think I might return to live in Framsden one day. I confess that the likelihood is slim because of the unexpected dip in the property market in Norfolk. I add that I would like to have stayed but that my plans were somewhat optimistic. Lord Tollemache gives me a wry smile and we leave it at that. Inside the Hall, we enter yet another room that I have never visited before, clad with dark panelling and protected from the still-bright invasion of a summer evening. Lord Tollemache switches on the picture lights, and there she is. The oil portrait of Catherine Tollemache was painted in 1597. She is more beautiful than I had concluded already from my view of digital images. I stand gratefully, silently, committing every detail to memory.

A professional from the Norwich Museum of Costume and Textiles took great trouble to explain each item of clothing to me, and she was working from a digital image, too. I look closely at the dark cap, barely discernible on the back of Catherine's head of dark, possibly auburn, hair. The Museum described this not as a hat but as an integral part of the way her hair was dressed in the 'sweetheart' style. I wonder how long it took to dress her hair, to don the layers of clothing that make up her dress: her petticoat, vastguard, sleeves, kirtle. The accounts I have been transcribing reveal to me that she was particular about her sleeves. She paid to have them cut locally, even though they were made by her London tailor. I recall reading a letter in the archives in which the tailor castigates her mildly for her taste in unfashionable sleeves. Diplomatically, she found a way to achieve what she wanted. My resepct for her is magnified here, where she lived, where she raised her seven children, lost two more, wrote the recipes that that I am about to share with 60, 70, 80 – how many people?

Lord Tollemache is patient with me until, with practised ease, he tells me it is time we should leave because people will be returning soon for the talk. Half-way across the moat, he stops and drops a bombshell. Dr John Blatchly, who is one of Suffolk's most highly-respected and active historians, and is also Lord Tollemache's Honorary Librarian, will be in the audience. I swallow hard. I have not met him. I will be introduced.

There is no time for nerves: anxiety in the Coach House seems more pronounced than when we left. The organiser, in touch by mobile phone with her spies out and about in the garden, reports that people are arriving late and still joining the tour.

'How many do we have so far?'

'At least 90, My Lord.'

'Well then, we'll need to get more chairs in here.'

The doors close on 104 people. Lord Tollemache welcomes everyone, including me. It is all a blur. I can't remember whether I thank him or not, but I recall standing there looking at this sea of faces. Somewhere there are friends, colleagues, the John Innes presentation team; but I recognise no-one. I take a deep breath, smile and say: 'Well, who'd have thought that forty-two recipes would create such excitement!' Mercifully, people laugh and I relax.

For the next hour, I open the 16th-century recipe book and its secrets spill out as *Food to Impress, Perfumes to Delight and Colours to Astonish*. One hundred and four people gasp at the price of sugar; the exotic ingredients used to make soap; at the fact that there was a Soap House dedicated to the task here at the Hall; at the quantities of roses purchased for the distillation of rose-water; but most of all, given the presentation earlier of the

John Innes rose, they are amazed to hear Catherine Tollemache's 400-year-old instructions 'To make flowers grow of any colour'. I follow this with an image that was sent to me the day before by one of the John Innes team: it shows a 'new' multi-coloured rose. That one brings the house down and there we end.

Lord Tollemache gives a final thank-you. He has, he says, lived with these recipes for years but has never seen them in this light before. People are invited to ask questions, but, politely, or maybe because they are roasting in the crush and their tongues hanging out for a drink, they do not. Lord Tollemache reminds people why we are here: to raise money to reinforce the bell-frame in St Mary's church. Much has been raised from various sources of funding, but the project needs more. He thanks everyone for contributing, simply by being here tonight, and invites them to enjoy their drinks and nibbles. The rush is little short of a stampede. The room empties and I release my grip on the projector, exhale in relief. But I am not alone. A lady is advancing on me, papers in hand.

'Hello', she says, introducing herself as Tina. 'I wonder – are you writing a book on all this, and if so, do you have a publisher?'

It is the second time I have been asked that question since I returned from Framsden. Perhaps it is about time I gave the answer.

Above: Blackie, Editor in Chief, 'Fruitful Endeavours', January 2012.

The book (below) was published in August 2012.

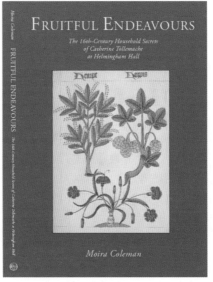

Author's images

12: Finding my voice

From somewhere, I hear myself say: 'Yes, I am writing a book, but no, I do not yet have a publisher...' I learn that Tina is a designer who works frequently for one of Suffolk's most prestigious publishing houses. They specialise in history. She thinks my material would make for an interesting book. She suggests that I submit a proposal.

On the drive back to Attleborough later that night, I reflect less on the hectic event than its outcome. Perhaps what I have needed all along is evidence that someone might be interested in reading this book that I have not yet written.

I download a submission form from the publishers' website. There are many questions about my academic tenure and my published works. About the only box I can complete positively is the 100-word synopsis. I have that sinking feeling that my work is not going to be what they want under any circumstances.

I'm right.

It sounds, they tell me, as though it might be a very interesting topic. However, with such a limited local focus and with no offer of a significant financial contribution from me, they regret, &c., &c....

❈ ❈ ❈

Tina has another request: she asks if I will write an article for the Suffolk Gardens Trust newsletter, and also whether I will give a presentation to the Trust's members. I say yes to both but sadly manage to fulfil only the first. It will be one of many losses post-Framsden.

The remit for the article is that it must relate to the gardens of Helmingham Hall rather than its historic archives, although clearly these can be mentioned, especially the recipes, where there is an obvious connection with the garden. I e-mail Lady Tollemache, and ask her if I might 'borrow' her Head Gardener's expertise before I put pen to paper. Her response is generous: of course I may talk to Roy. Better still, here's his direct phone number. Arrange to come and meet him in the gardens. As it happens, he has recently made a complete list of all the heritage apple varieties in the garden, so that might be a good thing to write about, might it not?

This is the first time since leaving Framsden that I have driven past St John's Row without making that right turn through the break in the hedge. I glance and glance away, keeping my eyes on the road. I am a visitor now, not a tenant.

Roy and I meet in the walled garden at Helmingham Hall. There is a vicious and capricious wind accompanied by a scudding rainstorm that comes suddenly, forcing us to raise collars and take shelter. The storm ceases as quickly as it began and sunlight dances on the raindrops as they skitter off the leaves, hastened by the occasional gust of wind. By the time we reach the Apple Walk, the wind is rising again. Embryonic fruit is hurled to the ground on all sides, and I take a photograph of Roy, baby apples falling about him and his trouser bottoms whipping around his ankles. He is smiling broadly and looks for all the world like an impressive figurehead, which is exactly what he is at Helmingham Hall Gardens. We return to the shelter of the Walled Garden and he leads me through the cropping calendar and its idiosyncracies.

There are early apricots that fruit late, and vice versa. Then there are greengages: Roy tells me that one variety here is a historic descendant of the earliest introductions into England, nurtured not 30 miles from here at Hengrave Hall. Hengrave was home to Sir William Gage who gave his name to the green plum known as *Reine Claude* in France, where he found it. We move around the entire perimeter of the walled garden, inside and out. Each side of the wall supports fruit. There are plums, apples, pears and cherries on the outer faces; figs, peaches, nectarines and more basking and burgeoning in the protective warmth of the inner side.

Roy leads me through the Apple Walk as though reading from the pages of Debrett's Peerage. One by one, he introduces me to *King of the Pippins* (early C19th), *Duchess of Oldenburg* (c.1817-24), *Lady Sudeley* (raised 1849, originally known as 'Jacob's Strawberry', re-named 1884). Then we come to a tree and a family I recognise from my own research: *Lady Henniker,* with its distinctive Y-shaped form, was raised at Thornham Hall, Suffolk, between the 1840s and 1850s by the then Head Gardener, John Perkins, and introduced to the Royal Horticultural Society by him in 1873. This talented man also wrote and published a beautifully illustrated book entitled *Floral Decorations for the Table,* dedicated to Lady Henniker. It was a guide for ladies of her ilk who were responsible for ensuring that tables for breakfast, luncheon, dinner, tea, supper, weddings, harvest festivals, cricket games and hunts were decorated with seasonal foliage, fruits, vegetables and flowers, artistically arranged. One of my favourites is the autumn table. Fresh figs are to be laid on vine leaves, each resplendent with colour, to surround each place setting. Running the length of the table centre are epergnes, vases, candlesticks and, of course, the food.

The Apple Walk offers more toothsome history with *Bramley's Seedling* (raised 1809-13, introduced 1865), *Kerry Pippin* (1819-20), *Blenheim Orange,* (discovered 1740, exhibited 1822), *Cox's Pomona* (raised 1825, introduced 1850*)* and *Golden Reinette* (known England mid-1600s), and *Irish Peach* (1819). With the loss of mature cedar trees in the 1987 storm, the Apple Walk was extended in 1992 at its eastern end to run parallel with the Parterre (which itself holds mature black mulberry and quince trees), adding more historic varieties to the roll-call: *Pitmaston Pine Apple* (raised 1785, exhibited 1845), *Egremont Russet* (recorded 1872, exhibited 1883), *Brownlees' Russet* (1848*),* [*Laxton's*]

Epicure (1809), *Margil* (reputedly late 17th century and undoubtedly stocked in large quantities by George London of Brompton Park Nursery by 1750), *Laxton's Royalty* (raised 1908, introduced 1932), *Cornish Aromatic* (1813 but probably much earlier origin), *Gravenstein* (origins claimed in Europe in the 1600s, introduced 1820s), *Devonshire Quarrenden* (recorded 1676), *Ashmead's Kernel* (raised c. 1700 but not widely planted until mid-19[th] century) and *Rosemary Russet* (described 1831). *Scrumptious* is the most modern variety, raised in the 1980s, and there is one pear, *Winter Ne[l]lis* (late 19[th]-century, ripe as late as November at Helmingham).

By the time I leave, my soggy, wind-tattered notebook is filled with species, varieties, fruiting dates, characteristics and more. I can look along the walls and be certain that is a Brown Turkey fig lurking in the delicious warmth of the right angle. I can look at Coe's Early Drop and know that it fruits late. And most of all, I can look at Roy Balaam and marvel that he holds it all together and has done so for almost sixty years. He shares his knowledge easily and generously. I am inspired. I write my article and call it: 'Rooted in History'.

❋ ❋ ❋

In August 2010, Jeremy and I move a mile down the road to our new urban dwelling, a name that sticks. I am living next door to my most valued friends, John and Sue. I have, after much prevarication that taxes John's patience to the limit, signed on the dotted line, purchased the fruit of his efforts.

❋ ❋ ❋

A few weeks before my purchasers complete, I receive news that building work is scheduled to commence nearby in a few months' time. I pass the news to my solicitor so that she can tell the purchasers' solicitor. I hold my breath. All is well.

❋ ❋ ❋

However, writing this retrospectively, I am saddened but not surprised to learn that despite significant levels of objection (again), the local planning authority has given permission for 375 houses and an industrial estate on what was agricultural land immediately behind the houses facing my Attleborough cottage. I think of all my neighbours on that side of the road: they have nurtured their gardens and encouraged wildlife. They have lived, as I did at Framsden, surrounded by farmland. I cannot imagine what they are going through now, although the signs are apparent every time I browse 'Rightmove' (old habits die hard).

❋ ❋ ❋

At the urban dwelling, I ask for John's help in setting out a series of trellis divisions to make the small rear garden seem larger. The Framsden greengage is fan-trained against one of them and thrives, fruiting heavily.

Ironically, Jeremy has returned to where he used to live before I adopted him. Despite the changes, he sniffs his way around, dispenses with hiding, resumes normal service and settles readily.

I have to hope I am equally adaptable, but I wonder if I will ever get Framsden out of my mind. As it is, I find myself with little time to fret about anything – except frequent attacks of stage fright before the delivery of every new presentation and day school, of which there are many.

The late Summer of 2010 seems to be bursting with opportunity. The WEA are keen to have another day school. Curiously, just as the Oxburgh one took place around the time a buyer emerged for my Norfolk cottage, so the 'Roses on a Plate' day school occurs less than a week before I move out. The blessing is that it takes place in Attleborough. Peter Beales Roses has kindly agreed to collaborate on this day, which will take place in the midst of their Classic Roses Garden less than half a mile from where I live.

'Roses on a Plate' presents the rose not as a plant but as a resource. Half the day looks at how it was used in history: all those roses in lieu of rent have an interested audience at last. Then we explore the practical applications of the rose in medicines, perfumes and in food. The second half of the day is in the hands of Peter Beales Roses staff. Because Catherine Reynolds and Sarah Wilmot are attending, representing the John Innes Centre, I asked if the Peter Beales team will explain how the centenary rose, the bi-coloured *Rosa John Innes* was developed. The marquee is filled with bent heads as people struggle to make a clean cut, then struggle more to create a graft. Everyone has even greater appreciation for rose-breeders than they had already. The day ends with a tour of the sumptuous National Collection of Classic Roses and is a resounding success.

❋ ❋ ❋

Sadly, a few years later, the Beales rose dynasty loses three of its gifted family in a short space of time. Joan, wife of Peter, died in September 2012, Peter, the firm's founder, honoured throughout the world for his expertise, in January 2013; and their daughter, Amanda, rose-breeder and author, in August 2013.

Their roses live on as a lasting tribute.

❋ ❋ ❋

Summer 2010 passes in a blur of short local talks. Autumn is even more demanding with two major presentations. One is the National Trust event at Oxburgh Hall, a half day based on a selection of Catherine Tollemache's recipes. The second fulfils a long-awaited opportunity to work with my friends at Strangers' Hall Museum. As part of the Museum's 'Tudor Month' celebrations, we create a day of discovery. My role is to reveal a selection of Catherine Tollemache's recipes in the morning at the wonderful vaulted lecture theatre of Norwich Castle, and then move the group to Strangers' Hall Museum in the afternoon to introduce them to Tudor household linen, furniture and culinary equipment, examples of which they can see on display.

Bethan, resplendant in her Tudor costume, ends the day by producing Tudor food, including a 'subtletie' created as a ship full of sailors, wittily designed and highly coloured. I am not there to see it. Exhaustion claims me.

I look at the growing list of invitations for 2011 and cancel the lot. It was a tough decision and an unpleasant thing to do. I hate to let people down, but it was essential. I had to recharge the batteries.

❈ ❈ ❈

Rest does not come naturally to me. Building myself up to full power is one thing, but mental stagnation is not part of the plan.

I look at all the things I have not done. At the top of the list is that unwritten book.

The question 'Are you writing a book?' is about to receive a credible response; and I am about to be tested on my answer.

❈ ❈ ❈

I draft the first few chapters tentatively. A good and trusted friend, who has been honoured for his professional work in the field of history and archives, offers to review this effort before I submit it to a publisher. I send him my opening chapter, the one that sets the scene for all the rest. It is long, detailed and weighty with footnotes. There isn't an illustration in sight.

'There's no doubting the credibility of your research', he says, 'but… well, you don't have to work so hard to prove it. You're not submitting a thesis – or are you? Is that what you really want to do? You don't seem clear who it is you are writing *for*.'

I recognise and acknowledge my own confusion.

'Frankly I'm not sure I know how else to write. You've written books: can you give me any guidance?'

'Yes', he says, 'I think you need to loosen its stays a bit.'

❈ ❈ ❈

I approach Phillimore & Co. directly. The firm has a long-established reputation for publishing English local history. My shelves are full of their titles. They invite me to submit a detailed proposal and a sample chapter.

'It's a biography', their commissioning editor says when she first replies.

'No it's not', I respond.

Instantly, I come up against the first principle of writing a book. What is it about?

'May I submit a fresh proposal to you?' I venture. Yes, do that. And this is how it begins. First, I re-submit a proposal for the same book but with a different title and emphasis. That goes forward for consideration. I wait anxiously.

A few weeks later, in a long telephone call, the patient and courteous Noel Osborne, Chairman of Phillimore & Co., draws me out, encourages me to talk about my passion. In retrospect, I recognise that the discussion was far less about the book than it was about my research and the ways in which I have used it so far. He has practical recommendations: abandon the weighty tome you thought you were going to write. Instead, focus on what you can bring to life – the household and the recipes of that remarkable woman, for example. You can talk about her with enthusiasm, so inject that same enthusiasm into your book. And think about including illustrations. They will make the book more appealing. Importantly, identify your target market clearly and write for your readers. Where have I heard that before? When I've done all that, suggests Noel Osborne, send him another synopsis. He has more practical advice to offer: don't waste the material you exclude from the book: try to find academic outlets for it, submit articles for inclusion in the publications of special-interest societies, for example.

The greatest challenge is to identify my target market. I am perplexed. Surely it consists of people like me? Surely not, my critical friends tell me when I harangue them endlessly with this dilemma. Eventually, I set up an e-mail reading group of people with diverse interests, all of whom are willing to be honest with me. I send them sample chapters. I receive their comments and gradually loosen the stays. As I do, my readers' comments begin to coalesce and I begin to recognise my target market. Phillimores receive and accept a new proposal for a book with the working title of *Fruitful Endeavours: the 16th-century household secrets of Catherine Tollemache at Helmingham Hall.* I sign a contract that commits me to contributing to the cost of production with author sponsorship. The piggy bank empties again. As with my silver gap year, I tell myself this is an investment, even though it will take years to recover and is equally full of risk.

By the end of 2011, I am well on the way to completing my first book. The foreword is written by Lord Tollemache, who also gives permission to reproduce the portrait of Catherine Tollemache. There are to be fourteen colour illustrations, including contributions from the John Innes team and Strangers' Hall Museum. Five, including the book cover, are sumptuous images from a certain Tudor pattern book, the illuminated manuscript in the Bodleian Library; the very one that motivated my interest in plants at Framsden three years ago. I dedicate the book to the Open University. Life is restored to what I wanted it to be, full of challenge and anticipation, deadlines and decision-making.

✵ ✿ ✵

Then sadness shatters this silvered mirror of euphoria. Jeremy, that pernickity ball of grey fur, dies suddenly in November 2011.

✵ ✿ ✵

Undaunted, I decide to adopt another adult cat within weeks. A local vet recommends one just streets away from where I live. His owners are moving into sheltered accommodation and cannot take him with them. We meet.

Blackie, coal-black, satin smooth, sleek and sphinx-like, moves in with me two days before Christmas 2011. He settles remarkably quickly. He is adoring, up-close and personal. He likes to put his head on my shoulder. I sing Christmas carols to him and he purrs and sighs with pleasure. He likes to be involved. As the pages of my first draft print-out of *Fruitful Endeavours* emerge, and I place them in a box ready for reading and editing, he climbs in and sits on them, an imposing Editor in Chief if ever there was. He is an ever-present sentinel as I write doggedly, determined to meet the submission deadline.

On the appointed day, 26 January 2012, I package up the DVD containing the completed first full draft and take it to the Post Office to arrange special delivery. Just before I leave the house, I send my design editor a frivolous e-mail: 'Hi Andrew, It's done! Unless I get squashed by a bus between here and the Post Office, you will have *Fruitful Endeavours* on your desk tomorrow morning'.

✾ ✾ ✾

It was not me, but Blackie. He met his end that evening, racing across the busy road outside the urban dwelling.

✾ ✾ ✾

Life goes on. Between January and July 2012, *Fruitful Endeavours: the 16th-century household secrets of Catherine Tollemache at Helmingham Hall* emerges relatively unscathed from copy editing. I learn that it is St Mary's church, not Church; stepfather, not step-father; rose-water, not rosewater; I am warned of an over-use of some words and phrases: alternatives are left to me. I raise three cheers for the 'Find' facility in 'Word'. Did I really say 'In the event' 27 times? In the skilful hands of Phillimore's design editor, Andrew Illes, the book that I wrote emerges as something more tactile and beautiful than its 'paperback' description suggests.

We talk marketing. Noel Osborne recommends that given the book's local focus, I should take responsibility for this since I can probably identify, reach out and touch my market. So, while the book goes through the production process, I turn my attention to how I will sell it. This is new to me (unless you count all those boot sales).

I set up a website, www.fruitfulendeavours.co.uk, with e-commerce facilities for purchasers. The gift-shop at Helmingham Hall will be my first retail customer. I reserve pitches at forthcoming history fairs and anywhere else I think my market might congregate. I circulate hundreds of flyers through special interest societies across Suffolk and Norfolk. I pester every contact I can possibly exploit. I persuade some local libraries and museums to place pre-publication orders.

I'm all set.

✾ ✾ ✾

In August 2012, within a year of that encouraging telephone call from Noel Osborne, I take delivery of a pallet containing five hundred copies of my first book. The question that has been asked for the past four years has been answered.

The book is launched at Helmingham Hall at a fund-raising event for the church - they are still paying for those bells. The air is filled with exotic fragrances: Dave Hart, the research scientist who brought the recipes to life at the 'From Plant to Plate' day school in Norwich in 2010, repeats the performance. He improves on it by sourcing additional rare ingredients that were specified by Catherine Tollemache. We moisten our hands in rose-water and roll these hot little balls of fragrance to create beads. We make a hole 'with a bodkin', all as directed. There is applause as Dave presents to Lady Tollemache a perfumed pomander, a bracelet of beads made to her husband's ancestor's 400-year old recipe.

Over drinks and nibbles (mercifully enough to go around this time), people come to have their book signed. As they read the publicity on the back cover, several of them say to me:

'Oh! You lived here on the Estate for a year. That must have been a wonderful experience. Are you going to write a book about that?'

❖ ❖ ❖

Ironically, although *Fruitful Endeavours* sells well, I am in demand again for the public events I thought I could avoid: the diary fills two years in advance with requests for presentations and talks: two years of quaking in my boots all over again. I do find the courage to decline some invitations, particularly if they involve hours of cross-country driving at night or in the winter. Groups are understanding and some are able to offer alternatives. It upset me deeply to let people down in 2011 and I tell myself it is far better for all concerned if I say no when I mean no.

Happily, there is more writing to do, too. Taking Noel Osborne's advice, I produce a long, detailed article for *Suffolk Review*, published by Suffolk Local History Council. Others are in the pipeline.

❖ ❖ ❖

Fruitful Endeavours finds favour in the USA, where there is a strong appetite for English domestic and culinary history. Cindy Renfrow, an American food historian whose *Take a thousand Eggs* I admire and acknowledge in *Fruitful Endeavours,* makes contact. Cindy transcribed an English medieval manuscript to create her book and it is a remarkable piece of work. She tells me she has a daughter who works in a publishing house in New York. Constance and I make contact and I discover an ardent fan of Victorian England and English literature. She is writing a novel. We correspond. Constance thinks I ought to write a book about my silver gap year.

She offers to read it, chapter by chapter, scrutinises it, advises me.

All the same, the usual provisos apply: the buck stops here.

❖ ❖ ❖

On 22nd July 2013, one of the hottest days on record in England to date, the Duke and Duchess of Cambridge welcome George, their first son who is third in line to the throne. Tomorrow, we will say 'history was made yesterday'.

Before the news broke that day, I was at Helmingham Hall, doing what I love to do, touching the family's history on paper, parchment and vellum. I still struggle with dates, muddle my monarchs and get excited with every new discovery. Lord Tollemache's current Honorary Archivist, Vic, who took over when Bill Serjeant retired, is an endlessly patient man. Vic takes all my excited blustering in his stride while pointing me gently in the right direction. It is just like old times.

Today, in one of those 'incidents of coincidence', as I think of them (never fate, never destiny), I view a document relating to a swan mark. I learn that in 1638, Sir Henry Bedingfeld of Oxburgh sold his 'Catherine wheel' swan mark to Sir Lionel Tollemache, 2nd baronet, who is Catherine Tollemache's son. At the time, the 2nd baronet and his wife had a newly-acquired second seat at Fakenham Magna in Suffolk, not far from Euston Hall. It may not have been where Sir Lionel kept his swans, but it was well situated for proximity to the historically important swan-keeping areas of the fenlands of Norfolk and Cambridgeshire, lying to the north and west.

I turn the document. There, in the centre, is a clear drawing of the Catherine wheel swan mark. I smile, make some small noise of recognition.

'Hmm?', says Vic, looking up from his own work.

'Oh, it's this swan mark. In February this year I gave a talk to Oxburgh Garden Club. I showed them this very mark while we explored Oxburgh's gardens and compared their development with another garden of Tudor origin'.

'Let me guess: was the other garden here, at Helmingham?'

'Yes it was, and the Oxburgh group came for a follow-up visit in May.'

'And you didn't know then about the sale of the swan mark from their Sir Henry to Catherine's son, the 2nd Sir Lionel?'

'No, not then. I didn't discover it until today. I must e-mail Barbara, my contact in the Oxburgh Garden Club. She will be very excited!'

'How did you come to be interested in the history of swan-keeping?'

'Oh, it began with a request from the WEA. I led a day school for them in 2010 based on the Oxburgh Hall water-gardens, long gone now. I've spent many happy hours at Norfolk Record Office. Apart from other swan-related treasures, they hold records of the annual swan-upping for Catherine Tollemache's family, the Cromwells of North Elmham, from 1671 to 1675.'

'Annual swan-upping? How did that work?'

'The swanherd had to walk the extent of the breeding area of the swans once a year, count and record the breeding state of all the family's marked swans.'

'How far afield did the swans go – how far did the swanherd have to walk, or row, to find them?'

'The area was extensive, from water just north of North Elmham, right down to an area south of Norwich.'

'I'm amazed! I'd better not get too interested otherwise today's work will never get done. Let's break for a walk ourselves, shall we?'

The grounds are quiet today, not open to public visitors. I see Chris, wearing a soft hat to protect his head and shade his eyes from the intense glare of the sun. He looks up from his work, recognises me from some distance, waves his hat and calls a greeting. I tell Vic that Chris was the previous tenant of the cottage I occupied just along the road in Framsden. Vic gives me a long look, says: 'It must have had a lovely garden'.

I do no more than nod. We return to the welcome coolness of the Hall where I let today's task absorb me.

✦ ✦ ✦

I may have lost Framsden but I have gained a deeper understanding of my place in the past. I will not relinquish the live end of history again.

✦ ✦ ✦

Where will it end?

✦ ✦ ✦

My first book, *Fruitful Endeavours,* is having its first reprint. To coincide with delivery of the new stock, I have permission from the Bodleian Library to reproduce five images that appear already in the book. From these images, I propose eight designs for stationery. The designs are based on illustrations of plants from that inspirational medieval illuminated manuscript once at Helmingham Hall, the one whose facsimile copy almost bankrupted me five years ago in my silver gap year. Each card will incorporate a story about the plant and its use in the 16th century.

The limited edition range is being marketed as 'Fruitful Endeavours History Bites: designed for you to send a little message with a lot of history.'

The plan is not without risk, but I see it as an investment.

Sounds familiar, don't you think?